'How has America responded to China's rise? What is the China factor in America's major decisions for the next decade? What's at stake for America across our government, economy and society? Eric Heikkila gives fine analyses on a vast scale. Given the Chinese juggernaut, and its impacts on the American economy and government, this book is essential reading for understanding China, and ourselves, in the next decade and more.'

Glenn Shive, *Chinese University of Hong Kong*

'The U.S. and China are intertwined in ways unimaginable twenty, let alone forty years ago. Prof. Heikkila's new book helps us understand the many ways that China's rise affects the U.S. and the ways the two governments interact. Anyone interested in this vital relationship and how its evolution will affect both countries and the world at large will benefit from reading this important book.'

Clayton Dube, *Executive Director, US–China Institute,*
University of Southern California

CHINA FROM A U.S. POLICY PERSPECTIVE

In this book, Eric J. Heikkila explores a truly important question that has not been adequately analyzed to date: how the rise of China alters the context in which the broad spectrum of policies in the United States should be assessed. Here, the policy domain of the U.S. government is carved into three broad spheres:

- economic policies: fiscal policy and deficits, trade policy, and employment and income
- sustainability policies: climate change, urban policy, and energy policy
- geopolitical policies: homeland security, defense policy, and foreign relations.

For each domain, Heikkila assesses the key policy issues and tradeoffs, examining how the balance of such tradeoffs shifts due to China's rise. In doing so, he demonstrates how a rising China exerts its gravitation pull on U.S. policy, not so much through lobbying or negotiation, but through the very nature of its being. A concluding chapter presents a workable synthesis derived from these diverse perspectives.

At a time of increasing tensions, it is all the more important for U.S. policy makers to focus on the many substantive policy questions that are impacted by China's rise. *China from a U.S. Policy Perspective* will be of key interest to scholars, practitioners, and students of policy analysis, U.S. politics, Chinese politics, and International Relations.

Eric J. Heikkila is a Professor at the USC Price School of Public Policy at the University of Southern California, Los Angeles, where he also serves on the

Executive Committee of the USC US–China Institute. Dr. Heikkila is the founding Executive Secretary of the Pacific Rim Council on Urban Development, and has had visiting appointments at Peking University, National Taiwan University, the Chinese University of Hong Kong, Nanyang Technological University in Singapore and the Graduate Research Institute for Policy Studies in Tokyo. Trained initially as an economist, he has a strong record of scholarly publications in urban development and public policy, many with a focus on China. As Director of Global Engagement for the USC Price School of Public Policy, he helped maintain institutional ties with partner institutions in China and elsewhere.

CHINA FROM A U.S. POLICY PERSPECTIVE

Eric J. Heikkila

Routledge
Taylor & Francis Group

NEW YORK AND LONDON

First published 2021
by Routledge
52 Vanderbilt Avenue, New York, NY 10017

and by Routledge
2 Park Square, Milton Park, Abingdon, Oxon, OX14 4RN

Routledge is an imprint of the Taylor & Francis Group, an informa business

Library of Congress Cataloging-in-Publication Data
Names: Heikkila, Eric John, author.
Title: China from a U.S. policy perspective / Eric J. Heikkila.
Other titles: China from a United States policy perspective
Description: New York, NY : Routledge, 2020. | Includes
bibliographical references and index.
Identifiers: LCCN 2020014807 (print) | LCCN 2020014808 (ebook) |
ISBN 9780367897970 (hardback) | ISBN 9780367897963 (paperback) |
ISBN 9781003021209 (ebook) | ISBN 9781000174021 (adobe pdf) |
ISBN 9781000174052 (mobi) | ISBN 9781000174083 (epub)
Subjects: LCSH: United States–Foreign relations–China. | China–
Foreign relations–United States. | United States–Economic policy. |
United States–Energy policy. | United States–Military policy. |
China–Strategic aspects.
Classification: LCC E183.8.C5 H45 2020 (print) | LCC E183.8.C5
(ebook) | DDC 327.73051–dc23
LC record available at https://lccn.loc.gov/2020014807
LC ebook record available at https://lccn.loc.gov/2020014808

ISBN: 978-0-367-89797-0 (hbk)
ISBN: 978-0-367-89796-3 (pbk)
ISBN: 978-1-003-02120-9 (ebk)

Typeset in Bembo
by Wearset Ltd, Boldon, Tyne and Wear

To my father, Walter Heikkila, whose auroral arc will always inspire.

CONTENTS

List of Figures   xi
List of Tables   xii
Preface   xiii
Acknowledgments   xv
List of Abbreviations   xviii

1 Introduction   1

PART I
Economic Policy Perspectives   **11**

2 Fiscal Policy and Deficits   13

3 Trade Policy   33

4 Employment and Income   52

PART II
Sustainability Policy Perspectives   **69**

5 Climate Change   71

6 Urban Policy   91

7 Energy Policy   108

PART III

Geopolitical Policy Perspectives   **129**

  8 Homeland Security   131

  9 Defense Policy   151

10 Foreign Relations   173

11 Synthesis and Conclusions   196

Index   209

FIGURES

1.1	US–China comparisons: GDP, CO_2 and defense	4
2.1	Federal deficit, 1990–2030	14
4.1	Manufacturing employment vs. import penetration ratio, 1960–2019	55
5.1	Comparing CO_2 emissions (megatons per year)	73
5.2a	Carbon tax	85
5.2b	Cap and trade	85
6.1	Urban regions and climate change	94
6.2	Cargo container route shares, NE Asia to U.S. East Coast	98
6.3	Foreign purchases of U.S. residential real estate ($ billions)	101
7.1	Crude oil prices, 1968–2019 (in constant 2010 $)	109
7.2a	Price increase induced by shift of demand curve	110
7.2b	Price increase induced by shift of supply curve	110
7.3	S-shaped energy use trajectory	113
7.4	U.S. energy exports and imports, 1990–2050	117
8.1	Progression of homeland security concerns	132
10.1	China and U.S. trade with East Asia and the Pacific, 2001 and 2017 (in constant 2010 $)	187
11.1	Linked policy domains	197

TABLES

1.1	U.S. policy realms	2
3.1	Top sources of U.S. merchandise trade imbalances, 2018 (in $ billions)	35
4.1	Widening income disparities, 1980–2018	54
5.1	Agencies involved in the Interagency Working Group on Social Cost of Carbon	79
6.1	Urban population, in thousands (and as percentage of total population)	91
8.1	Critical infrastructure sectors	144
9.1	Defense expenditures by country, 2018	154

PREFACE

Some years ago (more than I care to confess), I was participating in an Executive Committee meeting of the U.S.–China Institute at my home institution, the University of Southern California. Chaired by Dr. Clayton Dube, our committee members had diverse disciplinary interests, but we were all drawn together by a shared interest in the U.S.–China relationship. One member of our committee was participating via video call from Washington, DC, where he told us about the excellent conference room and other facilities that USC maintained there. Stimulated by this news, I began to reflect upon how our Institute might make use of this fine facility, noting that so many U.S. federal departments had an interest in China. Expounding upon this further, I suggested that we could perhaps organize a seminar series that drew upon federal officials with appropriate interests and expertise. My fellow committee members responded politely but non-committally, and we moved on to the next agenda items. It dawned on me that if it was going to happen, I should be the one to do it – after all, I was the sole person on the committee who was billed as a professor of public policy. I was in no position to expect someone else to do it if I would not do so myself.

I then set about putting together a graduate seminar as a special topics course. Even then, I was thinking that if the course went well, I might consider undertaking a book project along the same lines. I was fortunate that this seminar drew a really special group of graduate students who dug into the topics with enthusiasm and acumen. By the time the semester was over, I had decided to take the plunge. I continued to offer the course on a fairly regular basis over subsequent years. Initially, the course readings, lectures, and discussions helped me to frame the ideas in the book. Once the book had gotten well underway, it in turn supported my teaching of the course. I feel confident that many people may learn a great deal by reading this book, but I am certain that no one will learn as much from reading it as I have learned from writing it. It has been a most valuable endeavor. I am grateful to many people who helped and encouraged me along the way, as amplified in the Acknowledgments.

During the time that I was busy working on this book, the world has changed in fundamental ways. The U.S. and China are locked in an acrimonious trade war; we have all been engulfed in a devastating viral pandemic that had its origins in China; global efforts to combat climate change have faltered badly; Hong Kong is in the throes of divisiveness as China asserts its sovereignty in more overt terms; global institutions are being steadily undermined; and, here in the U.S., democracy is steadily giving way to demagoguery. I am convinced that this book examining China's rise from a U.S. policy perspective is increasingly important – but for all the wrong reasons. Now, more than ever, we need to approach these issues from a reasoned perspective that is grounded in sober, clear-minded policy analysis. I hope this modest effort can help point the way.

ACKNOWLEDGMENTS

Institutions matter, and people matter – and this proposition certainly holds true in terms of seeing this book through to its completion. The anchor institution, for me, is the University of Southern California, located in Los Angeles. With its ambitious agenda, entrepreneurial spirit, lofty goals, and high expectations, it is an institution that encourages each one of us to set the bar high. It also is the umbrella institution for many fine schools, including the USC Price School of Public Policy, which has been my academic home for decades. I am grateful to my Dean, Jack H. Knott, for making it clear to me, emphatically, that this project is one that I *must* complete, and for helping me to prioritize accordingly. I also thank my department head, Marlon Boarnet, for his support, especially during my sabbatical leave. I benefited also from conversations with colleagues and students at the Price School, especially those students who enrolled in the graduate seminar I taught on several occasions on this topic.

I am also blessed to have been Director of the Price School's Global Engagement Office (GEO), which gave me ample opportunity to engage with China and the world. My highly accomplished colleague, Ginger Li, as Deputy Director, has held up much more than half the sky in that capacity, along with her capable team, thereby giving me more opportunity to focus on this book.

I have also been greatly assisted by USC's inspiring, enduring and tangible commitment to a global outlook, and this attitude permeates the entire institution. Colleagues affiliated with the East Asian Studies Center welcomed my interest in China when I first arrived at USC, even though I lacked any formal training in area studies. USC's support for the U.S.–China Institute, as I explained in the Preface, was instrumental to my decision to embark on this project. The single person to whom I owe the most gratitude is my friend and colleague, Clayton Dube. As USCI's Executive Director, he has put on the most amazing programming, covering so many diverse aspects of the U.S.–China relationship. His immense network of colleagues with relevant expertise matches his own extraordinary depth of knowledge and penetrating insights. From the outset, he has consistently cheered me on, provided numerous guest lectures, and made me feel that I am not alone in this endeavor. Stanley Rosen, another esteemed USCI-affiliated colleague, has also been most generous with his time and astute advice.

It was during the 2019/20 academic year that I was given sabbatical leave by USC so that I could finish the almost-completed manuscript and pull everything together in one big final push. Here again, institutions and people made a big, appreciable difference. My friend and colleague, Mikitaka Masuyama, Executive Vice President of the Graduate Research Institute for Policy Studies in Tokyo, made it possible for me to finally come to GRIPS. Likewise, my friend and colleague, Hong Liu, Head of the School of Social Sciences at Nanyang Technological University in Singapore, arranged a most kind invitation for me. Combined, these visits gave me the space I needed to devote myself fully to the final stages of this endeavor, and I am so grateful for that. John Burns, recently retired as Dean of Social Sciences at Hong Kong University, gave me critical feedback on an early draft that prompted me to reshape it in important ways. Glenn Shive, Executive Director of the Hong Kong-America Center enthused over the project while offering wide-ranging and helpful advice. I am grateful to my friend and colleague, Thomas Zearley, who helped link me to work that he and others at the World Bank office in China were engaged in, and I benefited from insightful conversations with then-Country Directors David Dollar and, subsequently, Bert Hofman. I also benefited from the beautifully nuanced and astute observations of Dingli Shen, former Dean of the Center for American Studies at Fudan University in Shanghai. While these and other colleagues were highly inspiring, it is my fault, not theirs, if the final outcome falls short in any way.

Another institution that I feel a debt of gratitude is one where I know no one, and I presume that no one who works there knows me. Any reader of this book will quickly see that almost every chapter makes extensive references to reports produced by the Congressional Research Service (CRS). So, although I have never met anyone who works there – and, indeed, CRS appears to shun contacts from outside because they are rightfully focused on serving members of Congress and their staffs – I have come to admire the professional and non-partisan approach that is a hallmark of those well-written, balanced, and informative reports.

Routledge, as part of the Taylor and Francis Group, has been terrific to work with. Natalja Mortensen, a Senior Acquisitions Editor there, acted swiftly and decisively to move the project along from beginning to end, assisted by her capable Editorial Assistant, Charlie Baker. Her colleague, Kathryn Schell, generously helped to bring my initial proposal to Natalja's attention.

Finally, I am profoundly grateful to acknowledge the inspiring influence of my father, Walter Heikkila, a retired professor of physics, to whom I have dedicated this book. And at home, my wife Sylvia has long held up much more than half the sky, enabling me to indulge my whims and follies.

ABBREVIATIONS

A2/AD	anti-access/area denial
ADIZ	air-defence identification zone
AI	Artificial Intelligence
AIIB	Asian Infrastructure Investment Bank
AML	anti-money laundering
APT-1	Advanced Persistent Threat, Level 1
ASA	Air Service Agreements
BRI	Belt and Road Initiative
BRICS	Brazil, Russia, India, China, and South Africa
Btu	British thermal unit
CAA	Clean Air Act
CCS	carbon capture and sequestration
CDC	Centers for Disease Control and Prevention
CDM	Clean Development Mechanism
CFIUS	Committee on Foreign Investment in the United States
CIC	China Investment Corporation
CISA	Cybersecurity and Infrastructure Security Agency
CNOOC	Chinese National Offshore Oil Corporation
CNPC	China National Petroleum Corporation
CPP	Chinese Communist Party
CRS	Congressional Research Service
DEU	defective end user
DHS	Department of Homeland Security
DPP	Democratic Progressive Party
EAP	East Asia and Pacific
EAR	Export Administration Regulations

EET	emissions in trade
EPA	Environmental Protection Agency
ETA	Employment and Training Agency
FATF	Financial Action Task Force
FCCC	Framework Convention on Climate Change
FDA	Food & Drug Administration
FDI	foreign direct investment
FSMA	Food Safety Modernization Act
FSOC	Financial Stability Oversight Council
GATT	General Agreement on Tariffs and Trade
GDP	gross domestic product
GDPR	General Data Protection Regulation
GHG	greenhouse gas
GVC	global value chain
HHS	Health & Human Services
IBRD	International Bank for Reconstruction and Development
ICS	industrial control system
ICSID	International Centre for Settlement of Investment Disputes
IDA	International Development Association
IEA	International Energy Agency
IFC	International Finance Corporation
IMF	International Monetary Fund
IoT	Internet-of-Things
IPCC	Intergovernmental Panel on Climate Change
IPR	import penetration ratio
IPR	intellectual property right
IRTS	increasing returns to scale
ITO	International Trade Organization
LNG	liquified natural gas
MAD	mutually assured destruction
mboe/d	million barrels of oil equivalent per day
MIGA	Multilateral Investment Guarantee Agency
MPOs	Metropolitan Planning Organizations
NAFTA	North American Free Trade Agreement
NCA	National Climate Assessment
NG	natural gas
NMSCO	National Military Strategy for Cyber Operations
NOC	national oil companies
OPEC	Organization of Petroleum Exporting Countries
PCT	Patent Cooperation Treaty
PHEIC	Public Health Emergency of International Concern
PLA	People's Liberation Army
R&D	research & development

RCEP	Regional Comprehensive Economic Partnership
RGGI	Regional Greenhouse Gas Initiative
RMB	renminbi
SAMs	surface-to-air missiles
SAR	Special Administrative Region
SCC	social cost of carbon
SCO	Shanghai Cooperation Organization
SPR	Social Policy Research Associates
STEM	science, technology, engineering and mathematics
TAA	Trade Adjustment Assistance
TARP	Troubled Asset Relief Program
TEU	twenty-foot equivalent unit
THAAD	Terminal High Altitude Area Defence
TPP	Trans-Pacific Partnership
TRIPS	Trade-Related Aspects of Intellectual Property Rights
UHNW	ultra-high-net-worth
UNCLOS	United Nations Convention on the Law of the Sea
UNDR	Universal Declaration of Human Rights
UNFCCC	United Nations Framework Convention on Climate Change
U.S.	United States
USMCA	United States-Mexico-Canada Agreement
USTR	United States Trade Representative
WHO	World Health Organization
WIPO	World Intellectual Property Organization
WTO	World Trade Organization

1

INTRODUCTION

Statement of Aims

This book is about *policy analysis* in the United States in the era of a rising China. Policy analysis is distinct from the political processes by which policies are formulated, enacted, and implemented. Policy analysis focuses on the *substance* of policies themselves. For the purposes of this book, the policy domain of the U.S. government is carved into three broad spheres: economic policies, sustainability policies, and geopolitical policies. At a time of increasing tensions between the United States and China, it is all the more important for U.S. policy makers to focus less on rhetorical flourishes and more on the many important and substantive policy questions that are prompted by China's rise.

Policy analysis is contextual. Policies that are compelling in one time and place may be wholly inappropriate in another. The changing context that is the focus of this book is the rise of China, but the book is *not* about China per se – it is about how the rise of China alters the context in which the broad spectrum of policies in the United States should be assessed. From a U.S. perspective, the rise of China is certainly consequential, but the nature of those consequences varies by policy sphere. The rise of China looks very different from a U.S. employment and income perspective, for example, than it does from a U.S. climate change or homeland security perspective.

The analytical method applied here is essentially what economists refer to as comparative statics. For each policy domain, the book sets out the key policy issues and tradeoffs that need to be assessed, and it then examines how the balance of such tradeoffs shifts due to China's rise. That shift in the balance of policy tradeoffs is, by definition, the impact of China from a U.S. policy perspective. It is analogous, in a somewhat poetic way, to the influence of the moon on the Earth's tides. Even if one's interest is strictly earthbound, to properly analyze what is happening here on Earth, one must consider how the moon's movements pull the equilibrium in one direction or another. Likewise, the focus of this book is on how a rising China exerts its gravitational pull on U.S. policy, not so much through lobbying or negotiation, but through the very nature of its *gravitas*.

This book does not seek to compete with current news cycles, but instead articulates more enduring policy fundamentals. Administrations come and go and the views of one may be diametrically opposed to those of its predecessor, but the underlying tradeoffs do not change so abruptly, whether the topic in question is climate change, trade tariffs, or relations with Taiwan. The book strives to be neutral, to the extent that it is indeed possible to allow policy analysis to inform and shape one's thinking, rather than the converse. In this sense, it shares a certain kinship with reports produced by the Congressional Research Service that strive for the same objective: to set out the relevant policy tradeoffs in a clear, informative, well-researched, and balanced manner. Notwithstanding this balanced approach, the book does not shy away from staking out a firm viewpoint wherever that is warranted.

In order to take on a full range of policy issues in the United States impacted by China's rise, it is necessary to carve up the policy domain of the United States government in some meaningful way. To a certain extent there is an unavoidable arbitrariness to this task. Policy domains in fact lie more along a continuum rather than in discrete packets neatly labeled "Energy," "Employment," or "Defense." We take as a first cut the actual policy spheres that are set out explicitly in the structure of the Executive branch of the United States government, and in particular those corresponding to U.S. federal departments with Cabinet-level appointments. There is actually good reason for this, insofar as these Cabinet positions are themselves *endogenous* to the collective policy making process at the federal level in the United States, as these governmental structures are negotiated outcomes ratified by Congress and enacted into law. The focus of this book is on the policies themselves rather than the departments. Accordingly, the book is thus grouped into three main Parts comprising the policy domains shown in Table 1.1.

Other pertinent policy domains are tucked away within these groups. Agriculture policy as pertains to China, for example, is subsumed under trade policy.

TABLE 1.1 U.S. policy realms

Economic policies	*Sustainability policies*	*Geopolitical policies*
• Fiscal policy & deficits	• Environmental protection	• Homeland security
• Trade policy	• Urban & transport policies	• Defense policy
• Employment & income	• Energy policy	• Foreign relations

Policies entailing domestic transfer payments (Social Security benefits, Medicare and the like) are not included here because such internal transfers are not directly impacted by the rise of China. The fiscal dimensions of such payments are addressed via fiscal policy and deficits. Policies linked to food and drug safety and to disease control are subsumed under homeland security. Similarly, policy issues of a judicial nature that may be linked to the rise of China here fall under foreign relations. Finally, transportation policies are considered here in conjunction with housing and other urban policies. In all cases, these changes are intended to add analytical clarity to the overall whole.

A central premise underpinning the entire book is that there is no single U.S. policy perspective on the rise of China. Each of the topical areas outlined above has earned a meaningful place in public policy discourse within the United States. As this book makes emphatically clear, the rise of China looks very different through each one of these policy lenses. This accords with the adage that "Where I stand depends on where I sit." Each of these perspectives has validity and importance in its own right, and this is the book's foundational principle. In its chapters, the public policy issues for each of these perspectives are analyzed and assessed on their own terms. Ultimately, however, it is necessary to have a workable synthesis derived from these diverse perspectives, and the final chapter of the book is dedicated to that task.

An Overview of China's Rise

China's remarkable transformation over the past several decades has been one of the most remarkable and significant global events of our time, or indeed of any time. It is also the impetus for an examination of U.S. policy responses to this compelling phenomenon that is reshaping the economic, ecological, and geo-political contours of the globe. While each of the subsequent nine chapters examines in much more detail the relevant aspects of China's rise as they impact relevant policy domains of the United States, it is useful here to take a quick preview. Figure 1.1 sets out a sampling of three aspects of China's rise over the past three decades. To enhance comparability, the corresponding U.S. figure for the year 1990 in each case is indexed to 100.

The first graph indicates total gross domestic product (GDP) in constant 2010 U.S. dollars. Subsequent to 1990, GDP in the United States has doubled, while that of China increased thirteen-fold. China's total GDP in 1990 was a mere 9.2 percent of that of the United States, but by 2018 it was more that 60 percent. The economic impacts of China's rise are felt in terms of trade, global supply chains, deficits, and labor dislocations. Those and other economic policy realms are dealt with in Chapters 2–4. The second graph in Figure 1.1 shows total CO_2 emissions in China, again benchmarked against U.S. counterparts. Three decades ago, China's emissions were less than half of those in the U.S., but are now well over double. During this same period,

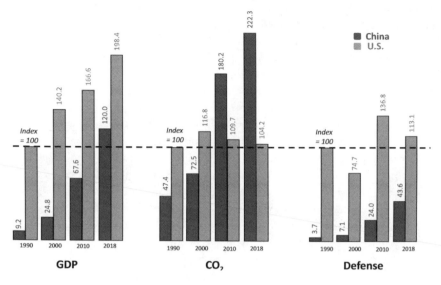

FIGURE 1.1 US–China comparisons: GDP, CO_2 and defense

Source: Based on data retrieved from:

- GDP – In constant 2010 US$, World Bank (n.d.)
- CO_2 – In million tons, Crippa et al. (2019).
- Defense – In constant 2017 US$, Stockholm International Peace Research Institute (n.d.).

U.S. emissions rose initially but then decreased gradually and are now roughly unchanged from three decades earlier. These developments have had a momentous impact on global attempts to meet the severe challenges posed by climate change. That in turn has important implications for energy and transportation policies and for the broad set of policies at the federal and more local levels that impact the day-to-day lifestyles of everyone residing in the United States. These policy implications are examined in detail in Chapters 5–7. The third graph in Figure 1.1 compares military expenditures between China and the United States. It is instructive not only to compare the two countries over time but also the corresponding shares of military expenditures as a proportion of GDP. In 1990, China's military expenditures were a mere 3.7 percent of those in the United States, but are now well over 40 percent. The growth in China's military expenditures has been more or less proportionate to the corresponding growth in China's GDP, and in that sense reflect a growing economic base. In the U.S., in contrast, military expenditures (in constant dollar terms) have scarcely grown over the past 30 years, while GDP has doubled, so the military budget in the U.S. comprises about one half of the share of GDP that it did at the outset.

Part I Economic Policy Perspectives on China's Rise

The policy focus of Chapter 2 (Fiscal Policy and Deficits) is on fiscal policy generally, and maintaining the creditworthiness of the U.S. government. This necessarily entails an examination of U.S. federal deficits, trade deficits, savings deficits, and the relationship between them. Historical trends show striking patterns in the variable growth of U.S. deficits. An appendix includes a primer on the national income accounts. The analysis shows that while the rise of China has facilitated U.S. trade deficits, a more fundamental cause lies in U.S. policies that encourage consumption in excess of production.

Chapter 3 (Trade Policy) shifts the policy focus from the U.S. deficits to trade policy. A key element of this is establishing international agreements, both bilateral and multilateral, that set the rules within which international trade is undertaken. The World Trade Organization (WTO) and other institutions for managing global trade are struggling to remain relevant in the face of rapidly evolving trade patterns. With proliferating global supply chains, international trade is increasingly between the Global North and Global South. Where the WTO has failed to produce comprehensive trade agreements, there has been a tendency to default to a plethora of bilateral or regional agreements. One positive aspect of the WTO has been the incorporation of Trade-Related Aspects of Intellectual Property Rights (TRIPS). These trade issues with China have been compounded by enforcement issues, so even where agreements are in place, they may have relatively little effect in practice. A careful examination of the renminbi (RMB) exchange rate policy suggests that the root cause of U.S. trade problems lie elsewhere.

Chapter 4 (Employment and Income) begins with an overview of the labor movement and of trends in employment and income disparities in the United States. These trends are linked to parallel developments and transformations in the modes of production of the U.S. and the global economy, with special emphasis on the more recent trend toward global value chains. The analysis then extends to the displacement of jobs in the U.S. attributable to the importation of goods from abroad, especially from China. The evidence suggests that such impacts are more likely to be in low-skilled jobs in sectors confronting significant competition from imports. This is consistent with economic theory that links wage growth to labor productivity. From this perspective, a more dynamic and forward-looking solution is to encourage investment in human capital and the high-wage jobs that skilled labor can command. Enhanced labor mobility within the U.S. can also help to redeploy individuals to those sectors that offer the best opportunities for gainful employment. The penultimate section of this chapter examines the cost-effectiveness of training and education programs, such as the Trade Adjustment Assistance Program, to boost wages. Evidence here suggests that enhancing labor mobility may be the more effective solution. Finally, the chapter concludes that consumer gains from imported goods, in the aggregate, likely outweigh negative wage impacts, but the distribution of those gains and losses may be problematic.

Part II Sustainability Policy Perspectives on China's Rise

Chapter 5 (Climate Change) begins by recounting the formation of the U.S. Environmental Protection Agency and its contentious origins in the budding environmental movement in the late 1960s. It frames environmental policies as a classical problem of regulation in the context of externalities, whereby pollutants are an unintended consequence of economic processes. The policy challenge is how to encourage productive economic activity while minimizing these negative externalities. These challenges are compounded in the context of global warming, where the requisite levels of international cooperation are difficult to sustain. From this perspective, the rise of China magnifies and intensifies the problem because it has quickly emerged as the world's leading emitter of greenhouse gases. From an environmental perspective, the rise of China is a global problem. The chapter examines the institutional challenges of coordinating an effective global response to climate change. It also delves into the underlying economic aspects of regulatory approaches within the U.S., and includes an appendix offering a primer explaining the pros and cons of a carbon tax versus the cap-and-trade approach.

More than 83 percent of Americans reside in urban areas, and Chapter 6 (Urban Policy) begins with an overview of the complexities of managing cities. China's rise impacts our cities in several ways. As China adds its immense weight to the global burden of climate change, our cities will be stressed by both adaptation and mitigation measures. The policy challenges are compounded because there is no single or unified locus of decision making that can address these challenges. These myriad individual responses are likely to impact urban life in the U.S., including travel behavior and goods movement.

China's rise also manifests itself through the global transport of people and of goods, and that has important implications for U.S. infrastructure investment in roads, seaports, airports, and rail links. China's rise is also reflected in the changing face of U.S. cities, especially those that receive concentrated inflows of people and commerce, thus posing a different set of policy challenges, from building codes to urban densities and lifestyle changes.

Chapter 7 (Energy Policy) describes the lynchpin role of energy policies and their inextricable links to economic, lifestyle, environmental, and geopolitical considerations. China's rise impacts each of these dimensions. The discussion begins with an historical overview of volatile oil and other energy prices, and the demand and supply factors that contribute to those trends. As China's economy grows, the demand for energy shifts commensurately, outstripping any parallel increases in energy supply from China. Increases in energy prices are an inevitable outcome unless additional U.S. and global supplies are forthcoming.

New technologies and methods such as fracking have added substantially to oil supplies but with likely detrimental environmental impacts. Thus, the rise of China leads to some combination of higher energy prices and increasing environmental costs here in the U.S. and elsewhere. An additional geopolitical factor arises when global supplies become fragmented or segmented into distinct nonoverlapping markets. Notwithstanding these complications, energy policies could be a positive means by which to foster across-the-board cooperation with China because both the U.S. and China have a mutual interest in seeing global energy supplies increase and global energy demand reduced.

Part III Geopolitical Policy Perspectives on China's Rise

Chapter 8 (Homeland Security) explores policies geared to the protection of the United States against a range of potential invasive threats, short of military conflict. Imported food and pharmaceuticals are doubly invasive because, in addition to crossing national borders, they are biologically invasive. It is difficult to provide the same level of regulatory oversight to such products imported from China that would apply to comparable domestic products. In the case of communicable diseases, matters are further complicated by the infectious nature of the invasive threat. As in the case of SARS and now COVID-19, communicable diseases may spread through what otherwise could be perfectly innocent interactions between Chinese and Americans. These difficulties are ratcheted up further in the case of bioterrorism, where the potential threat is linked to malignant intent, whether it be by state or rogue agents. Such viral threats can also enter the cyber realm and may target critical infrastructure. Just as nations must safeguard against the possibility of war, however unlikely or unwanted, homeland security policies are geared to potential threats from China or other potential adversaries. As China grows economically and in terms of technological sophistication, the onus is on the United States to take precautionary measures accordingly. The chapter argues in favor of working directly with China and others to develop a set of collective security protocols that address the full range of such potential homeland security concerns.

Chapter 9 (Defense Policy) begins by tracing how the stature and position of the U.S. as a global power have moved in parallel with significant military events, from the American War of Independence, the Civil War, the two World Wars and subsequent engagements in Korea, Vietnam, and elsewhere. This overview also compares U.S. military strength with other countries, noting the absolute primacy that we still maintain. It then delves into current military doctrine, as the U.S. transitions from a position of sole dominance among any number of others to a position of clear dominance but with a small number of near contenders, notably Russia and China. The analysis then examines the manner in which the rise of China impacts U.S. defense policy with a focus on three potential hot spots in the western Pacific region: North-east Asia (centered on Korea), the South

China Sea, and Taiwan. Although the U.S. continues to maintain absolute military command of the global commons, the geographic contours of the commons will inevitably be reshaped through China's rise. The defense policy challenge for the U.S. is how to adapt steadily and pragmatically to this evolving context so that we continue to protect core interests while avoiding unnecessary and potentially devastating conflict.

Chapter 10 (Foreign Relations) begins with an historical overview of America's role in the world, with a focus on the Bretton Woods era that was the foundation for the post-World War II global order. It examines the evolving role of the United Nations, the World Bank, and the International Monetary Fund (IMF) over subsequent decades along with the Cold War era and the emergence of a more assertive Global South. It also examines the role of the United States in the context of a global shift in influence, in relative terms, from West to East, and from government to non-state actors. The rise of China both contributes to and derives momentum from these developments. China's ambitious Belt and Road Initiative, together with ancillary institutions such as the Asian Infrastructure Investment Bank, set in place an alternative development paradigm to that inscribed by the Bretton Woods institutions, and this poses an implicit challenge to U.S. policies of statecraft. The rise of a more assertive China also poses policy questions for the U.S. regarding our response to developments in Taiwan, Hong Kong, Xinjiang, and other contested areas within China's core sphere of influence pertinent to its own perceived territorial integrity. The chapter also assesses the full range of global influence of China versus the United States in terms of formal alliances and institutions, economic clout, and competing models of soft power, including human rights and other aspirational endeavors.

The Trump Effect

From the outset, this book was intended to focus on the core policy challenges that *any* presidential Administration would have to contend with, and not be drawn into an overtly partisan rendering of such policy analyses. Although different administrations might respond quite differently, the underlying policy tradeoffs are essentially the same and so a robust policy analysis should apply in either case. The advent of the Trump Administration, however, may be the ultimate challenge for any such erstwhile objectivism. One reason is that policy analysis, while unavoidably political for any administration, has seemingly become quite untethered from objective analysis under Trump. Whether it be climate change, trade policy, or defense, any policy analysis that does not conform to a pre-determined ideological or partisan view is summarily dismissed in the most scathing terms. A second and related reason is that the ultimate Trump legacy may be one of undermining the very institutions that are the foundation of our system of government. For all its myriad imperfections, there is something uniquely inspiring about a carefully crafted balance of power between the three essential branches of government in the United States – and the proposition that an informed citizenry can be responsible for governing itself through democratic processes. This denigration of institutions is even more pronounced at the international level, where there is less institutional cohesion to begin with.

While these developments are indeed sobering, they also magnify the importance and necessity of a book such as this. Now is the time, more than ever, for more reasoned and reasonable voices to make themselves heard. Now is also the time for all of us, as citizens and stakeholders of democracy, to take such responsibility upon ourselves. In a democracy, it is the electorate rather than politicians who must bear the burden of blame or earn justifiable praise. It is up to us to make informed judgments. That is the premise of democratic governance, and this is an era in which that premise is being put to the test. If this book can help to frame a responsible discourse about the impacts of a rising China on public policy issues in the United States, then it will have served its intended purpose.

Intended Audience

This book aims to address the interests of several distinct groups of readers, including university students in related disciplines. There are many books about China, but this book is unique in that it describes how different U.S. policy spheres perceive the rise of China. The analysis is framed in terms of fundamental policy mandates and principles, so it should have enduring value beyond short-term current events. It is written at the level of advanced undergraduate or Master's students, and is scholarly yet highly accessible. I teach a graduate seminar on this same topic, and have been gratified by the response.

The book is also targeted to U.S. policy makers, as it provides a uniquely comprehensive assessment of how the rise of China filters through a full range of U.S. policy lenses. It should also appeal to a broader reading public, especially those with an interest in China and in public policy issues generally – especially now, as China-related issues come increasingly to the fore. Finally, this subject matter should reverberate within China itself, as many Chinese have an acute interest in how they are perceived by the United States.

References

Crippa, M., Oreggioni, G., Guizzardi, D., et al. (2019). *Fossil CO_2 and GHG Emissions of All World Countries, 2019*, Report, EUR 29849 EN, Publications Office of the European Union, Luxembourg, doi:10.2760/687800. Available at: https://edgar.jrc. ec.europa.eu/overview.php?v=booklet2019&dst=CO2emi

Stockholm International Peace Research Institute (Sipri) (n.d.). Available at: www.sipri. org/databases/milex/

World Bank (n.d.). Available at: https://data.worldbank.org

PART I

Economic Policy Perspectives

2

FISCAL POLICY AND DEFICITS

Creditworthiness

The Department of the Treasury is responsible for maintaining the full faith and credit of the United States of America as a governmental entity, as well as for ensuring the creditworthiness of the banking system and other financial institutions within the country. Creditworthiness is the key to the viability of the nation as a whole. The first U.S. Secretary of the Treasury, Alexander Hamilton recognized this "plain and undeniable truth" when he insisted that any public debt issued by the United States government should be accompanied by a clear and credible plan for its repayment. The precedent and rationale for this were set out in brilliant fashion by Hamilton in his *Report on Public Credit.*

> And as on the one hand, the necessity for borrowing in particular emergencies cannot be doubted, so on the other, it is equally evident, that to be able to borrow upon good terms, it is essential that the credit of a nation should be well established.... For when the credit of a country is in any degree questionable, it never fails to give an extravagant premium, in one shape or another, upon all the loans it has occasion to make. Nor does the evil end here; the same disadvantage must be sustained upon whatever is to be bought on terms of future payment. From this constant necessity of borrowing and buying dear, it is easy to conceive how immensely the expenses of a nation, in a course of time, will be augmented by an unsound state of the public credit.
>
> *(Hamilton, [1790] 1961–1979)*

The United States government has struggled to follow Hamilton's wise dictum. As shown in Figure 2.1, from the turn of this century, a seemingly inexorable trend has been steadily increasing federal budget deficits, and the Congressional Budget Office projects that this trend will continue for the next decade. The outsized impact of the financial crisis of 2007–2008 is vividly apparent, as the budget deficit plunged (in terms of its depiction on the graph) from $160.7 billion in 2007 to $1,412.7 billion just two years later. The deficit was then steadily reduced until 2015 whereupon it once again resumed its precipitous descent. Each year that the U.S. government runs a deficit, that shortfall is added to the public debt, which is now approaching $20 trillion, or $20 *million million*. Currently, the total public debt in the United States exceeds $50,000 per capita, or $130,000 per household. Because the public debt is growing much faster than the economy as a whole, the cumulative effect is more sobering yet. At the turn of this century, total public debt was 33.7 percent of GDP. Ten years later it grew to 60.8 percent and is now at 80.8 percent. The Congressional Budget Office projects that the federal debt will continue to rise gradually over the next decade, and it is expected to reach 98.3 percent of GDP. Alexander Hamilton would be aghast.

The mechanism by which the U.S. government borrows funds is the sale of promissory notes by the Department of Treasury, typically with denominations of $1,000.[1] Clearly, a very large volume of such securities (notes, bills, or bonds) must be sold to the public in order to raise sufficient funds to cover such enormous deficits. This is where Hamilton's admonition about creditworthiness is so crucial. The inherent value of a promissory note is derived from the credibility

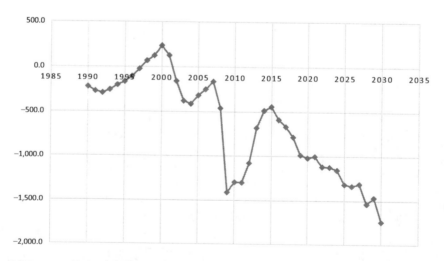

FIGURE 2.1   Federal deficit, 1990–2030

Source: Congressional Budget Office.

of the person or institutional entity that is making the promise to repay. At stake is not only with the creditworthiness of the U.S. government, but also of the entire banking and financial system, and its mandate reflects this concern. Congress is ultimately responsible for passing laws that shape the financial sector. For example, in 2010, following the most acute and severe financial crisis that the United States had undergone in almost a century, Congress passed the *Dodd–Frank Wall Street Reform and Consumer Protection Act* which mandated a sweeping set of reforms to the manner in which the financial sector is regulated. In the area of financial sector stability, for example, this entails stronger oversight by the Department of the Treasury of large interconnected firms, enhanced coordination with state-level regulators and their international counterparts, ongoing research on issues of financial stability, addressing executive compensation in the financial sector, limiting the scope of non-core activities by banks, and regulating the manner in which mortgage securities are packaged and traded. A similar scope of activities for the Department of the Treasury is mandated by Dodd–Frank regarding consumer protection.[2]

The U.S. Department of the Treasury also is actively engaged in helping to manage the global financial system. The United States has by far the largest economy in the world, roughly equivalent to the next two largest (China and Japan) combined. Moreover, the U.S. and global economies are increasingly intertwined through trade of goods and services and through corresponding financial flows and transfers. The basic architecture of the current system is a legacy of the Bretton Woods conference of 1944, which established the International Monetary Fund (IMF) and the International Bank for Reconstruction and Development (IBRD, now the World Bank). While some of the specific concerns motivating the principal actors of that time have lapsed into history, many fundamental issues of managing a highly inter-connected international financial system have remained, evolved, and intensified. One central issue is managing a system of currency exchange, international banking, and financial flows that encourages free trade while supporting stability and avoiding systemic crises. The complexity of these issues is evidenced by the persistence of repeated financial crises throughout the world, including the Eurozone. The Department of the Treasury has a direct interest in anticipating and, where possible, averting such crises because the interconnectedness of the global system heightens the risk of contagion from one region to another. For example, if U.S. financial institutions hold assets in banks abroad, and if those banks fail, their troubles can quickly rebound back home. Although the fundamental concern from a U.S. Treasury perspective is the creditworthiness and stability of U.S. financial institutions, its purview is necessarily global in scope. Likewise, issues of fraud and money laundering fall within the Treasury's ambit, including in the context of the war on terrorism. To manage these international responsibilities the Department of Treasury works in part through the IMF and the World Bank, in part through multiparty forums such as G7 or

G20, and in part through bilateral talks and direct intervention, for example, monitoring and regulation of financial flows.

Attention: Deficit Disorder

As noted above, it is the past accumulation of federal government deficits that is now approaching $20 trillion in U.S. government debt held by the public. It is useful to examine this in more detail because it is so fundamental to the credit-worthiness of the United States government and the viability of the nation's Treasury. It is also important for understanding where China fits into the picture. A most fundamental point is that the U.S. federal deficit and the nation's trade deficit are linked. In fact, this has been a notable topic of research among macroeconomists who address the so-called twin deficit hypothesis. This issue emerged initially during the Reagan years when the U.S. federal deficit and the current account (trade) deficit both grew in tandem. The twin deficit hypothesis subsequently received renewed attention for similar reasons (Bartolini and Lahiri, 2006). Empirical research has led to mixed findings, but there is a general consensus that if these federal and current account deficits are not twins, they are at least "cousins." This point is reinforced by virtue of the way in which the national income accounts are defined.

As explained in more technical detail in the Appendix to this chapter, there is an intrinsic and unshakeable relationship between deficits that arise in different sectors of the economy. That is, the current account deficit (essentially, the excess of imports over exports) in the U.S.[3] will *always* be equal to the sum of the federal deficit plus the shortfall of domestic savings relative to private sector investment. This recognition arises from the fact that any income received as part of the country's Gross National Product is either consumed directly or set aside (in the form of taxes or savings) to support public sector expenditures and private sector investment. If the amount set aside is insufficient, the balance can only be restored through net imports. Stated starkly: if we "eat" more than we produce, we must borrow the differential from abroad. This is why some policy analysts advocate measures to increase savings, such as a tax on consumption, as a means of reducing pressure arising from large government sector deficits without having to increase the current account deficit. It bears repeating that if any one sector (government, private, or external trade) is out of balance, the others must and will compensate.[4]

Budgets and Stakeholders

The preceding sections have outlined the overall responsibilities of the U.S. government within the context of the federal debt and the viability of the financial system as a whole. Clearly, the composition and size of the federal budget are of considerable concern to a great many stakeholders from all corners of society. The two basic options for reducing the deficit are to either reduce outlays or increase revenues. The politics either way are seemingly intractable, as expressed well by the Bowles–Simpson Report that assessed the likely response to any broad proposal to address the deficit: "countless advocacy groups and special interests will try mightily through expensive, dramatic, and heart-wrenching media assaults to exempt themselves from shared sacrifice and common purpose" (2010, Preface).

A closer examination of the federal budget sheds light on the nature of the challenge. Total outlays are projected by the Congressional Budget Office to rise from $4.6 trillion in 2020 to $7.5 trillion ten years later, for an increase of $2.9 trillion. The lion's share of this increase (all but $0.4 trillion) is attributed to *non-discretionary* budget items, such as net interest payments on prior debt and mandatory programs, such as Social Security, Medicare, and Medicaid. The entitlements stemming from these programs are specified by law, based on age and medical condition of recipients and similar factors beyond the immediate purview of the budget process. The share of discretionary outlays, which comprised 30 percent of the total in 2020, will fall to less than 24 percent by 2030. Moreover, defense expenditures account for roughly half of all discretionary outlays. That provides precious little room for reducing the budget deficit under current laws regarding mandatory outlays.

Because the federal deficit is such a sizeable proportion of the budget, there is little hope for reducing the deficit without some combination of steep spending cuts or major increases in tax revenues. Demographic trends are not helping. Baby Boomers will be retiring in droves over the next decade or more, with the Census Bureau[5] projecting the number of elderly (defined as 65 years of age and older) to jump from 56.1 million in 2020 to 80.8 million just 20 years later, and then to 94.7 million by 2060. This is a major factor driving the increase in mandatory outlays on Social Security, Medicare, and Medicaid. That is a strong demographic current to swim against while striving to shore up the budget. The size of the Baby Boomer generation is significant not only from a budgetary perspective but also politically. Older citizens tend to vote in larger proportions than their younger counterparts, and they also tend to be highly protective of Social Security, Medicare, and other benefits that are geared to elderly segments of the population.

By 2030, more than seven–eighths of the federal budget will be composed of mandatory entitlement programs, interest rates, or defense. Hence, only one-eighth of the federal budget is categorized as discretionary non-defense programs. Even if all such programs were eliminated *in their entirety*, it would not be sufficient to eliminate the deficit. This leaves little option but to raise tax revenues, but this can also be a perilous path for political leaders, especially during periods of economic uncertainty. Calls for tax reform and revisions to the tax code are not readily acted upon through corresponding legislation. Much is at stake in many of the arcane provisions of the federal tax code, and

Washington, DC, is crowded with lobbyists who are keen to see their favored tax breaks secured. Populist agitation against tax increases has a long-storied tradition throughout the history of the country, and their vehemence is no less than that of those who insist upon a continuation of the entitlements that they feel are only their fair due.

Because of the political difficulties in reducing government outlays or raising tax revenues, it may be that comprehensive political accords are more likely to be passed than piecemeal efforts that may fall prey to special interests. One example of such an attempt, as alluded to earlier, is the National Commission on Fiscal Responsibility and Reform of 2010, known as the Bowles–Simpson Commission, after its two co-Chairs. The bi-partisan commission was appointed with a view to incorporating a wide range of perspectives and interests into one comprehensive proposal for reducing the federal debt and restoring a sound fiscal basis for the U.S. government. Thus, 14 of the 18 members were required to vote their approval of the final report in order for it to be forwarded to Congress. That did not occur, but 11 of 18 Commission members did manage to reach a compromise in support of a report that outlined six broad policy recommendations:

1   Undertake discretionary spending cuts on government outlays.
2   Reform the tax code to broaden the tax base while lowering tax rates.
3   Reduce health care costs.
4   Restore fiscal integrity to the Social Security program.
5   Lower the costs of other mandatory programs.
6   Improve the budgetary process.

The lack of consensus within the Commission on these measures led to a political stalemate that was broken only by more drastic sequestration measures specified by the *Budget Control Act* of 2011. Sequestration is a process by which across-the-board cuts in non-exempt programs, including defense, are automatically enforced (Lynch, 2013). In effect, U.S. federal budget issues have become so contentious politically that compromise is increasingly untenable and automation trumps seasoned judgment or reason. Ultimately, some compromise along the lines of the Bowles–Simpson Commission is needed in order to address the budget deficit effectively in a thoughtful and far-reaching manner. Otherwise, as the Commission Report warns, "If the U.S. does not put its house in order, the reckoning will be sure and the devastation severe." It is sobering to recognize that the potential scope for bipartisan cooperation is even less likely now than it was ten years ago.

A somewhat different political landscape envelopes the policy realm of financial regulation. The trick is to find the right balance in any regulatory framework. Too much regulation of the financial sector stifles innovation, restricts the flow of financial capital, limits the opportunity for higher rates of return on investments, and undercuts the inherent dynamism of market processes. Too little regulation leaves vulnerable groups exposed to underhanded practices of potentially unscrupulous lenders and other purveyors of financial services. The financial crisis of 2008 in the United States created a sea change in the public perception of the appropriate balance. As Warren (2010, p. 391) wrote during the aftermath, "The consumer credit market is broken. Businesses have learned to exploit customers' systematic cognitive errors, selling complex credit products that are loaded with tricks and traps." More broadly, a problematic combination of financial flows and regulatory practices contributed during the first decade of this century to a large volume of mortgage loans being purveyed to homeowners whose ability to repay was questionable. The wholesale commodification of mortgages exacerbated the problem, as there was no longer a simple or direct relationship between borrower and lender. Instead, myriad promised income streams to be generated by repayment of those loans were rearranged and repackaged as mortgage-backed securities brokered by Wall Street firms and supported by a range of financial and regulatory institutions, both public and private. As Baily, Klein, and Schardin observe:

> Poorly underwritten mortgages, predatory and misleading lending practices, and overly complex mortgage products served to inflate the asset bubble that ultimately created the financial crisis. Such products and practices were allowed to proliferate in part because oversight was fragmented among several regulatory agencies, leading to "significant gaps and weaknesses" in supervision.
>
> *(2017, p. 29)*

The Dodd–Frank Act of 2010[6] responded to the aftermath of the ensuing financial crisis by, among other things, consolidating dispersed regulatory responsibilities under one newly created Financial Stability Oversight Council (FSOC). As one of the most articulate and effective advocates for such reform, Warren wrote:

> With no single agency or set of laws to provide a meaningful regulatory foundation, a new approach to consumer financial regulation is in order: a single, new commission aimed at regulating consumer financial products. Such an agency could develop expertise and make regulatory changes to respond to market innovations. [It] would have the authority to cover all relevant products – all home mortgages, all credit cards, all payday loans, etc. – thereby ending the spotty regulation that depends on whether the product was issued by a state bank, federal bank, a thrift, a credit union, or a group of private investors.
>
> *(2010, p. 392)*

It remains to be seen whether this new set of institutions will ultimately be successful in avoiding future financial crises. Professor Charles Murdock (2011) provides a thorough and thoughtful analysis of the provisions of Dodd–Frank, concluding that had it been in effect a decade earlier, it would have helped mitigate significant aspects of the financial crisis, but not in all regards. He finds that Dodd–Frank does not fully address risks of moral hazard due to asymmetric knowledge regarding the intrinsic quality of financial assets, and he is quite scathing of ratings agencies that, in effect, sold their integrity. Murdoch's final assessment bears repeating:

> Overall, Dodd–Frank is a substantial step in the right direction, but additional steps still need to be taken. The overall key to avoiding financial crises is integrity and courage. The corporate culture needs to reject the ethic reflected in '[let's] hope we are all wealthy and retired by the time this house of cards falters.' Moreover, politicians need the courage to stand up to lobbying pressure and do what is necessary to curb the concentration of power in our financial system and management incentives for short-term profits.
>
> *(Ibid., p. 1325)*

China's Growing Foreign Reserves

The rise of China enters this picture in several ways, most notably through its financing of a significant portion of the U.S. government debt through its purchase of securities (bills and notes) auctioned by the U.S. Department of the Treasury. As explained earlier, the sale of these promissory notes is the operational means by which the government of the United States borrows funds to cover the federal deficit. Those securities are financial assets that can be bought and sold in the open market. As recently as 1970, no more than 5 percent of publicly held federal debt was in the hands of foreigners.[7] That proportion is now at about 40 percent, up from almost half a decade ago. China is the nation with the largest holdings, accounting for over 18 percent of the foreign total,[8] which puts China's share of all publicly held U.S. debt at just over 7 percent. China's position vis-à-vis U.S. federal debt is viewed with alarm by some. A central concern is that the U.S. economy may be increasingly vulnerable to severe disruption if China should decide to sell off a large portion of its substantial holdings of U.S. Treasury securities. If China were to flood the market with Treasury bills and notes, it surely would have a depressive effect on the price of these assets, and this translates immediately into an effective increase in the interest rates paid by the U.S. government.[9] That is, in order to borrow a specified amount to cover the federal deficit, the Department of the Treasury would have to promise more to lenders in return.

To assess the validity of this concern, it is useful to consider the issue first from China's perspective. One begins with the recognition that China's foreign exchange reserves, at over $3 trillion,[10] are now *by far* the largest in the world, and are roughly 2.5 times the value held by second-place Japan. The growth in these reserves is directly correlated to the trade surplus that China has maintained over many years now as part of its export-led growth strategy. Chinese exporters are paid in their own currency, Chinese renminbi (RMB), while those abroad who are importing Chinese goods are typically paying in U.S. dollars or some other foreign currency. For each transaction, the Bank of China accepts payments in foreign exchange from the importer and provides an equivalent value in RMB to the exporter, calculated at the official exchange rate. The reverse transaction occurs when China imports goods from abroad. Each year China continues to run trade surpluses, the Bank of China amasses a larger pool of foreign reserves.

The People's Bank of China also accumulates foreign reserves through its interventions in foreign exchange markets to stabilize the value of its currency, the yuan (RMB).[11] This has been another contentious issue from a U.S. perspective, and is discussed in more detail in Chapter 3 (Trade Policy). An important element of the monetary policy for any country outside the U.S., including China, is whether and how to set the value of its currency relative to the U.S. dollar and other currencies. One option is to adopt a flexible exchange rate policy that relies on foreign exchange markets to set the value through free exchange. Although flexible exchange rates are advocated by many economists, one disadvantage is that currency fluctuations may introduce an unwanted element of uncertainty, especially for those engaged in import and export activities.[12] National policy makers may have other reasons for wanting to keep their currency at a specified level, based on internal political and economic considerations. In the case of China, the value of the yuan has not been determined through flexible exchange rates but has instead been managed through purposeful foreign exchange operations conducted by the People's Bank of China. For more than a decade until 2005, US$100 was sufficient to purchase over 800 RMB, but by early 2014 that same US$100 was scarcely sufficient to purchase 600 RMB. Subsequently, the RMB has depreciated to the point that by 2020 US$100 could purchase about 700 RMB. When the official exchange rate specifies a value of the yuan that is too low relative to market valuations, as has been the case for much of this time, demand for the yuan will normally exceed the available supply. To prevent this excess demand from raising the value of the yuan, the People's Bank of China can print additional renminbi and use them to purchase (or "sop up") the extra U.S. dollars and other foreign currencies that are on offer in foreign exchange markets to purchase Chinese yuan at the official exchange rate. This is in fact what China has done when the value of the RMB is relatively low, and this added significantly to the pace at which China accumulated foreign reserves – even more quickly than can be attributed to its very large net export earnings over that same period.

One immediate consequence of this rapid accumulation of foreign reserves by the People's Bank of China is a direct and equivalent increase in China's domestic money supply. For each purchase of a U.S. dollar the People's Bank issues an equivalent amount of its own currency that is then injected into the Chinese domestic economy. This increase in the money supply tends to have an inflationary effect as more money is bidding for the available goods and services. That in turn makes Chinese products more expensive relative to those abroad. Thus, the inflationary consequences of accumulating foreign reserves may partially undermine the initial rationale for intervening in foreign exchange markets in the first place. To counteract this effect, the People's Bank could sell securities (the Chinese counterpart to U.S. Treasury securities discussed above), thereby withdrawing renminbi from the domestic economy.[13] As the supply of those securities increases, their price will fall and so the interest rate will rise.

A closely related issue is the valuation of the RMB relative to the U.S. dollar. We examine this issue in more detail in Chapter 3, from the perspective of U.S. trade policy. The valuation of the RMB relative to the U.S. dollar is also of keen interest to the U.S. because it affects financial flows above and beyond those directly associated with goods trade. If the valuation of the RMB is kept artificially low, then the price of financial assets denominated in U.S. dollars will be correspondingly high. From an investment perspective, however, the calibration of one currency unit to another is somewhat arbitrary and not so crucial. For investors, what is more important is the *rate of change* in this valuation. As we have seen, the RMB has appreciated in value over the past 15 years relative to the U.S. dollar, and conversely, the dollar has depreciated commensurately relative to the Chinese yuan. This depreciation in the value of the U.S. dollar relative to the yuan lowers the rate of return realized by Chinese investors in U.S. denominated assets.

China's foreign reserve holdings have become so immense that they cannot be viewed as merely an operational account to facilitate China's ongoing currency operations. These foreign reserves at $3 trillion constitute a substantial store of wealth in their own right and thus should be managed as such. It is for this reason that China in 2007 created a sovereign wealth fund with an initial registered capital of $200 billion, the China Investment Corporation (CIC), which, by the end of 2018, had a total net asset value of over US$856 billion. These assets are acquired by CIC through special bonds issued by the Finance Ministry.[14] In accordance with the so-called "Santiago Principles," a set of generally accepted principles and practices articulated by the International Working Group of the International Forum of Sovereign Wealth Funds (IWG, 2008), the CIC undertakes a longer-term portfolio wealth management strategy. This entails investments in financial and real assets that CIC deems to have enduring growth potential, with more than half of its investments in 2018 directed to the United States (CIC, 2018).

Co-dependence of Creditor and Debtor

It is in this context that we may assess the concern that the U.S. economy might be vulnerable to offloading by China of U.S. securities that it holds. If China were to do so, it would in effect be exchanging one type of asset (namely, U.S. Treasury securities) for some other store of wealth. The alternatives for China are somewhat limited. According to the International Monetary Fund, U.S. dollar denominated securities comprise more than 60 percent of allocated world foreign exchange holdings, with Euro holdings next at about 20 percent. No other foreign currency comes close. Because its foreign reserve holdings are so immense, it would not be practical for China to shift the bulk of its portfolio to euro or Japanese yen denominated securities – it would engulf those markets. Moreover, the impacts of a massive sell-off of U.S. Treasury securities would be damaging to China's own interests. From a portfolio perspective, the depressive effect on those U.S. securities prices caused by the commencement of a sell-off could translate into a substantial loss of financial wealth for China's portfolio as a whole. In the face of a sell-off, the U.S. Treasury would have little alternative in the short run but to lower the price of securities in order to meet the borrowing requirements arising from the federal government deficit. As we have seen, that in turn corresponds immediately and directly to a sharp increase in the effective rate of interest. China might decide to switch a portion of its wealth holdings from U.S. securities to tangible wealth, such as real estate, equity shares of publicly listed companies, or other forms of direct investment in the United States. As described above, China is indeed beginning to do more of this through its sovereign wealth fund. It is doing so, however, as a supplement rather than as an alternative to its growing foreign reserves.

Thus, China is also in a bind, and it is in effect the same bind that the U.S. is in. As McKinnon puts it:

> China with its stable dollar exchange rate is key in holding the world's dollar-based monetary system together. If the People's Bank of China wearies of seemingly unending purchases of low yield dollar assets in order to stabilize its exchange rate, other emerging markets would surely follow. The result would be catastrophic, not only for the United States itself, but also for China and other emerging markets which would face a precipitate fall in their exports to their most important trading partner.
>
> *(2013, p. 458)*

A Parable

China's situation is analogous to that of a shopkeeper or factory owner who habitually extends loans to her best customer, Uncle Sam. In certain regards things don't look so bad. The factory owner is able to keep her employees busy producing wares that she ships to her customer, while she herself is accumulating an impressive stock of financial wealth in the form of IOUs from a customer whose credit is well established within the broader community. The customer in turn appears to be content issuing IOUs in exchange for goods produced and sold by the factory owner, though in the back of his mind he must surely know that a day of reckoning cannot be postponed indefinitely. At some point, the factory owner and her employees are going to need more than IOUs to sustain themselves. The employees have been very productive, exceeding their own consumption levels. If the factory owner declines to accept any more IOUs, the customer would be forced to retrench with a sharp reduction in goods purchased, perhaps compelling the factory owner to begin laying off staff. Both the customer and the factory owner may see it in their interests, therefore, in the short run at least, to maintain the fiction that these IOUs are worth more than they really are, when in fact the claims on tangible wealth exceed the wealth to be had. So long as the broader community continues to treat these IOUs as a commonly accepted medium of exchange, the game can continue.

At some point a clever factory owner may work out an arrangement to compensate her employees directly with the product of their own labor, keeping a cut for herself in return for her entrepreneurial role. The workers will be better off than before because they are now able to earn a larger portion of the output that they themselves produced. The factory owner will be better off with a smaller share of real output rather than a larger share of dubious claims on future output. Another option the factory owner may have is to begin acquiring real property owned by the customer (perhaps even the shirt off his back, assuming it fits her) in lieu of IOUs. If these are consumable goods, then the customer will find his consumption reduced commensurately. If the real property acquired by the factory owner is in the form of productive assets, then future output derived from these properties will belong to the factory owner rather than the customer. Either way, the customer will have little choice but to learn to live within reduced means.

This parable, though quite simplified, does capture the essence of the co-dependency that has bound the economic fates of the United States and China to each other. In effect, the United States is consuming more than it produces, while China is doing the reverse. Bernanke (2005) emphasized the role of a "global savings glut" as a primary causal factor behind these trends, contending that the root of the U.S. trade deficit lies outside the United States. From his perspective, the U.S. current account deficit is the "tail of the dog" – that is, he believes it is primarily the *outcome* of savings (net of investments) from China and elsewhere. This large volume of global savings enters the United States in search of investment opportunities, thus driving down interest rates and culminating in an abundance of liquidity, thereby bolstering the value of real and financial assets. This buoyancy in asset prices coupled with lax financial regulations prior to the financial crisis encouraged a high degree of leveraging, i.e., debt to equity ratios. In the housing market, this led to the issuance of a substantial volume of mortgage-backed financial securities that promised a stream of mortgage payments that ultimately was not forthcoming, thus leading to the financial crisis of 2008. This entailed not only a collapse of housing markets but also of many of the financial institutions that dealt in such securities.

China and the U.S. Asset Bubble

In the aftermath of the financial crisis, the Federal Reserve Board undertook a policy of "quantitative easing" in an attempt to shore up asset prices. As explained by Joyce et al. (2012), this is an unconventional approach to monetary policy that under more normal circumstances would focus on setting short-term interest rates through lending operations within the banking system. Because of the severity of the financial crisis, the emphasis of quantitative easing instead was for the Fed to purchase large volumes of financial assets (both Treasury securities and corporate bonds) to stem if not to reverse their wholesale decline in value. This was coupled with a Troubled Asset Relief Program (TARP) established by the Department of the Treasury to take steps to keep households and businesses afloat. The combination of foreign and domestic holdings, supplemented by the Federal Reserve's accelerated purchases, was essential for financing the mushrooming total federal debt. According to Martin Feldstein (2013b), this approach is fraught with difficulties, and will lead inevitably to an increase in U.S. interest rates:

> Long-term interest rates are now unsustainably low, implying bubbles in the prices of bonds and other securities. When interest rates rise, as they surely will, the bubbles will burst, the prices of those securities will fall, and anyone holding them will be hurt. To the extent that banks and other highly leveraged financial institutions hold them, the bursting bubbles could cause bankruptcies and financial-market breakdown.

Chinese (Money) Laundering?

One final issue to note here in the financial context of the rise of China is that of illicit financial flows. In the aftermath of 9/11, this has risen as a priority in the United States. Most forms of organized criminal activities – including a full range that includes terrorism, drug trade, or white-collar crimes – entail a significant flow of money. As with any kind of enterprise, financing of one kind or another is the very bloodstream of the corpus of such organizations and networks. If the U.S. Treasury Department can cut off their flow of funds, it may be possible to incapacitate them. Internationally, the focus of such enforcement is an anti-money laundering (AML) regime with a Financial Action Task Force (FATF) at its core. As the world's second largest economy, China's financial networks and flows interpenetrate increasingly with that of the international economy, and the United States in particular. Consequently, the potential for the flow of illicit funds increases commensurately. China became a full member of FATF in June 2007, and indeed it has its own reasons to be vigilant regarding money laundering. As Heilmann and Schulte-Kulkmann (2011, p. 643) point out, "Combating money laundering [in China] is inseparably connected to the sensitive policy domain of 'countercorruption and discipline inspection.'" But as they point out as well, FATF has no capacity to sanction member states, so China may have an incentive to implement commended best practices on a selective basis.

A Tale of Two Perspectives

How the United States might best respond to the fiscal policy challenges posed by the rise of China depends on one's understanding of the underlying causal mechanisms. As we have seen, there are two distinct views on this question. One view, generally termed the expenditure perspective, emphasizes the combined U.S. federal deficit and trade deficit. The other view, as articulated by Bernanke (2005), emphasizes the importance of a global surplus of savings relative to investment expenditures outside the U.S., and especially within China. These two perspectives are not mutually exclusive or contradictory, and in fact both are derived from the same fundamental accounting relationships. They are two sides of the same coin of the realm, so to speak, but they do emphasize different underlying causes with correspondingly different policy responses. If one views the problem primarily in terms of a "global savings glut," then the logical policy response is to find ways to reduce savings – or, equivalently, to increase consumption rates – abroad. Several factors are likely in play, including interest rates, demographic trends, trade barriers, and institutional considerations. For example, individual Chinese have a strong motivation to save for their old age because of the dearth of state-sponsored retirement income or health care. Moreover, as a consequence of its longstanding one-child policy, only recently set aside, China has an ageing population, with a typical child having an *exclusive* claim, as it were, on both parents and all four grandparents.

Another contributing factor to the outflow of savings from China is that financial institutions there do not allocate savings effectively. China's macroeconomic policies compel households to endure artificially low interest rates on bank deposits so that subsidised capital can be lent to state-owned enterprises. This in turn spawns an active shadow banking system as described by Ayyagari et al.:

> Historically, a large share of bank funding has gone to state-controlled companies, leaving companies in the private sector to rely more heavily on alternative financing channels.... The corporate bond market in China

is crippled by excessive government regulation and the lack of institutional investors and credit rating agencies to help price the debt accurately.

(2010, p. 3052)

Because financial institutions in China are unable to allocate savings effectively there is extra incentive to send those savings abroad. As Bernanke (2005) points out, the Chinese government itself acts effectively as a financial intermediary by issuing bonds to soak up domestic savings and then using the proceeds to purchase U.S. Treasury securities. Tsui (2011) points to another problem with financial institutions in China, based on a highly leveraged nexus between local government infrastructure investments, land acquisition, and bank lending. All of these considerations, and more, may help to explain why China contributes in such large measure to a "global savings glut" that in turn seeks out investment opportunities in the United States, where there is a corresponding deficiency in savings. If this channel of causality is seen as primal, then there is strong incentive for the U.S. to call for changes within China that would favor consumer spending over savings. Ultimately, of course, it is up to the Chinese government to determine whether a reduction in net savings is in its own interests. Our focus here is on U.S. policy.

This brings us to the "homegrown" perspective on U.S. deficits. Rather than emphasizing a savings glut overseas, this view focuses on the persistence of federal and current account deficits within the United States. From a policy perspective, the challenge is to increase tax revenues relative to government expenditures and/or to increase domestic savings relative to investments. As we have already discussed, the "twin deficits" hypothesis is one variant of this approach. It draws on the empirical observation that the federal and the current account deficits in the United States grew in tandem to one another during the 1980s and then again during the past decade or more. It is clear from an understanding of the national income accounts, however, that the observed empirical correlation between these two deficits does not imply a direct or necessary underlying causal link. As we have seen, there are three distinct surpluses/deficits that must balance out in the aggregate:

- federal deficit – the excess of government expenditures over taxes;
- current account deficit – the excess of imports over exports;
- savings deficit – the excess of investment over savings.

To the extent that the aggregate of taxes and savings falls short of the corresponding aggregate of government expenditures and investment, net imports must make up the shortfall.[15] As Bergsten (2009, p. 34) puts it, "budget rectitude is the only reliable instrument for preserving a viable level of external deficit." Ultimately, the best way for the United States to address the challenge posed by the rise of China is to take measures to put our own house in order. Some variation of the recommendations of the Bowles–Simpson Commission are required to reduce federal government outlays on social security and health care while reforming the Federal Tax Code to broaden the tax base. At a more macroeconomic level, measures to increase aggregate savings in the United States are also in order. This entails a shift away from an economic model that relies so heavily on consumer expenditures to sustain aggregate demand. Some countries, such as Singapore and Australia, have introduced mandatory savings programs to boost savings while others have relied on a consumption tax. In the end, the problem is not that China has accumulated a pool of savings that the United States borrows from. The problem is that the United States runs deficits that result in its need to borrow.

Appendix: A Primer on the National Income Accounts

Imagine an economy in which there were no government sector and no foreign trade – only households and businesses. Total expenditures on U.S. produced goods and services comprise two corresponding elements: consumption expenditures (C) by households and investment expenditures (I) by businesses. Of course, because each transaction involves two parties, for every dollar of expenditure over the course of the year, there is an equivalent amount received as income. This total income will have been disposed of in either of two ways: consumption (C) or set aside as savings (S). Thus, the complement to consumption from an expenditure perspective is investment, while the complement to consumption from an income perspective is savings. But, because total expenditure is equivalent to total income, it follows immediately that investment equals savings ($I = S$).

Now, if we add a government sector to this economy the same idea applies but in a broader way. Specifically, we must add government outlays (G) to the expenditure side of the story. And, on the income side, we recognize that some income may be taxed away by the government. So now, on the expenditure side, it is investment and government outlays combined ($I + G$) that form the complement to consumption. Likewise, on the income side, savings and taxes (T) combined ($S + T$) are the complement to consumption. But, as before, we know that every dollar expended was received as income, so now we have it that investment and government outlays combined must equal savings and taxes combined:

$$(I + G) = (S + T)$$

From this, it immediately follows that any government deficit must be counter-manded by an equivalent surplus of savings over investment, so that

$$(S - I) = (G - T)$$

Note that this is an *identity*,[16] and so it is true by definition. In that sense it is akin to saying that whatever is not "eaten" by one sector is left over for another.

We have demonstrated that in a closed economy with no foreign sector, the government sector can run a deficit only if the private sector sets aside sufficient savings to accommodate it. But of course the United States is in fact a decidedly open economy and so we must now consider how to include the foreign trade sector into this same analysis. We begin by considering expenditures by foreigners on products or services produced in the United States. These exports (X) from the United States abroad are now included as an expenditure item on U.S. goods and services along with consumption, investment and government outlays. Now it is the combination of $(I + G + X)$ that constitutes the complement to consumption on the expenditure side of the economy. Likewise, we can add imports (M) to the United States from abroad as another means of disposing of income, alongside savings and taxes as the complement to consumption. As before, every dollar expended is also a dollar earned, so now we have

$$(I + G + X) = (S + T + M)$$

Equivalently, we see that

$$(G - T) = (S - I) + (M - X)$$

Prior to the introduction of a foreign sector, we had seen that for the government sector to run a deficit, the private sector had to leave an equivalent amount on the table. Now, with the introduction of the foreign sector, we see that the government sector deficit may be compensated for either by an excess of savings over investment, *or* by an excess of imports over exports receipts, *or* by some combination of the above.

The previous equation is often rearranged simply as

$$(G - T) + (I - S) + (X - M) = 0$$

This is a rather beautiful expression because it sets out quite concisely a fundamental truth about the economy. It refers to three distinct sectors, respectively: the government sector, the private sector, and the foreign trade sector. It shows clearly and succinctly that an imbalance in any one sector must be compensated for somehow by the others. They are mutually interdependent, so any analysis that relies on only a partial view (e.g., by focusing on foreign trade alone) is likely to be flawed and/or misleading.

Discussion Questions

1   We have seen that for any deficit in the trade sector $(X-M)$, there will always be an offsetting surplus in the government $(G-T)$ and/or private sector $(I-S)$. In order to reduce the U.S. trade deficit, which do you think is the better option: to reduce government expenditures relative to taxes $(G-T)$ or increase private savings relative to investment $(I-S)$? What are the policy levers you might call upon to attain such outcomes? Which option is more politically feasible?

2   Can you provide a persuasive argument supporting the hypothesis that persistent U.S. trade deficits are sustainable over the long run? If yes, would you advocate in favor of doing so? If not, what will have to "give" to make it work? In other words, what mounting economic stresses or strains will make it impossible to sustain those trade deficits?

3   The chapter uses a simple shopkeeper analogy to depict the trade relationship between the United States (customer) and China (shopkeeper). Is this analogy too simplistic? If yes, what key aspects of the true relationship are missing, and why do they matter? If not, what does this tell us about the fundamentally asymmetric economic relationship between the two countries?

Notes

1   Online purchases of Treasury securities are available in increments of $100. See www. treasurydirect.gov.

2   More detailed information about Dodd–Frank in the context of the Department of Treasury is available at www.treasury.gov/initiatives/wsr/Pages/facts.aspx. See also Baily, Klein and Schardin (2017).

3   These fundamental national accounting relationships hold true for *any* country, but our focus here is on the U.S. economy.

4   Interested readers are referred to the Appendix for a more detailed explanation of these fundamental national income relationships.

5   See also Vincent and Velkoff (2010).

6   It is officially called the *Dodd–Frank Wall Street Reform and Consumer Protection Act*.

7   See Table 4–7 in OMB (2019).

8   Japan's holdings are comparable to China's, at 17 (versus 18) percent of all foreign holdings of U.S. debt. See, also, Labonte and Nagel (2015).

9   To use a simple example, consider a note issued by the U.S. Department of Treasury promising to pay the bearer of that note $1,000 one year hence. Suppose that initially the market price for this financial asset were $950. That translates into an effective interest rate of 5.3 percent, which equals a return of $50 on an initial investment of $950. If the market price were suddenly depressed to $900, the effective interest rate rises substantially, to 11.1 percent, which reflects a return of $100 on an initial investment of $900.

10   China's foreign exchange reserves, now at about $3 trillion, peaked at almost $4 trillion in 2014. See https://tradingeconomics.com/china/foreign-exchange-reserves.

11   The term yuan and renminbi may be used more or less interchangeably. Both refer to the official currency of the People's Republic of China.

12   Many economists would argue that financial risk derived from uncertainty over flexible exchange rates may be addressed most effectively through a futures contract

that guarantees an indicated rate of exchange for a specific quantity to be exchanged on a given future date.

13 This counteracting strategy is commonly referred to as "sterilization." See Higgins and Klitgaard (1998, 2004) for a clear explanation.

14 See Caixin Online (2013).

15 Or, as indicated in the Appendix: $(I-S) + (G-T) \equiv (M-X)$.

16 More formally, a relationship that is identically true (i.e., true by definition) should use a three-pronged equals sign ($\equiv$) rather than the usual two-pronged sign ($=$).

References

Ayyagari, Meghana, Asli Demirguc-Kunt, and Vjislav Masimovic (2010). "Formal versus Informal Finance: Evidence from China," *The Review of Financial Studies*, 23(8), 3048–3097.

Baily, Martin, Aaron Klein, and Justin Schardin (2017). "The Impact of the Dodd–Frank Act on Financial Stability and Economic Growth," *The Russell Sage Foundation Journal of the Social Sciences*, 3(1), 20–47.

Bartolini, Leonardo and Amartya Lahiri (2006), "Twin Deficits, Twenty Years Later," *Current Issues in Economics and Finance*, 12(7).

Bergsten, C. Fred (2009). "The Dollar and the Deficits: How Washington Can Prevent the Next Crisis," *Foreign Affairs*, 88(6), 20–38.

Bernanke, Ben (2005). "The Global Saving Glut and the U.S. Current Account Deficit," Homer Jones Lecture, U.S. Federal Reserve Board, Washington, DC.

Bowles–Simpson (2010). *The Moment of Truth: Report of the National Commission on Fiscal Responsibility and Reform*, Washington, DC: The White House.

Caixin Online (2013). "Putting China's Forex Reserves to Better Use," *Wall Street Journal*, Market Watch, 23 July.

CBO (2015). *The Budget and Economic Outlook: 2015 to 2025*, Washington, DC: Congressional Budget Office.

CIC (2018). *Annual Report*, Beijing: China Investment Corporation.

Feldstein, Martin (2013a). "America's Misplaced Deficit Complacency," commentary on *Project Syndicate*. Available at: www.project-syndicate.org.

Feldstein, Martin (2013b). "When Interest Rates Rise," commentary on *Project Syndicate*. Available at: www.project-syndicate.org.

Hamilton, Alexander ([1790] 1961–1979). *The Papers of Alexander Hamilton*. Edited by Harold C. Syrett, et al. 26 vols. New York: Columbia University Press.

Heilmann, Sebastian and Nicole Schulte-Kulkmann (2011). "The Limits of Policy Diffusion: Introducing International Norms of Anti-Money Laundering into China's Legal System," *Governance*, 24(4), 639–664.

Higgins, Matthew and Thomas Klitgaard (1998). "Viewing the Current Account Deficit as a Capital Inflow," *Current Issues in Economics and Finance*, 4(13), December.

Higgins, Matthew and Thomas Klitgaard (2004). "Reserve Accumulation: Implications for Global Capital Flows and Financial Markets," *Current Issues in Economics and Finance*, 10(10), September/October.

IWG (2008). *Sovereign Wealth Funds: Generally Accepted Principles and Practices*, International Working Group of the International Forum of Sovereign Wealth Funds.

Joyce, Michael, David Miles, Andrew Scott, and Dimitri Vayanos (2012). "Quantitative Easing and Unconventional Monetary Policy: An Introduction," *Economic Journal*, 122, 271–288.

Labonte, Marc and Jared Nagel (2015). *Foreign Holdings of Federal Debt*, CRS Report RS22331, Washington, DC: Congressional Research Service.

Lynch, Megan S. (2013). *Sequestration as a Budget Enforcement Process: Frequently Asked Questions*, Washington, DC: Congressional Research Service.

McKinnon, Ronald (2013). "The U.S. Saving Deficiency, Current Account Deficits, and Deindustrialization: Implications for China," *Journal of Policy Modeling*, 35, 449–458.

Murdock, Charles (2011). "The Dodd–Frank Wall Street Reform and Consumer Protection Act: What Caused the Financial Crisis and Will Dodd–Frank Prevent Future Crises?," *SMU Law Review*, 64, 1243–1328.

OMB (2019). *Analytical Perspectives: Budget of the U.S. Government, Fiscal Year 2020*, Washington, DC: Office of Management and Budget.

Tsui, Kai Yuen (2011). "China's Infrastructure Investment Boom and Local Debt Crisis," *Eurasian Geography and Economics*, 52(5), 686–711.

Vincent, Gregory and Victoria Velkoff (2010). *The Next Four Decades: The Older Population in the United States, 2010 to 2050*, Washington, DC: U.S. Census Bureau.

Warren, Elizabeth (2010). "Redesigning Regulation: A Case Study from the Consumer Credit Market," in Edward Balleisen and David Moss (Eds.), *Government and Markets: Toward a New Theory of Regulation*, Cambridge: Cambridge University Press, pp. 391–418.

3

TRADE POLICY

Tricks of the Trade

President Calvin Coolidge is famously reputed to have declared that "[T]he chief business of the American people is business. They are profoundly concerned with producing, buying, selling, investing and prospering in the world."[1] Nearly one hundred years later, trade policy has resumed a position of prominence as President Trump has assailed perennial U.S. trade deficits with friends and rivals alike, but especially with China. The trade data are indeed quite startling; for decades, the United States has routinely run the biggest trade deficits in the world, up to $627 billion in 2018, according to U.S. Census data. China looms very large in this regard, both as our largest trading partner (alongside Canada and Mexico) and, most especially, as the single country that accounts for two-thirds of the total U.S. trade deficit. The immense size of the United States economy gives rise to a seeming contradiction. Although the U.S. is the largest trading nation on Earth, with a total merchandise trade in excess of $4 trillion in 2018, merchandise trade is nonetheless a relatively small proportion (20.8 percent) of total GDP compared with Japan (29.9 percent), China (34.0 percent), Germany (72.1 percent) and the world as a whole (46.1 percent).[2] U.S. trade is a big deal, but U.S. investment, government expenditures, and especially consumer spending are even more so.

As noted by Williams and Donnelly (2012), U.S. trade issues enter the policy domain in several important ways. As a key component of gross domestic product, trade flows are intrinsic to *macroeconomic* debates. This was especially evident in our prior discussion in Chapter 2 (Fiscal Policy and Deficits) of the pivotal role of balance of payments in the national income accounts. U.S. trade issues also have an important *strategic* dimension as a means of fostering bilateral and global alliances through free trade agreements and the like. At a *micro-economic* level, trade flows, including those of intermediate goods, extend the supply chains that underlie production and distribution of goods and services. At a *household* level, trade flows expand the range of goods and services available to consumers while also altering the employment landscape. It is not surprising, therefore, that trade issues can be multifaceted and contentious within the sphere of U.S. policy debates.

U.S. merchandise trade, both inbound and outbound, impacts a wide range of economic sectors. Leading the list of U.S. exports are aircraft and spacecraft, cereals, other grains and seeds, plastics, miscellaneous chemicals, meat, animal feed, fabrics, optics, and medical instruments. Conversely, the U.S. imports large quantities of mineral fuel and oil, electrical machinery, motor vehicles, machinery, apparel, furniture, toys, and organic chemicals.[3] Additionally, U.S. trade in *services* has risen slowly but steadily over the past ten years, from 5 percent to 7 percent of GDP. This trend reflects the fact that the U.S. economy is itself increasingly dominated by services, and advancing telecommunications technology enables such services to be delivered instantaneously on a global scale. Part of this trend, too, entails services whereby the United States appears to be "importing" tourists or students from abroad, but from an economic trade perspective we are in fact exporting tourism or education services – the recipients are just coming to the U.S. to take delivery of their purchases!

Two principal economic drivers of trade are comparative advantage and economies of scale. The former concept dates back to the early nineteenth-century British economist, David Ricardo, who famously articulated the principle by which gains of trade can make both trading partners better off even when one country may enjoy an absolute advantage, more prowess as it were, in all goods. His fundamental insight was that comparative advantage is based on the opportunity cost associated with the underlying production technologies and resource endowments. This Ricardian principle would help explain, in particular, why nations with very different technologies and endowments might find mutual benefit through trade, where each specializes in sectors that build on its respective comparative advantage. Notwithstanding this fundamental insight, during much of the twentieth century, intra–industry trade was conducted increasingly between nations with *similar* production technologies and endowments. For example, trade between the United States and Europe dominated much of the twentieth-century global trade, with similar advanced manufactured goods being traded back and forth. To explain this, economists pointed to increasing returns to scale (IRTS), together with consumer preferences for variation in product types within sectors. Rather than having each nation produce a small share of every type of good, specialization combined with trade could generate additional gains from trade in the aggregate. Paul Krugman, a leading proponent of this IRTS approach, in a paper based on his Nobel Prize acceptance speech, observes that in recent years the world appears to be returning to a more classical scenario of trade based on differences: "For the last two decades, however, the trend has been in the other direction, with rapidly rising trade between advanced economies and much poorer, lower-wage economies, especially China.... The old trade theory has regained relevance" (Krugman, 2009, p. 569).

Reflecting this trend, multilateral trade negotiations through the World Trade Organization (WTO) and other venues have focused increasingly on these "North–South" issues, as discussed in more detail below. From the perspective of many developing countries, the current system favors the industrialized countries. Trade based on comparative advantage tends to perpetuate the technological edge already enjoyed by the more developed countries. This view is reflected to varying degrees in notions of the "development of under-development," popularized by Andre Gunder Frank (1966) in the context of U.S. trade with Latin America in the mid-twentieth century or "flying geese" formations, originally attributed to Kaname Akamatsu of Japan in the 1930s but popularized decades later, whereby a hierarchy of national economies is maintained through progressive stages of development (see Kojima, 2000, for an account).

From a U.S. perspective, persistent and growing trade deficits are widely interpreted as a sign of economic decline, with a particular concern for the consequences of trade for domestic employment. Trade imbalances are seen as evidence that the U.S. is "exporting jobs" to China, a topic that we explore in much more detail in Chapter 4 (Employment and Income). The prominence of China in this context is evident in Table 3.1, where the U.S. merchandise trade imbalance with China in 2018 ($419.5 billion) is almost precisely equivalent to the next ten largest countries *combined*. Evolving patterns of trade flows reflect an ongoing economic restructuring, but the causes of restructuring are rooted

TABLE 3.1 Top sources of U.S. merchandise trade imbalances, 2018 (in $ billions)

China	*−419.5*
Next ten countries:	*−419.7*
Mexico	−80.7
Germany	−68.1
Japan	−67.2
Ireland	−46.7
Vietnam	−39.5
Italy	−31.9
Malaysia	−26.3
India	−20.8
Thailand	−19.4
Canada	−19.1

Source: International Trade Administration, U.S. Department of Commerce.

more in developments that are internal to the economy (Hornbeck, 2013). Notwithstanding this point, trade is often viewed in contentious terms. Fordham and Kleinberg (2011) analyze survey data to reach the unsurprising conclusion that Americans' views of China as a geo-political power are often directly linked to their own perceived self-interests regarding trade.

Several issues arise in this context. One is to understand the source of these very large and persistent merchandise trade deficits, and to what extent China is in some sense to blame. Following on that is the question of remedial action, and in particular what kinds of specific actions against China, if any, may be warranted. These questions in turn are set within the larger context of what institutions and mechanism are the appropriate venue for the United States in responding to U.S.–China trade imbalances.

Is China to Blame for U.S. Merchandise Trade Deficits?

Does China Play by the Rules?

As explained below in more detail, the World Trade Organization (WTO) embodies the rules of the game regarding international trade. Its 164 members[4] are expected to ascribe to its rules and regulations, and they in turn receive membership benefits flowing from the relatively free trade that it promotes. China acceded to the WTO in 2001, a milestone event that was widely expected at the time to accelerate China's transition to a more Western-style economy, promoting economic development and reforms within China while creating bountiful opportunities for the United States and other countries to benefit from trade with China. By most accounts that has not happened. As summarized by a recent Congressional Research Service report:

> Major areas of concern expressed by U.S. policymakers and stakeholders include China's alleged widespread cyber economic espionage against U.S. firms; relatively ineffective record of enforcing intellectual property rights (IPR); discriminatory innovation policies; mixed record on implementing its World Trade Organization (WTO) obligations; extensive use of industrial policies (such as subsidies and trade and investment barriers) to promote and protect industries favored by the government; and interventionist policies to influence the value of its currency.
>
> *(Morrison, 2018, p. i)*

While the Trump Administration began protesting China's perceived shortcoming in this area in a much more amplified manner, a review of past annual reports by the United States Trade Representative's (USTR) office clearly indicates that the perceived problems with China's compliance date back to previous administrations as well. For example, in 2012, a USTR report summarized a range of grievances pertaining to intellectual property rights:

> A wide spectrum of U.S. rights holders reports serious obstacles to effective protection and enforcement of all forms of IPR in China, including patents, trademarks, copyrights, trade secrets, and protection of pharmaceutical test data. Compounding these obstacles is the troubling direction that China's policies in the IPR area have taken recently. These policies include China's efforts to link eligibility for government preferences to the national origin of the IPR in products. In addition, many companies are concerned that Chinese government agencies are inappropriately using market access and investment approvals as a means to compel foreign firms to license or sell their IPR to domestic Chinese entities. Further, for many industries, sales of IP-intensive goods and services in China remain disproportionately low when compared to sales in similar markets that provide stronger environments for IPR protection and more open market access. These concerns, coupled with the size of China both as a consumer marketplace as well as a globally significant producer of a wide array of products, mean that China's protection and enforcement of IPR must remain key priorities for U.S. trade policy.
>
> *(USTR, 2012, p. 26)*

Keupp et al. (2009), in their survey of U.S. and other foreign firms operating in China, found that Chinese courts were not an effective means for securing IPR protection, and that a range of informal strategies were used instead by such firms, including technological specialization, de facto secrecy, internal and external "*guanxi*" (relations), and customer education. Such measures constitute a kind of rearguard action by which foreign firms in China attempt to ward off systematic attempts by Chinese institutions to trade market access for transfer of intellectual property while awaiting whatever additional protection might be wrought through other remedies.

It is clear that a fairly strong bipartisan consensus has emerged within the U.S. that China is not playing by WTO rules, and this has been borne out as well by actions brought against China by the U.S. and others through WTO dispute resolution mechanisms. China's trade-related violations, when viewed comprehensively in the aggregate over a sustained period of time, strongly suggest that China's policies are intended to promote its own economic developmental aspirations while taking full advantage of its WTO membership. Some observers view China as a "free rider" in this context, whereby it seeks to reap the benefits of liberalized trade but without doing its fair share in promoting and supporting the underlying principles espoused by WTO (Morrison, 2018). One might argue that every country, including the United States, seeks to promote its own trade agenda within WTO and is not above bending the rules as part of an ongoing strategic interplay. What makes China unique, however, is not only its enormous size as a global trading partner, but also its fundamentally different political, economic, and institutional configurations. Rules of the game that might implicitly presume a liberal democratic set of driving values may not fit China's circumstances. We return to this topic below.

Is China a Currency Manipulator?

Another recurring accusation is that China is a currency manipulator, though this is one charge that the Trump Administration actually dropped in early 2020 during the course of its trade negotiations with China. The IMF's *Annual Report on Exchange Arrangements and Exchange Restrictions* details a bewildering collection of currency regimes among the 190 member countries and territories falling within its purview. There are conventional pegs, crawling pegs, crawl-like arrangements, pegged exchange rates, floating exchange rates, currency boards, stabilized arrangements, and more. The variety across countries seems to be as richly diverse as the languages one finds across the world. Exchange rates are a means of "translating" between these currencies. But just as there are a few dominant languages that stand above all others, there are also a relatively small number of dominant currencies and their associated economic regions. The United States and 43 other countries or territories constitute an effective U.S. dollar domain, comprising two-ninths of the world's GDP. Then there is the Eurozone, of almost comparable size. Next is China's renminbi, with an economic domain roughly half the size of the U.S. in terms of GDP. The Japanese yen, the British pound and myriad other currency zones follow in rapidly diminishing magnitudes. The currency zones are in effect *relative price regimes*, especially of traded goods, because they are the bases for converting values from one zone into those of another. As noted above, there are distinctly different approaches for managing how any such price regime interacts with others. The U.S. dollar and the euro are free floating, so that the relative price of these currencies is determined through market transactions on foreign currency exchanges.

In the case of China, the exchange value of the renminbi is managed through what the IMF terms a "crawl-like arrangement," and this has been the source of considerable friction with the United States and other countries that argue that the RMB's upward "crawl" has been too slow. They have charged China with "currency manipulation" through deliberate efforts to undervalue the RMB as a means of boosting Chinese exports and limiting its imports from abroad. From this perspective, persistent U.S. deficits are caused at least in part by underpricing of Chinese products in global markets. Cline (2010) and Bergsten (2009) are representative of this viewpoint.

It is helpful to trace through the logical sequence of events arising from an appreciation of the Chinese yuan. At root, this is a price effect – in the initial instance, prior to other adjustments that might arise – as goods from China become more expensive relative to their foreign counterparts while, conversely, imports from abroad become more affordable to those operating within the Chinese RMB zone. The RMB has appreciated over the past decade relative to the dollar by roughly a 4 to 3 ratio. In the first instance, this implies a 33 percent price increase to U.S. importers of Chinese export goods denominated in RMB.[5] Normally, one would expect reduced demand for such imports in response to an effective price increase such as this. In fact, however, the U.S. trade deficit with China *increased* substantially during this same period, so it may be that other factors are in play. For example, it is possible that the demand for imports from China is inelastic, especially in the short run, in which case an increase in the RMB would actually lead to an *increase* in total U.S. expenditures on Chinese imports – the so-called J-curve effect. The OPEC oil crisis in the 1970s is a dramatic illustration of such an effect, where a quadrupling of oil prices caused U.S. total expenditures on imported oil to rise, not fall, because oil imports did not fall sufficiently to offset the increase in oil prices. Thus, calling for an appreciation of the RMB in order to reduce the U.S. trade deficit with China presumes that the U.S. demand for such imports is relatively elastic. That is an empirical question that is not clear *a priori* either way, and the literature is quite mixed on this point. A related consideration pertains to the substitution effect. As the RMB appreciates in value, the U.S. may switch to imports from other countries that compete with China, such as Vietnam, Thailand, Indonesia, India, or even Mexico. If these countries were almost competitive with China prior to the rise of the RMB, they might be well positioned to step in and fill the gap as exports from China begin to wane. Again, the extent to which substitution would occur is an empirical question that would need to be borne out by the evidence.

Thorbecke and Smith (2010) distinguish between "simple" and "processed" exports from China, where the latter refer to goods that are part of an integrated East Asian production chain. In such cases, comprising roughly half the total volume of exports from China, the higher value-added components are typically produced in Japan, Korea, or Taiwan, with final assembly occurring in China. A notable example of this is cited by Morrison (2013). Apple video iPods imported from China in recent years cost $144 to produce abroad, but only $4 (or 2.8 percent) of that value added was attributable to Chinese labor. The remaining $140 of value added was based on more advanced manufacturing processes and technologies in Japan, Taiwan, and elsewhere. Because the final stage of assembly was in China, however, the entire $144 for each item produced counts officially as a U.S. import from China. The item retailed in the United States for $299, so the lion's share of the value added was derived from U.S. distribution, retailing, and corporate earnings. Several lessons apply. One is that trade data can be quite misleading, so that items listed as imports from China may not be wholly so, especially in the case of complex global supply chains. Another point is that the prime beneficiaries of this process were in fact U.S. technology, distribution, and retail firms – as well as U.S. consumers. Thorbecke and Smith conclude that an appreciation of the RMB would only impact "simple" exports from China, such as toys or textiles. For processed goods, a concomitant appreciation of other Asian currencies would be required as well in order to reduce U.S. imports. Otherwise, the relatively small value-added components associated with China would just move elsewhere, with little impact on the overall U.S. balance of trade.

Yet another consideration pertains to internal adjustments within the Chinese economy in response to an appreciation of the yuan. Wage pressures within China might be reduced as workers enjoy enhanced purchasing power with their RMB-denominated incomes. Factory owners might find it more economical to import advanced machinery and equipment from abroad, thereby boosting productivity and cost efficiency for Chinese goods. These and other internal adjustments within China could mitigate the effects of an appreciation of the Chinese yuan. It is also important to distinguish between nominal and real changes in the exchange rate. For example, suppose that all prices and wages in China were to double over some period of time due to inflation while prices in the U.S. and the dollar–RMB exchange rate remained unchanged. In such a case, one U.S. dollar would still buy the same quantity of Chinese yuan, but the latter would now purchase fewer goods. Thus, even though the nominal exchange rate remains unchanged in this example, the effective purchasing power of the U.S. dollar has diminished relative to the yuan. Likewise, by similar reasoning, U.S. goods become more attractive to people holding Chinese yuan. This example is not merely hypothetical, as inflation rates in China have exceeded those in the U.S. in recent years, so that the nominal appreciation of the RMB has been augmented by this purchasing power effect.

Currency and trade issues should also be considered within the broader context of industrial policy and economic development, especially with respect to developing countries. The most notable success stories from the past half-century have been countries that invested heavily in promoting advanced industries, thereby bootstrapping themselves up to a higher level of productivity and global competitiveness. According to Rodrik's (2010, p. 90) succinct summary: "poor countries become rich by producing what rich countries produce." He argues that economic transformation within developing countries is often hampered by institutional barriers, incomplete information, deficient capital markets, and other market failures. It is for this reason that Japan, Taiwan, Korea, and other economic success stories entailed strong policy interventions designed to allocate resources to these transformative sectors. Prior to 2001, China also engaged a full range of such measures that were necessarily curtailed after its accession to the WTO. Short of that, intervening in foreign exchange markets to keep the value of the renminbi low is a kind of second-best policy option for China to sustain its economic transformation. Again, Rodrik says:

The reason that undervaluation of the currency works as a powerful force for economic growth is that it acts as a kind of industrial policy. By raising the domestic relative price of tradable economic activities, it increases the profitability of such activities, and spurs capacity and employment generation in the modern industrial sectors that are key to growth.

(Ibid., p. 90)

The question, of course, is whether such a strategy of *currency devaluation cum industrial policy* is permissible within the overarching WTO framework. This brings us full circle to the basic complaint by many that China is engaged in currency manipulation in order to promote exports and limit imports. A fundamental point here is that as a signatory to the WTO accord, the United States is not at liberty to impose punitive measures arbitrarily in response to perceived currency manipulation by China. Instead, it must seek recourse through the established WTO mechanisms. According to Staiger and Sykes, who combine economic and legal reasoning in their assessment of this point:

The only provision of WTO law specifically relating to currency practices is to be found in Article XV(4), concerning "exchange action" that would "frustrate the intent" of GATT. To discern whether the intent of GATT is frustrated, it is necessary to ascertain whether currency practices in fact have effects that are equivalent to the effects of measures that GATT/ WTO law prohibits, an issue on which any complaining nation has the burden of proof.

(2010, p. 586)

In their carefully argued analysis, they conclude that "the claim that China has engaged in currency manipulation in violation of IMF law is dubious and quite possibly impossible to prove regardless of the merits" (ibid., p. 592). Several considerations contribute to this conclusion. One interesting point addresses reasonable expectations about what the exchange rate ought to be. At the time that China joined WTO, the RMB had been effectively pegged to the dollar for many years. Subsequent to that, the RMB has only appreciated relative to the dollar, whereas prior experience might have suggested a continuation of the peg. This makes it difficult to argue *prima facie* that "the intent of GATT is frustrated." Prior expectations aside, an economic analysis of the impacts of exchange rate effects hinges on a seemingly arcane technical point regarding the invoicing practices of Chinese exporting firms. It is often the case that firms invoice in U.S. dollars or third country currencies rather than in renminbi, in which case the effect of any alleged currency manipulation is muted. A related point concerns alleged damages to the U.S. economy that might form the basis for redress. As Morrison and Labonte point out:

> According to economic theory, a society's economic well-being is usually measured not by how much it can produce, but how much it can consume ... the lasting effect of an undervalued RMB is to increase the purchasing power of U.S. consumers.
>
> *(2013, p. 34f.)*

Finally, one should not lose sight of the root cause of persistent U.S. deficits. As Hornbeck (2013, p. 6) puts it, "The fundamental cause of the U.S. trade deficit is excess spending by U.S. consumers, business, and government. In essence, Americans consume more than they produce." Those who argue that Chinese currency manipulation is to blame are not so different from a family who blames a department store sale for the household's insolvency.

What Is the Appropriate Institutional Venue for Responding to China?

The World Trade Organization

The WTO not only sets the rules of the game for international trade, it also provides a dispute mechanism for adjudicating trade disputes. There is a growing perception, however, that the WTO is not well equipped to do the job. As Wendy Cutler, a prominent former trade negotiator for the USTR, flatly asserts:

> The World Trade Organization (WTO) would ideally help reduce friction between the United States and China, but it is not up to the task given its outdated rules and governance challenges. The crisis ... points to this deeper problem: the failure to keep up with developments in the trading and investment landscape. An equally pressing issue is the WTO's slowness to respond to technological advancements, particularly the digital economy. Simply put, the trade regime is in trouble and in urgent need of reform.
>
> *(Cutler et al., 2019, p. 1)*

To assess this claim, it is useful to briefly review the original purpose of the WTO when founded on January 1, 1995, with the United States as one of 76 initial member countries. WTO membership subsequently has more than doubled, with China joining on December 11, 2001. The WTO is itself a successor to the General Agreement on Tariffs and Trade (GATT), founded shortly after World War II. At that time, over 50 countries were engaged in an attempt to create an International Trade Organization (ITO) that was to have been a third and complementary partner to the IMF and the International Bank for Reconstruction and Development (IBRD) (now the World Bank). Although the United States was active in those efforts, it proved impossible to pass ratifying legislation in the U.S. Congress, in effect causing the ITO to be still-born. From this historical perspective, the WTO can be seen as the living rein-carnation of the ITO.

Much of the twentieth century entails a concerted effort to reduce tariff rates through multiparty negotiations between countries, especially between the United States and Europe. As Robert Baldwin (2009) recounts, U.S. tariff rates peaked shortly after the Smoot–Hawley Tariff Act of 1930 and fell steadily afterwards, from 51.2 percent in 1931, to 26.3 percent as the first round of GATT negotiations got underway in 1946, to 12.2 percent in 1960 just prior to the Kennedy Round of trade negotiations, to just 4.8 percent in 2004 during the Doha Round of negotiations. Recent decades have also witnessed a steady increase in the value of merchandise trade (defined as the sum of exports and imports) as a proportion of gross domestic product. For the world as a whole, merchandise trade rose steadily from 29.9 percent of global GDP in 1985 to 46.1 percent by 2018. For the United States, the trade proportion increased from 13.1 percent to 20.8 percent over the same interval. In the case of China, merchandise trade grew from 22.6 percent of its GDP in 1985 to 62.7 percent by 2005, before falling back to 34.0 percent by 2018. Part of the observed decline in merchandise trade in China relative to Chinese GDP from 2005 to 2018 may be attributed to the rising value of the RMB over that same interval, as the value of China's GDP would be enhanced in U.S. dollar terms. China's total merchant trade is now comparable to that of the United States[6] – with twice the proportion for an economy that is half the size.

The transition from the GATT to the WTO in 1995 marked a significant milestone in global trade. Although the WTO is a direct outgrowth of the Uruguay Round final agreements, and the WTO inherited all the prior GATT agreements and protocols, the creation of the WTO marked what one observer at the time call a "dramatic departure from international trade practice" and "an entirely new legal system for international trade dispute resolution that [may] greatly erode traditional concepts of state sovereignty" (Shell, 1995, pp. 833, 831). The WTO's Dispute Settlement Body is, by mutual agreement of all WTO members, the final arbiter of any trade disputes that may arise between countries. The dispute settlement process is intended to move swiftly – relative to GATT standards – to a final and binding resolution. By joining, WTO member countries agree to abide by the rulings of the Dispute Settlement Body in responding to any disputes they may have with trading partners. In turn, by virtue of mutuality, each member country benefits from the fact that other countries also cede such rights.

Intellectual Property Rights: TRIPS Abroad

The same Uruguay Round of GATT negotiations that led to the creation of the WTO also gave rise to the Trade-Related Aspects of Intellectual Property

Rights (TRIPS) agreement that came into effect under the WTO auspices in 1995. With TRIPS, for the first time, intellectual property rights were incorporated under a full-scale multilateral accord. The United States had been a strong advocate for such an agreement, as befits its status as the world's technological leader.[7] According to one early observer, "TRIPS has teeth. It contains detailed, comprehensive substantive rules and is linked to the WTO's comparatively hard-edged dispute settlement system in which treaty bargains are enforced through mandatory adjudication backed up by the threat of retaliatory sanctions" (Helfer, 2004, p. 2). Although TRIPS was a significant milestone in terms of formal international recognition of intellectual property rights (IPR), the formal protection of IPR dates back to Venetian laws passed almost 500 years earlier. From the outset, the incentives for passing such laws stemmed less from an interest in protecting the rights of individual inventors and more from a desire to link innovation to economic development interests of the state by fostering a competitive advantage (May, 2002).

From an economic standpoint, intellectual property is like most any other property or asset that has income-producing potential. It is analogous in certain regards to having secured early ownership of a well-located property in a growing metropolis. Those who arrive later have little choice but to pay high rents to those who secured the initial property rights. The relationship between early and late arrivals can perpetuate itself as the owners of key properties can use the economic rents thus derived to invest in further capital accumulation. Advocates for IPR protection argue that without such protections, there would be less incentive to innovate. This debate over IPR is particularly poignant in the area of pharmaceuticals. On the one hand, research & development (R&D) costs can be very high for new pharmaceuticals, with substantial downside risks, and so there is a strong case for incentivizing R&D companies through IPR protection. On the other hand, there are compelling moral grounds for making such products widely available to people suffering from afflictions that could be cured or alleviated by such products, regardless of their ability to pay. At a practical level, Archibugi and Filippetti (2010) argue that Western nations should focus more on fostering ongoing innovation rather than impeding developing nations from acquiring knowledge associated with past innovations. They point out that for many industrial processes, it is the tacit knowledge surrounding leading technologies that is most essential, rather than the codified knowledge embodied in IPRs. They report that pharmaceuticals, however, are a notable exception to this rule. The TRIPS Agreement also does provide some accommodation to governments that might be faced with public health or other emergencies.

In recent years China has emerged as a significant holder of intellectual property in its own right, with significant growth year by year. Only the United States, Japan, and Germany have registered more global intellectual property filings under the Patent Cooperation Treaty in recent years. All indications are that technology transfer is an important priority for China as part of its overall economic growth and development strategy. In some respects, these are favorable trends from a U.S. perspective. First, China is a party to TRIPS and so is obliged under these international treaties to provide effective IPR protection within its jurisdiction, and to do so in a manner that does not discriminate against foreign entities. As more Chinese firms develop intellectual property, China has increasing incentive to provide additional IPR protections through its court systems and related institutions. Notwithstanding these factors, however, IPR protection in China continues to pose a significant problem for U.S. and other foreign investors in China.

From a rational choice perspective, WTO membership can be seen to benefit members through an institutionalized process for negotiating and enforcing broad agreements on tariffs, merchandise trade, trade in services, intellectual property rights, and related trade issues. Of course, the real test is whether the "value added" from this process is perceived by each member to exceed the cost of limitations imposed. If that test is not met, then the WTO framework is more likely to be replaced by the emergence of regional trading blocs or unilateral action.

Unilateral Action

While the dominant trend for global trade over the past few decades has been toward a multilateral approach as embodied by the World Trade Organization, the Trump Administration moved abruptly toward an overtly unilateral approach. While this was a departure from past practices (Morrison, 2019), it can be viewed as a sign of growing dissatisfaction with the perceived ineffectiveness of WTO's dispute resolution mechanism, especially with regard to China. In a 2019 report to Congress reviewing China's WTO compliance, the U.S. Trade Representative argued that:

> It is unrealistic to believe that actions at the WTO alone would ever be sufficient to force or persuade China to make fundamental changes to its trade regime. [No] matter how many cases are brought at the WTO, China can always find a way to engage in market-distorting practices.... Accordingly, while the United States will use the WTO where possible – and will continue efforts to encourage other countries to work with us at the WTO – the United States must also take action outside the WTO to encourage China to move in a more open and market oriented direction.
>
> *(USTR, 2019, pp. 10–11)*

To address China's compulsory expropriation of intellectual property from U.S. companies, the Trump Administration turned to Section 301 of the U.S. Trade Act of 1974. Its "procedures apply to foreign acts, policies, and practices that the USTR determines either (1) violate, or are inconsistent with, a trade agreement; or (2) are unjustifiable and burden or restrict U.S. commerce" (Morrison, 2019, p. 1). As Harper (2018) points out, Section 301 and the WTO dispute mechanism are alternative mechanisms – one unilateral and the other multilateral – for addressing trade grievances. Another unilateral mechanism, one that the Trump Administration used to impose steel tariffs, is Section 232 of the Trade Expansion Act of 1962, which pins its rationale on national security concerns (Fefer and Jones, 2020). China responded with counter-measures, which led to a "trade war" that became a defining aspect of the Trump Administration's posture toward China. These tariffs and related measures were then used as leverage in direct bilateral negotiations with China.

Another perceived problem with the WTO regime is that it is oriented towards statutes and processes rather than outcomes. As Harper (2018, p. 129) relates, "Even if the WTO makes a finding against the offending nation, they will not force a nation to take any specific action, instead allowing the nation to come up with their own method for correcting the issue." This leaves China wiggle room, the USTR contends, to pretend to comply with WTO rulings while not fundamentally changing its approach to trade. This has led the Trump Administration to emphasize outcomes rather than procedures in its trade negotiations with China. While there is a certain pragmatic quality to such a "managed trade" approach, it also has some serious drawbacks. Even if the negotiated bilateral trade outcomes are attainable, which is not a given, those outcomes may come at the direct expense of other trading partners, including important allies of the United States. For example, for China to meet its negotiated commitments of increased agricultural imports from the United States, it may do so through commensurate reductions in agricultural imports from Brazil, Canada, and others. This could quickly lead to a chain reaction of additional managed trade agreements between China and many competing trading partners, with no assurance that the negotiated commitments will "add up" in the aggregate. (Bown, 2020; Hofman, 2020). An additional irony is that at the same time that the United States is insisting that China import more U.S. merchandise, it is also strengthening procedures for prohibiting sales to China on national security grounds of an increasing number of goods categories.[8] As Bown (2020, p. 13) aptly points out, "China cannot increase imports of products that the United States refuses to export."

Unilateral measures can be an attractive option when the WTO and other multilateral alternatives are seen to be ineffective and time-consuming. Many observers, however, point to the negative longer-term consequences of undermining a multilateral system that the United States and others put so much effort into constructing (Fefer and Jones, 2020; Harper, 2018; Koh, 2019; Williams, 2019). Such measures to address U.S. trade deficits with China are no doubt helpful on the margin, but as we saw in our prior discussion of fiscal policy and deficits, the fundamental source of the U.S. balance of trade deficit lies in the fact that Americans consume more than they produce. As Hornbeck

(2013, p. 9) aptly summarizes, "It is ironic that the most effective method of reducing the trade deficit is through monetary and fiscal policy, yet monetary and fiscal policy is rarely determined by the trade deficit."

Trade Blocs as Clubs

If one thinks of the WTO as a club, China may be a different kind of club member, and this begs the question of what terms of membership, if any, ought to apply. Club theory is a sub-field within economics that may be applicable to addressing such questions. From this perspective, a club comprises a group of entities (people, organizations, or, in this case, countries) that benefit from mutual association. While the theoretical underpinnings can entail a certain degree of mathematical rigor and complexity (Cornes and Sandler, 1996), the basic ideas are quite easy to grasp intuitively using the real-world analogy of clubs. Depending upon the intended purpose, some clubs may thrive on a diverse membership. An example could be some social clubs that promote knowledge about different languages and cultures. A diverse membership from many parts of the world could help individual members to establish contacts abroad more readily. Other clubs, in contrast, may be better suited to a membership comprising individuals with similar interests and abilities. Chess clubs are an example where individual members are normally keen to associate with others who not only enjoy chess, but who also play at comparable levels of skill. Social media platforms such as Facebook or WeChat also exhibit certain club-like characteristics. Political parties may also fit the paradigm.

Regional trade agreements such as the United States–Mexico–Canada Agreement (USMCA, formerly the North American Free Trade Agreement, NAFTA) also function as economic clubs. Often – as the term implies – the rationale for regional trade agreements is geographical, as countries within a specified region seek to remove trade barriers that might otherwise hamper mutually beneficial economic interchanges between neighboring countries. In other cases, the rationale for trade blocs may rely less on geographical proximity and more on similarity of institutions, political values, or levels of development. From this perspective, a problem with the World Trade Organization may be that it becomes somewhat of a hodgepodge, sacrificing unity of purpose for the sake of an expansive membership. It may be that the United States – and other countries as well – could benefit from focusing on trade alliances with truly like-minded countries. That way, more of our energies could be spent on trading, and less on struggling with recalcitrant erstwhile partners.

Trade and Developmental Trajectories

At this point, it is useful to take a step back to assess whether free trade should be an end in itself or a means to promote broader economic development objectives.

Figuratively speaking, it may be that the tail is wagging the dog. Earlier in this chapter we reviewed two mainstream theories that purport to explain the gains from trade. Both perspectives – the Ricardian comparative advantage principle and the increasing returns to scale explanation – are essentially static. Much of the current tension between the United States and China, however, arises from fundamental asymmetries between the two countries' respective levels of development, and these differences are best understood in terms of long-run development *trajectories* rather than static representations focusing on a moment in time. While the U.S. Trade Representative may be correct in charging China with not playing by the WTO rules of the game, those rules are not necessarily ones that promote meaningful development of China or other developing economies. Some would argue that the rules of the game are instead designed to reinforce the status quo. Free trade is not, or should not be, an end in itself. Free trade is a goal worth pursuing for any given country to the extent that it promotes that country's economic development or prosperity.

A similar and related point concerns the charge that China's actions are condemnable because they create market distortions. Market failures comprise a central theme in the study of economics, and they are especially rampant in developing economies with weak institutions. In all major developmental success stories from the last half-century – with China and the other so-called Asian Tigers being the notable standouts – strong state intervention was an essential factor leading to those remarkable developmental outcomes. State intervention, almost by definition, is a kind of market distortion. While there certainly are many kinds of state intervention that would be ill-advised, it would be foolish to argue that the only way to promote economic development over the long run is to avoid all market distortions.

This is not just an issue concerning China and the United States. Global trade is increasingly a North–South trade, and developing countries, including the influential BRICS[9] consortium, have become more assertive in advocating for trading regimes that are geared more directly to their developmental aspirations. From the outset, GATT negotiations provided certain concessions to developing countries, granting them additional protections from the negative impacts of trade and longer time horizons for reducing trade barriers. Nonetheless, during the early years, the primary focus for trade negotiations was between the United States and European countries that were re-establishing themselves in the aftermath of World War II, and this reflected global trade patterns at the time. More recently, however, much more merchandise trade flows between developed and developing countries. This in turn has altered the focus of multilateral negotiations within WTO.

This may actually present an opportunity for the United States and China, as the two principal leaders of the Global North and the Global South, respectively, but it is an opportunity that might just as readily be squandered. As we have seen, the global trading regime as embodied by the World Trade Organization is in a rather woeful state. It is slow and unwieldly; it is lagging behind important technological advances that are reshaping global trade patterns; and its increasingly diverse membership cannot agree on what fundamental changes are required. A similar dilemma arises in the context of climate change, a topic that is addressed in detail in Chapter 5. Notwithstanding mounting scientific evidence of a global imperative to reduce greenhouse gas emissions in the aggregate, it is exceedingly difficult to forge a broad consensus on burden-sharing. There too, the North–South divide presented a formidable chasm, with the United States and other developed countries of the Global North arguing that they have been reducing greenhouse gases (GHG) and that their counterparts in the Global South must make similar reductions. China and other countries of the Global South counter that GHG emissions are a largely unavoidable by-product of economic growth, and that they, too, have a right to pursue such growth. Global negotiations were at loggerheads until the United States and China forged a bilateral agreement in 2015 that become a guiding light for the 2016 Paris Accord.

This same principle could conceivably be applied in the case of global trade and the institutions that support it. While still exceedingly difficult, it is much easier for the United States and China to come to an agreement about trade principles that might span the North–South gap than it would be for 164 WTO members to reach such an agreement. Of course, the fact that the Trump Administration, after assuming power, promptly withdrew from the Paris Accord is a troubling counterpoint to what might otherwise be an optimistic refrain. If the United States and China cannot get it right, the prospects for a reasonably equitable and efficient global trading regime that bridges the North–South divide are dim indeed. The default option then devolves into a myriad piecemeal bilateral and multilateral agreements based on shifting power and temporary alliances, where the whole falls woefully short of the sum of parts.

Discussion Questions

1   Has the World Trade Organization outlived its usefulness, or does it still have an important role to play in adjudicating trade disputes? What WTO reforms, if any, are both necessary and attainable? What should be the role of the United States, and of China, in designing, advocating for, and implementing any such WTO reforms?

2   What are likely to be the longer-run consequences if a WTO-centric global trade order devolves into a myriad set of bilateral managed trade agreements? As the world's largest economy, is the United States likely to come out ahead by going it alone?

3   Most macroeconomists agree that U.S. trade deficits are ultimately a consequence of Americans consuming more than they produce. If so, what policy measures might be taken at the macroeconomic level to address these deficits?

Notes

1 See *The American Presidency Project*. Available at: www.presidency.ucsb.edu/ws/?pid=24180#axzz2g1CH6ktg.
2 These trade data are from the World Bank database, see http://data.worldbank.org/indicator/TG.VAL.TOTL.GD.ZS.
3 See Hornbeck (2013) and Morrison (2018).
4 In January 2020, the WTO website listed 164 states or fully autonomous customs regions as members.
5 An additional complication here is that imports from China might NOT be denominated in RMB, as noted by Staiger and Sykes (2010).
6 Merchandise trade data reported here are from http://data.worldbank.org/indicator/TG.VAL.TOTL.GD.ZS.
7 The U.S. routinely accounts for over one-quarter of all patent-filing applications under the Patent Cooperation Treaty (PCT), maintained by the UN's World Intellectual Property Organization (WIPO). See Ilias and Fergusson (2011).
8 One important mechanism for scrutinizing foreign direct investment from China or elsewhere into the United States is through the Committee on Foreign Investment in the United States (CFIUS).
9 BRICS is an acronym for Brazil, Russia, India, China, and South Africa.

References

Archibugi, Daniele and Andrea Filippetti (2010). "The Globalization of Intellectual Property Rights: Four Learned Lessons and Four Theses," *Global Policy*, 1(2), 137–149.
Baldwin, Robert E. (2009). "U.S. Trade Policy Since 1934: An Uneven Path Toward Greater Trade Liberalization", NBER Working Paper No. 15397, National Bureau of Economic Research, Cambridge, MA.
Bergsten, C. Fred (2009). "The Dollar and the Deficits: How Washington Can Prevent the Next Crisis," *Foreign Affairs*, 88(6), 20–38.
Bown, Chad (2019). "The Accumulating Self-Inflicted Wounds from Trump's Unilateral Trade Policy," in Ha Jiming and Adam Posen (Eds.), *US–China Economic Relations: From Conflict to Solutions*, Washington, DC: Peterson Institute for International Economics.
Bown, Chad (2020). "Unappreciated Hazards of the US–China Phase One Deal," in *Trade and Investment Policy Watch*, Washington, DC: Peterson Institute for International Economics.
Cline, William R. (2010). "Renminbi Undervaluation, China's Surplus, and the U.S. Trade Deficit," Policy Brief PB10-20, Washington, DC: Peterson Institute for International Economics.
Cornes, R. and Sandler, T. (1996). *The Theory of Externalities, Public Goods, and Club Goods*, Cambridge: Cambridge University Press.
Cutler, Wendy et al. (2019). "Trade in Trouble: How the Asia Pacific Can Step Up and Lead Reforms," Issue Paper, Asia Society Policy Institute.
Fefer, Rachel and Vivian Jones (2020). "Section 232 of the Trade Expansion Act of 1962," *In Focus*, IF10667, Washington, DC: Congressional Research Service.
Fordham, Benjamin O. and Katja B. Kleinberg (2011). "International Trade and U.S. Relations with China," *Foreign Policy Analysis*, 7, 217–236.
Frank, Andre Gunder (1966). "The Development of Underdevelopment," *Monthly Review*, September, 17–31.
Harper, Zachary (2018). "The Old Sheriff and the Vigilante: World Trade Organization

Dispute Settlement and Section 301 Investigations into Intellectual Property Disputes," *Trade, Law and Development*, 10, 107–134.

Helfer, Laurence R. (2004). "Regime Shifting: The TRIPs Agreement and New Dynamics of International Intellectual Property Lawmaking," *Yale Journal of International Law*, 29(1), 1–83.

Hofman, Bert (2020). "The Fallout of Phase One: What the Trade Agreement between the United States and China Means," *Newsletter*, 25 January 2020.

Hornbeck, J.F. (2013). *Trade Primer: Qs and As on Trade Concepts, Performance, and Policy*, CRS Report RL 33944, Washington, DC: Congressional Research Service.

Ilias, Shayerah, Ian F. Fergusson, Wayne Morrison, and M. Angeles Villarreal (2011). *Boosting U.S. Exports: Selected Issues for Congress*, Washington, DC: Congressional Research Service.

Keupp, Marcus, Angela Beckenbauer, and Oliver Gassmann (2009). "How Managers Protect Intellectual Property Rights in China Using De Facto Strategies," *R&D Management*, 39(2), 211–224.

Koh, Harold Hongju (2019). "Trump Change: Unilateralism and the 'Disruption Myth' in International Trade," *The Yale Journal of International Law*, 44, online.

Kojima, Kiyoshi (2000). "The 'Flying Geese' Model of Asian Economic Development: Origin, Theoretical Extensions, and Regional Policy Implications," *Journal of Asian Economics*, 11, 375–401.

Krugman, Paul (2009). "The Increasing Returns Revolution in Trade and Geography," *American Economic Review*, 99(3), 561–571.

May, Christopher (2002). "The Venetian Movement: New Technologies, Legal Innovation and the Institutional Origins of Intellectual Property," *Prometheus: Critical Studies in Innovation*, 20(2), 159–179.

Morrison, Wayne M. (2013). *China's Economic Rise: History, Trends, Challenges, and Implications for the United States*, CRS Report RL33534, Washington, DC: Congressional Research Service.

Morrison, Wayne M. (2018). *China-U.S. Trade Issues*, CRS Report RL33536, Washington, DC: Congressional Research Service.

Morrison, Wayne M. (2019). "Enforcing U.S. Trade Laws: Section 301 and China," *In Focus*, IF10708, Washington, DC: Congressional Research Service.

Morrison, Wayne M. and Marc Labonte (2013). *China's Currency Policy: An Analysis of the Economic Issues*, Washington, DC: Congressional Research Service.

Rodrik, Dani (2010). "Making Room for China in the World Economy," *American Economic Review: Papers & Proceedings*, 100(2), 89–93.

Shell, G. Richard (1995). "Trade Legalism and International Relations Theory: An Analysis of the World Trade Organization," *Duke Law Journal*, 44(5), 830–927.

Staiger, Robert W. and Alan O. Sykes (2010). "'Currency Manipulation' and World Trade," *World Trade Review*, 9(4), 583–627.

Thorbecke, Willem and Gordon Smith (2010). "How Would an Appreciation of the Renminbi and Other East Asian Currencies Affect China's Exports?" *Review of International Economics*, 18(1), 95–108.

USTR (2012). *2012 Special 301 Report*, Washington, DC: Office of the U.S. Trade Representative.

USTR (2019). *2019 Report to Congress on China's WTO Compliance*, Washington, DC: Office of the U.S. Trade Representative.

Williams, Brock R. and J. Michael Donnelly (2012). *U.S. International Trade: Trends and Forecasts*, CR Report RL 33577, Washington, DC: Congressional Research Service.

Williams, Nancy (2019). "The Resilience of Protectionism in U.S. Trade Policy," *Boston University Law Review*, 99, 683–719.

4

EMPLOYMENT AND INCOME

Labor Pains?

Current controversies regarding the impact of China's rise on employment and income in the United States, particularly in the manufacturing sector, can be usefully viewed from a longer-run perspective on the ever-changing character of labor and employment in the United States. The labor movement of the past century broadly reflects the evolving nature of economic production under advanced capitalist societies. The late nineteenth and early twentieth centuries marked an era of rapidly expanding industrial production in the United States, Great Britain, and other leading economies. It was during this era that a marked dichotomy between capital and labor emerged in political economic terms. The 1917 revolution in Russia that eventually ushered in the Soviet Union and a form of State-directed control of the means of production was ostensibly inspired by the works of Karl Marx, although he would most surely have been flummoxed to see what transpired under the banner bearing his name. Beginning in the next decade in China, a small band of Communist revolutionaries began to grow in strength until Mao Tse-Tung was finally able to proclaim the People's Republic of China in 1949. The inheritors of the mantle of leadership of the Chinese Communist Party continue to rule today. Although the mechanisms of Communist Party rule remain in force, and while some vestiges of Marxist rhetoric can still be found in leadership circles, the China of today with its own booming version of "Capitalism with Chinese characteristics"[1] is a far cry from what Marx or even Mao could have imagined. There is a certain irony, therefore, that contemporary and ostensibly Marxist China is now seen by some as a looming threat to the livelihoods of the American working class!

In the United States, the labor movement evolved in the context of a broader progressive movement beginning in the late nineteenth century, culminating in FDR's call for a New Deal for the American worker in the face of the Great Depression that epitomized the evident failures of capitalism, and the prominent appointment of Labor Secretary Frances Perkins, who played an active role in the shaping and implementation of many important New Deal initiatives, especially the enactment of Social Security. Labor union participation trends mirrored these developments. Union membership as a proportion of total employment rose steadily during the Progressive Era, through the Great Depression, and beyond World War II. After its peak in the mid-1950s, a steady decline in union membership rates ensued, continuing through the present date. By 2019, only 10.3 percent of all employees were represented by unions, compared with 28.3 percent in 1954.[2] This downward trend in labor union participation rates over past decades has been concomitant with a parallel decline in manufacturing's share of total U.S. employment. These trends in turn are best understood as manifestations of an ongoing historical transformation from a "Fordist" to a "post-Fordist" mode of capital accumulation. Professor David Harvey's (1990) classic text on *The Condition of Postmodernity* in turn sets this broad-brush economic transformation in the context of an even deeper historical transformation from an era of modernity to postmodernity. His thesis is too rich to describe here in any detail, but a key point is that the role of labor in the economy is an expression of the evolving modes of production and capital accumulation, while the latter are themselves part of a deeper metamorphosis of society. For our purposes, the transition from a Fordist to post-Fordist mode of production marks a decline of monolithic capital in opposition to monolithic labor. In recent decades, the economy has been characterized by increasingly flexible, geographically dispersed, loosely coupled production processes.

On a global scale, this process has attracted increasing attention. UNCTAD's *World Investment Report 2013*, for instance, focuses on the causes and consequence of these rapidly expanding global value chains (GVC). As discussed already in Chapter 3 (Trade Policy), the share of developing countries in global value-added trade and gross exports has increased substantially over recent decades. Thus, the post-Fordist trends discussed by Harvey a quarter of a century earlier are now much more pervasively global in scope through a persistent devolution of production to developing countries, including, of course, China. A conclusion of the *World Investment Report 2013* is that this expansion of global value chains has generally promoted employment growth, but that the employment impacts vary by country and by sector.

Another important trend affecting labor in the United States over the past decades concerns income *inequality*, which peaked during the Great Depression in the early 1930s, but fell sharply during the New Deal and in the post-war years as households shared in growing prosperity in more equal measure. Income inequality then began a steady climb upwards again beginning in the early 1970s,

TABLE 4.1 Widening income disparities, 1980–2018 (in constant 2018 $)

Year	1980 ($)	1990 ($)	2000 ($)	2010 ($)	2018 ($)	% increase 1980–2018
10th percentile limit	13,093	13,678	15,473	13,690	14,629	11.7
Median	51,528	55,952	61,399	56,873	63,179	22.6
90th percentile limit	119,008	138,465	163,771	160,174	184,292	54.9

Source: U.S. Census Bureau (2019).

continuing through the present time. As shown in Table 4.1, compiled using data from the U.S. Census Bureau (2019), the income gap between poor and rich households has been widening steadily over the past four decades. From 1980 to 2018, the income of poorer households at the 10th percentile limit rose by 11.7 percent in constant dollar terms. For households at the median, incomes rose almost twice as quickly, by 22.6 percent. For households at the upper reaches of the distribution (90th percentile), however, their incomes rose by a very robust 54.9 percent over the same interval. Economic inequality is even more pronounced in terms of wealth. The Federal Reserve Board's *Survey of Consumer Finances* (2016) finds that the top 10 percent of households own 78 percent of the wealth. Even within that upper group, there is pronounced inequality, with the top 1 percent of households owning as much (39 percent) of total wealth as the next 9 percent of wealthiest households (Stone et al., 2020).

Is the United States "Exporting" Jobs to China?

In the United States, these trends have been the cause of much concern, especially with reference to the rise of China and its impacts on American workers. Figure 4.1 illustrates the concern in stark fashion, showing a steady increase in the import penetration ratio[3] to the United States over recent decades from 6.2 percent in 1960 to a peak of 42.3 percent in 2008, from which it declined to 35.0 percent by 2019. Over these same decades the share of manufacturing in total U.S. employment has fallen steadily, from 28.4 percent in 1960 to a mere 8.5 percent by 2019. It is easy – perhaps too easy – to jump to the conclusion that the United States is "exporting" good manufacturing jobs to China and elsewhere, with profoundly negative consequences for U.S. labor. In fact, the decline in U.S. manufacturing employment had been a pervasive trend already underway for decades *prior to* the rise of China, so one must be cautious not to confuse correlation with causation.

One concern is off-shoring, a phenomenon whereby firms of one country open branches or facilities abroad. This can work in both directions, as the United States is both the largest foreign direct *investor* abroad as well as the largest *recipient* of foreign direct investment (FDI). According to a recent report

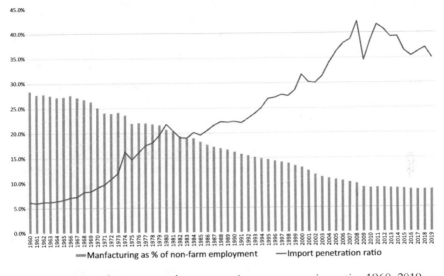

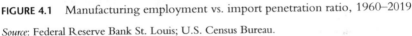

FIGURE 4.1 Manufacturing employment vs. import penetration ratio, 1960–2019

Source: Federal Reserve Bank St. Louis; U.S. Census Bureau.

by the Congressional Research Service (CRS), two-thirds of employees of U.S. overseas investors are in Europe or other highly developed economies with wage scales and standards of living that are comparable to the U.S. This is not the kind of FDI abroad that is likely to undercut U.S. employment or wage scales. The situation is changing rapidly, however, with employment levels of U.S. firms in China growing at a remarkable pace.[4] Even so, it is not clear whether off-shoring of U.S. companies leads to a reduction in U.S. employment at home. As the CRS report notes, after a careful consideration of the evidence:

> There appears to be no distinct pattern between the creation or loss of jobs within U.S. multinational companies and a commensurate loss or creation of jobs among the foreign affiliates of those companies … foreign direct investment may create jobs in the foreign affiliate that substitute for jobs in the parent company, but foreign investment may also positively affect job creation in both the parent company and the foreign affiliates.
>
> *(Jackson, 2013, p. 8)*

Conventional trade theory suggests that countries will trade in goods and services aligned with their comparative advantage. The United States is a country with a relative abundance of advanced capital, technology, and skilled labor. Data compiled by the U.S. Bureau of Labor Statistics show that manufacturing wages in the U.S. are higher than most other countries, with the notable exception of the Euro area. In many cases, however, manufacturing wages overseas have been rising relative to the U.S., which in part reflects the declining value of the U.S. dollar relative to other currencies. China's manufacturing wages remain low even in comparison with other relatively low-cost areas such as Mexico, Brazil, or Eastern Europe. It stands to reason, then, that a high wage economy such as the United States would shift away from manufacturing goods that are in direct competition with imports from low wage economies such as China.

Economic theory suggests that the U.S. economy will be more likely to retain those manufacturing activities that have sufficiently high productivity levels to compensate for its higher wages relative to China or other overseas competitors. This proposition is tested directly by Bernard et al. (2006). Drawing upon time series data extending over two decades through 1997, they follow the fates of hundreds of thousands of manufacturing plants exposed to increased competition from abroad. Their empirical investigation concludes that manufacturing plants are indeed more likely to shut down if they are located within industries that are more exposed to import competition from low-wage countries such as China. Moreover, within highly exposed manufacturing industries in the United States, those plants that employ higher skilled labor in conjunction with more plant capital are more likely to survive and thrive. As they conclude, "Low-wage country penetration is positively and significantly associated with plant death and, within industries, relative survival probabilities are higher for capital- and skill-intensive plants in the face of substantial low-wage country imports" (ibid., p. 231).

Autor et al. (2012), in their careful study, further examine the impacts of Chinese import competition on U.S. workers and the economy. In contrast to prior studies that focus exclusively on impacted manufacturing industries, they use *commuting zones* as their unit of analysis. These serve as proxies for localized labor markets. Variation in the degree of local market exposures to import competition provides the basis for their comparative empirical analysis. This approach allows them to examine some of the general equilibrium impacts beyond those industries that are immediately affected by import competition. To the extent that the U.S. labor force is highly mobile, and to the extent that U.S. labor markets are highly integrated, one would expect the impacts of import competition to be quite diffused throughout the United States. Conversely, to the extent that regional labor markets are relatively segmented from one another and to the extent that households are highly rooted to their geographical regions, then the impacts of import competition are more likely to be localized. Their study is based on an examination of those regional variations in impacts, noting that labor mobility is in fact relatively low for workers in the manufacturing sector – especially for those workers who lack post-secondary education. Housing market differentials may be part of the reason for this lack of mobility between regions.

Not surprisingly, the study by Autor et al. (2012) does find that increased exposure to import competition leads to a reduction in manufacturing employment. This would confirm that there is indeed a causal link underlying the correlation shown in Figure 4.1 between a rising import penetration from China and elsewhere and declining manufacturing employment in the United States in recent decades. Interestingly, however, they find that wage effects from import competition are not so much in the impacted manufacturing sectors but, rather, in the respective local labor markets more generally. Recall the findings of Bernard et al. (2006), discussed above, that plant closures and employment reductions are more likely to impact lower-skilled workers in plants with low levels of plant capital and thus lower productivity levels. Thus, as imports from China grow, local manufacturing *employment* declines but the average wages of those who remain employed are not adversely impacted. Instead, it is the effect of increasing unemployment levels that depresses wage levels generally within the localized region. This in turn leads to a sequence of adverse impacts:

> Through its effects on employment and earnings, rising import exposure spurs a substantial increase in government transfer payments to citizens in the form of increased disability, medical, income assistance, and unemployment benefit payments. These transfer payments vastly exceed the expenses of the [Labor Department's Trade Adjustment Assistance] program, which specifically targets workers who lose employment due to import competition.
>
> *(Autor et al., 2012, p. 30)*

The indirect "general equilibrium" effects of Chinese imports are also discussed by Acemoglu et al. (2013), which builds directly on the study by Autor et al. (2012). They investigate three channels through which such indirect effects can impact U.S. labor markets. One is input-output linkages, whereby reductions in demand in directly impacted industries propagate forward or backward through inter-industry supply chains. These may extend beyond the manufacturing sector. For example, the chemical and fertilizer mining industry in the U.S. sells 85 percent of its output to the manufacturing sector. The comparable figure is 92 percent for the iron and ferroalloy ores industry (Acemoglu et al., 2013, p. 19). When U.S. manufacturing is directly impacted by Chinese import penetration, these non-manufacturing sectors are likely to be impacted indirectly but substantially as well. Another channel of potential indirect impacts is through aggregate demand effects, as reduced wages lead to corresponding reductions in household expenditures. These reductions in demand are amplified throughout the economy in quintessential Keynesian fashion. A third indirect channel of impact, the reallocation effect, will offset somewhat the reduction in manufacturing employment as employees who lose their jobs may find alternative employment elsewhere, thus resulting in job creation that might not otherwise have occurred. To the extent that U.S. labor markets are "perfect" or robust, the domestic economy will quickly absorb employment losses in weak sectors and reallocate those workers to productive uses elsewhere. Evidence suggests, however, that labor market imperfections may cause unemployment to stagnate. Krueger et al. (2014, p. 4), for example, observe that "from 2008 to 2012, only 11 percent of those who were long-term unemployed in a given month returned to steady, full-time employment a year later."

The study by Acemoglu et al. (2013) develops estimates of all three channels of indirect impact, in addition to the direct impacts wrought by import penetration of Chinese goods in U.S. markets. They conclude: "The overall local impact is 591,000 jobs whose loss would have been averted through the absence of further increases in Chinese import competition after 1999" (ibid., p. 29). They go on to state that "Incorporating input–output linkages, we observe a larger impact of the rise in import competition from China, now accounting for an employment reduction of 1.3 million jobs (in manufacturing and non-manufacturing combined) between 1999 and 2011" (ibid., p. 31). This compares with Autor et al. (2012), who state that their "estimates imply a supply-shock driven net reduction in U.S. manufacturing employment of 548,000 workers between 1990 and 2000 and a further reduction of 982,000 workers between 2000 and 2007." Pierce and Schott (2014) attribute the decline in U.S. manufacturing to a policy decision to grant Permanent Normal Trade Relations status to China at the time of the latter's accession to the World Trade Organization.

An important caveat regarding any such estimates is that they are predicated upon a counterfactual premise that Chinese imports would have remained constant over the study period, rather than rising substantially as they had in fact done. It is of course necessary to formulate *some* counterfactual hypothesis in order to establish a baseline for comparison and a benchmark for impacts. Recall from Chapters 2 (Fiscal Policy and Deficits)[5] and 3 (Trade Policy), however, that net imports, whether they be from China or elsewhere, are a *necessary* counterpart to the large and persistent public and private sector deficits that the United States has maintained over this same period. Therefore, in order for the counterfactual hypothesis to be complete, one should clarify how these deficits are treated. If U.S. public and private sector deficits are presumed to remain intact, then the reduced imports from China will necessarily be replaced by imports from elsewhere. Alternatively, if one assumes that these U.S. deficits declined sufficiently to allow for a reduction in imports, one must also model the macroeconomic impacts of those very substantial fiscal contractions in order to capture the full general equilibrium outcomes of the counterfactual hypothesis. Stated simply, it is not realistic to assume that Chinese imports could be reduced in the absence of equally profound adjustments elsewhere in the economy. The studies cited above do not account for those. Nonetheless, these studies are certainly helpful in understanding the channels through which growing Chinese imports impact the U.S. economy, and their estimates are likely good partial equilibrium assessments of those impacts.

It is clear that the impacts of Chinese imports are not uniformly felt through-out the United States. Autor et al. (2012) state that the *aggregate* gains from trade are, on balance, positive. That is, the costs described above are offset by the gains to consumers and producers alike who benefit from lower cost imports. This knowledge is no doubt of small comfort to those who do bear the brunt of the cost of Chinese import penetration. The localized nature of these costs as described above will reverberate in adversely impacted industries and their respective communities. According to Acemoglu et al. (2013, p. 14):

> The sectors with the largest increase in Chinese import exposure from 1991 to 2011 were those intensive in the use of production workers, as would be expected given China's comparative advantage in labor intensive goods. These sectors include toys, sports equipment, and other products; apparel, leather (footwear), and textiles; and furniture and wood products. Also exposed [are] machinery, electrical machinery, and electronics, reflecting China's large global role in final assembly of consumer electronics. The least exposed sectors include food products, beverages and tobacco, chemical and petroleum products, and transportation equipment.

Holmes and Stevens (2012) provide another indication of industrial sectors in the U.S. economy that are most directly impacted by the mounting surge of Chinese imports. They show that the import share of shipments for these 17 industries rose from 34 percent to 70 percent over the ten-year interval, 1997–2007, with the Chinese share of those imports rising from 26 percent to 61 percent. During this same interval, U.S. employment declined by 66 percent over these industries, compared to a 5 percent growth in a control group of food and beverage industries that has a reasonably similar industrial structure but is less exposed to Chinese imports. Holmes and Stevens show that plant size also reduced sharply over this same period in these affected industries, from 63 to 30 workers per plant. In contrast, plant size remained relatively unchanged for the control group. This last observation would appear to affirm a central point advanced by Holmes and Stevens, as they argue:

> If a plant in the United States is huge, it is a signal that the plant is poten-tially vulnerable to competition from China. A huge plant is likely making something that can be traded across space – something that can be put in a container and shipped – as a local market would not likely be able to absorb all the output of a given huge plant.
>
> *(Ibid., p. 39)*

They argue that manufacturing plants more likely to withstand import competi-tion from China will have fewer but more highly skilled workers producing specialty or boutique products in distinctive market niches.

It is not only in the manufacturing sector that U.S. labor has concerns about increased competition from abroad. The global reach of telecommunications and internet connectivity has raised fears among some that overseas labor will compete directly with U.S. workers in service industries as well. Liu and Trefler (2008) argue that much of the expressed concern is unfounded and based on faulty analytics. Their own empirical analysis focuses specifically on U.S. off-shoring and "on-shoring" of services with low wage countries. By matching longitudinal Current Population Survey data with trade data, they estimate the impacts of industry exposure on U.S. wages and service employment by indus-try and occupation. They conclude that the effects of both off-shoring and on-shoring are small, but that the net outcomes favor U.S. workers. In other words, U.S. service industry employees on the whole gain more than they lose through such competition. They do find, however, that the U.S. workers who tend to be impacted more negatively are those with less education and who are working in less-skilled jobs. This negative finding regarding lower-skilled service sector workers exposed to competition from abroad echoes the findings we reviewed for the manufacturing sector. Thus, a central message that emerges from the empirical research is that, on the whole, competition from abroad is not such a bad thing for U.S. workers, except for those working in jobs that require little skill. This raises the question of how the United States might better equip its labor force to face competition from abroad.

Human Capital and the U.S. Labor Force

There are two fundamental alternatives to "upgrading" the U.S. labor force. One is to provide training or other interventions to improve the employment status of *existing workers* in the United States. The other policy approach is to encourage selective *immigration* to favor the in-migration of workers who already have the desired skill sets. These two approaches are not mutually exclu-sive, and in fact both are in play, but with rather different repercussions.

The analysis from the preceding section indicates that unskilled workers in the U.S. are most at risk from imports from China or other relatively low wage countries. This finding suggests that education or training – by adding skills to the unskilled – may might help "inoculate" U.S. labor from the adverse impacts of foreign competition. There is some evidence to support this proposition as income growth in the United States is strongly correlated with education attain-ment. It does not immediately follow, however, that education attainment is the cause of lower unemployment or higher salaries. As Michael Hout (2012, p. 380) observes, "The correlation between education and success might reflect positive selection bias in the educational system; schools treat those who will benefit from the treatment." Suppose, for example, that some people were natural "winners" while others were natural "losers." The same qualities that helped winners secure better jobs might have enabled them also to access better education opportunities. If that were the case, it would be difficult to attribute their subsequent economic success to education per se, rather than to the "winningness" of this fortuitous subset of the population. After reviewing the related literature and the attendant methodological challenges, Hout (ibid., p. 396) declares unambiguously that higher education does add value in this context, that "universities do not merely identify the young people who fit the desired [winning] profile, they disseminate skills and foster values." Another study, by Jepson et al. (2012), finds that this positive association between education and labor outcomes holds also for community college degrees, diplomas, and certificates.

While education *generally* may promote positive employment outcomes, imports from China have much more *specific* effects, as discussed already. These specific impacts prompt calls for more targeted policy responses. This is the intended purpose of the Trade Adjustment Assistance (TAA) program, established by the U.S. Trade Act of 1974. Administered by the Employment and Training Agency (ETA) of the Department of Labor, its intended purpose is to ease the transition to new employment opportunities for those workers whose jobs were lost due to foreign competition. According to the ETA website:

> The Trade Adjustment Assistance (TAA) Program is a federal entitlement program that assists U.S. workers who have lost or may lose their jobs as a result of foreign trade. This program seeks to provide adversely affected workers with opportunities to obtain the skills, credentials, resources, and support necessary to become reemployed.[6]

The TAA program has been studied in great depth, in particular by an exhaustive study commissioned by the ETA, and undertaken by researchers at the Social Policy Research Associates (SPR) and Mathematica Policy Research, Inc. In order to assess the impact of TAA-sponsored training on employment and related outcomes, the research team compared those outcomes for a sample of trainees with those of a control group of individuals who did not receive training but were otherwise similar to the "treatment group." As expected, earnings for younger workers in the treatment group dropped rather steeply over the first year or more as those workers received TAA-sponsored training. While they were in training, many of their counterparts in the control group were busy finding jobs and so earnings for the treatment group were negative by comparison. Over time, members of the treatment group completed their training and began earning more themselves. There is no evidence, however, that the incomes of the treatment group were sufficiently higher in these later years to compensate for the lost wages during training. In other words, laid-off workers who received TAA-sponsored training might have been better off by just returning to the job market and taking their chances. As summarized by the report, "Overall, although TAA participation substantially increased the receipt of reemployment and education and training services, these impacts had not yet translated into labor market gains during the four-year period following job loss" (Schochet et al., 2012, p. xviii). The outcome for older workers is even poorer, as members of the treatment group aged 60 and above fared consistently worse than their control group counterparts.

Jooyoun Park (2012) also assessed the impacts of TAA training. She notes that there is a relatively poor match between the occupational skills training that TAA participants receive compared to the occupations in which they are subsequently employed. Her study did find significantly higher incomes, however, for those participants whose occupation skill training *did* match their subsequent occupations. She concludes, therefore, that more emphasis should be placed on counseling and a careful front-end assessment of the appropriate kinds of training to provide. If the occupational matching could be improved from its current level of about 37 percent, that might result in a corresponding improvement of the economic outcomes resulting from such training. Galor (2011, p. 2) points to income inequality and imperfect capital markets as another possible barrier to workers' investment in their own human capital. He argues that

> In the presence of credit market imperfections and fixed costs associated with investment in education, occupational choices (and thus the efficient segmentation of the labor force between skilled and unskilled workers) are affected by the distribution of income. In particular, if the interest rate for borrowers is higher than that for lenders, inequality may result in an under-investment in human capital.

To recapitulate briefly, we have seen that imports from China *do* have repercussions for U.S. employment. Unlike the *benefits* of such imports on U.S. households in their dual capacity as consumers, which tend to be spread fairly evenly, the *negative impacts* of imports from China tend to be concentrated in certain industries, in certain geographical locations, and among certain segments of the labor force, especially the unskilled. There is some evidence to suggest that education and training policies can enhance the economic outlook of U.S. workers, thereby mitigating the negative repercussions of foreign imports. Policy responses such as the Trade Adjustment Assistance program, however well intentioned, appear to be inconsistent in their ability to deliver benefits commensurate with the costs. Displaced workers who do not receive TAA-sponsored training appear to be at least as resilient as their counterparts who did receive TAA training. This could be a good sign insofar as it suggests that the U.S. economy, despite its woes, is sufficiently dynamic that it can absorb displaced workers through standard labor market processes.

Recall that the second broad approach to upgrading the human capital of the U.S. labor force, rather than through direct education and training of existing workers, is by the use of selected immigration policies. In fact, this is quite common both in the United States and elsewhere, as preferences are given to prospective immigrants who possess targeted skill sets.[7] An obvious limitation of "importing" skilled labor is that this policy does not directly address the problems confronting unskilled labor in the U.S., nor does it purport to do so. According to a study by the Congressional Research Service on immigration policies geared to those with skills in science, technology, engineering and mathematics (STEM), "A broad consensus of business, academic, and policy leaders warn that the United States is on the verge of STEM workforce shortages, which will diminish U.S. global economic competitiveness" (Wasem, 2012, p. 24). Proponents of "STEM visas" argue that the United States should not be training the world's best and brightest, only to send them back to countries that are competing economically with the U.S. This view may reflect a narrow perspective on U.S. economic growth within a global context. It is quite possible that there will be more trade opportunities with China, India, and other countries as their own economies evolve. As shown in a study by Mattoo et al. (2008), moreover, there is not a reliable correspondence between the skill sets of highly qualified immigrants and their eventual occupations once they have settled in the United States. The authors attribute this under-placement to variations in the quality of training in the migrants' home countries. Immigrants from Latin America or Eastern Europe, for example, are less likely to be placed in high skilled occupations than their counterparts from Western Europe, India, or China – even after adjusting for differences in education, age, work experience, and other demographic indicators.

Laborers/Consumers

A balanced perspective on the impacts of China's rise on U.S. labor must include full consideration of the role of the laborer as consumer. The most direct link between the two is the *purchasing power* of wages received by households through labor. If Chinese imports cause U.S. consumer prices to fall, or to rise less swiftly than they might otherwise have done, this extends the effective purchasing power of wages. This effect tends to be diffused widely across the country, in contrast to the more localized impacts arising from worker displacement, as we have seen above. Thus, comparing costs and benefits of Chinese imports on U.S. households in their dual capacities as workers and consumers is analogous to comparing the volume of water in a shallow but vast pool of water to the volume of water in a number of isolated but relatively deep pools. This of course brings to mind the story about the statistician who drowned in a pool of water with an average depth of 1 meter – and all due cautions apply!

In assessing the magnitude of these effects, it is useful to bear in mind that the bulk of personal consumption expenditures in the United States is for services rather than merchandise, and services are predominantly domestic in content. As Hale and Hobijn (2011) point out, the United States is a relatively closed country despite its gigantic effect on world trade, with imports representing about 16 percent of GDP. Of this, Chinese imports represent only 2.7 percent of consumer spending in the United States, and of that only 1.2 percent represents the actual cost of those imports, with the remainder attributed to distribution and markups flowing to U.S. companies. The impacts of rising Chinese imports on consumers and laborers should be considered within that context.

There are several channels through which a rising China trade impacts consumer welfare in the U.S. (Feenstra and Weinstein, 2010). One is through the principle of *comparative advantage*, an idea that has dominated trade theory since David Ricardo, as discussed in Chapter 3 (Trade Policy) as well. Countries with different endowments of natural resources, labor, and production technologies are better suited to the production of correspondingly different goods. Aggregate output is maximized when each country specializes to some degree in those goods for which it has a comparative advantage. If the cost of trade is low, then the net gains from this increase in aggregate output should be shared among trading partners. A greater abundance of goods is a benign supply effect that should be reflected in lower consumer prices where competitive markets prevail.

Another mechanism by which U.S. consumers may benefit from a rising China trade is through an *expansion of import varieties*. Variety is said to be the spice of life, and trade may introduce a variety of spices – indeed, the spice trade was a powerful driving force of global trade in the seventeenth century. A broad class of models of monopolistic competition, dating back to a hugely influential paper by Dixit and Stiglitz (1977), is based on the premise that consumers do value a diverse selection of goods. This in turn encourages producers to find their own product market niches wherein they can benefit from *economies of scale* in production, which helps to lower average costs of production and hence consumer prices. Another channel through which a rising China trade can benefit U.S. consumers is through *reduced markups* in traded goods. These reduced markups are the outcome of what Feenstra and Weinstein (2010) term a pro-competitive effect.

Although the article by Autor et al. (2012) focuses on the negative repercussions of China trade through U.S. labor market disruptions, they do express the opinion that the aggregate gains from trade outweigh those negative impacts, so that the net effect is positive. A host of other authors seek to measure the positive welfare gains to U.S. consumers arising from trade with China. Amiti and Freund (2010) report that the growth of Chinese exports has for the most part been concentrated in existing goods, rather than through the introduction of new goods. This suggests a comparative advantage effect, which is further evidenced by the fall in the average price (of 1.6 percent per annum from 1997 to 2005) of U.S. imports from Chinese even as the price of imports from other countries rose (by 0.4 percent) over the same period. Handley and Limao (2013) estimate that prices in the U.S. would have been 3.3 percent higher had China not enhanced its U.S. trade through accession to the WTO, corresponding to what economists term a positive "welfare effect" of 0.8 percent of consumer real income.

Other authors attempt to estimate the welfare effects on U.S. consumers of China trade relative to a counterfactual "autarky scenario" in which there is no trade with China. In principle, this is the relevant benchmark if one seeks to understand the impacts of China trade. Di Giovanni et al. (2013) estimate a welfare gain of 0.11 percent for the U.S. as a result of China's trade.[8] They report substantially larger welfare gains under different scenarios for continued increases in Chinese productivity, as those are reflected in turn in lower prices for U.S. consumers. Feenstra and Weinstein (2010) estimate a cumulative welfare gain of 0.86 percent from 1992 to 2005 to U.S. consumers of lower markups and new varieties attributable to the China trade. Arkolakis et al. (2012) show that a broad class of monopolistic competition models point to estimates of gains from all trade (including non-China) to U.S. consumers of between 0.7 percent and 1.4 percent for a typical year. Finally, in an intriguing study, Fajgelbaum and Khandelwal (2013) conclude that the welfare gains from the China trade are much more concentrated among low-income Americans, as evidenced by differential consumption patterns among income groups.

To place these various studies and discussion points in some perspective, it may be helpful to use a simple comparison. Recall that Autor et al. (2012) attribute a reduction in U.S. manufacturing employment of 1.10 percentage points over the most recent decade of their study, with impacts falling primarily upon unskilled labor. As we saw in the study by Schochet et al. (2012), a sizeable proportion of those displaced workers do recover their employment and incomes over the next several years following their initial job loss – with or without TAA assistance. This employment and income recovery, which may well occur in non-manufacturing sectors, may substantially mitigate the negative impacts of the initial 1.10 percent employment loss in manufacturing. Suppose that mitigation effect was roughly equivalent to half, or 0.55 percent, then one might assess this loss against an aggregate welfare gain of between 0.70 and 1.40 percent, as suggested by the estimate provided by Feenstra and Weinstein (2010). Let us work with the midpoint of that interval, which is 1.05 percent. To simplify further, or to make the numbers more concrete, think of the 0.55 percent as 55 unemployed workers out of 10,000, as a result of China trade. Meanwhile, the 10,000 workers (including those 55 now unemployed) experience what is on average a welfare gain of 1.05 percent, which is equivalent to 105 out of 10,000. Intuitively, there ought to be some way for the 10,000 to draw upon their gain of 105 to compensate the 55 for their loss. Indeed, that is what Autor et al. (2012) observe as they find unemployment compensation and other forms of social insurance growing more in areas that are hardest hit by worker displacement. Thus, perhaps the real issue is not so much about China as it is about how we take care of our own here at home.

Discussion Questions

1   Are steep tariffs on imported goods from China, in effect, a tax on U.S. consumers used to subsidize low-productivity manufacturing jobs here?
2   Should people who lose their jobs in parts of the U.S. that are experiencing economic decline be encouraged to relocate to regions where they are more likely to find suitable employment?
3   How might "place-based" policies provide an alternative solution to relocation strategies as described in question 2?

Notes

1   The official slogan of course is "Socialism with Chinese Characteristics," but it is in fact equally "Capitalism with Chinese Characteristics."
2   1954 union membership rate as reported by Mayer (2004). The datum for 2019 is from the Bureau of Labor Statistics, see www.bls.gov/webapps/legacy/cpslutab1.htm.
3   The import penetration ratio (IPR) used here is a measure of the extent to which consumption of goods in the United States is reliant upon imports (M). The IPR data depicted in Figure 4.1 are calculated using the formula:

$$IPR = M / [GDP_{mfx} - X + M]$$

where GDP_{mfx} is the gross domestic product from the good producing sector and X and M represent the value of exports and imports, respectively.
4   During one surge, employment of U.S. firms in China rose 61 percent in just two years, from 2008 to 2010 (Jackson, 2013, p. 14).
5   The Appendix to Chapter 2 (Fiscal Policy and Deficits), in particular, discusses this important point in some detail.
6   See www.doleta.gov/tradeact/pdf/2011_brochure.pdf.
7   Indeed, by way of "full disclosure" and a case in point, I myself obtained permission to immigrate to the United States and assume my job here as a professor decades ago precisely because I was perceived (rightly or not) to have a skill set that was in short supply.
8   It is difficult to discern, for me at any rate, whether the 0.11 percent welfare gain reported by di Giovanni et al. (2013) is a mean annual increase or the cumulative effect over a decade.

References

Acemoglu, Daron, David Autor, David Dorn, and Gordon Hanson (2013). "Import Competition and the Great U.S. Employment Sag of the 2000s," *Society of Labor Economics*, September. Available at: www.sole-jole.org/14148.pdf.

Amiti, Mary and Caroline Freund (2010). "The Anatomy of China's Export Growth," in Robert Feenstra and Shang-Jin Wei (Eds.), *China's Growing Role in World Trade*, Chicago: University of Chicago Press.

Arkolakis, Costas, Arnaud Costinot, and Andres Rodriguez-Clare (2012). "New Trade Models, Same Old Gains?," *American Economic Review*, 102(1), 94–130.

Autor, David, David Dorn, and Gordon Hanson (2012). "The China Syndrome: Local Labor Market Effects of Import Competition in the United States," NBER Working Paper No. 18054, National Bureau of Economic Research, Cambridge, MA.

Bernard, Andrew, Bradford Jensen, and Peter Schott (2006). "Survival of the Best Fit: Exposure to Low-Wage Countries and the (Uneven) Growth of U.S. Manufacturing Plants," *Journal of International Economics*, 68, 219–237.

di Giovanni, Julian, Andrei A. Levchenko, and Jing Zhang (2013). "The Global Welfare Impact of China: Trade Integration and Technological Change," *American Economic Journal: Macroeconomics*, 6(3), 153–183.

Dixit, Avinash and Joseph Stiglitz (1977). "Monopolistic Competition and Optimum Product Diversity," *American Economic Review*, 67(3), 297–308.

Fajgelbaum, Pablo D. and Amit K. Khandelwal (2013). "Measuring the Unequal Gains from Trade." Available at: www.econ.ucla.edu/pfajgelbaum/MUGFT.pdf.

Federal Reserve Bank of St Louis. Available at: www.stlouisfed.org

Federal Reserve Board (2016). *Survey of Consumer Finances*. Available at: www.federal reserve.gov/econres/scfindex.htm

Feenstra, Robert C. and David E. Weinstein (2010). "Globalization, Markups, and the U.S. Price Level," NBER Working Paper No. 15749, National Bureau of Economic Research, Cambridge, MA.

Galor, Oded (2011). "Inequality, Human Capital Formation and the Process of Development," Working Paper No. 2011-7, Department of Economics, Brown University.

Hale, Galina and Bart Hobijn (2011). "The U.S. Content of 'Made in China'," *FRBSF Economic Letter*, 2011–25, Federal Reserve Bank of San Francisco.

Handley, Kyle and Nuno Limao (2013). "Policy Uncertainty, Trade and Welfare Theory and Evidence for China and the U.S.," NBER Working Paper No. 19376, National Bureau of Economic Research, Cambridge, MA.

Harvey, David (1990). *The Condition of Postmodernity*, Oxford: Blackwell.

Holmes, Thomas J. and John J. Stevens (2012). "An Alternative Theory of Plant Size Distribution, with Geography and Intra- and International Trade," NBER Working Paper, No. 15957, National Bureau of Economic Research, Cambridge, MA.

Hout, Michael (2012). "Social and Economic Returns to College Education in the United States," *Annual Review of Sociology*, 38, 379–400.

Jackson, James K. (2013). *Outsourcing and Insourcing Jobs in the U.S. Economy: Evidence Based on Foreign Investment Data*, CRS Report RL32461, Washington, DC: Congressional Research Service.

Jepson, Christopher, Kenneth Troske, and Paul Coomes (2012). "The Labor-Market Returns to Community College Degrees, Diplomas, and Certificates," Working Paper No. WP12/23, UCD Centre for Economic Research, University College Dublin, Dublin.

Krueger, Alan, Judd Cramer, and David Cho (2014). "Are the Long-Term Unemployed on the Margins of the Labor Market?," Paper presented at conference, Brookings Panel on Economic Activity.

Mattoo, Aaditya, Ileana Cristina Neagu, and Caglar Ozden (2008). "Brain Waste? Educated Immigrants in the U.S. Labor Market," *Journal of Development Economics*, 87, 255–269.

Mayer, Gerald (2004). *Union Membership Trends in the United States*, CRS Report RL32553, Washington, DC, Congressional Research Service.

Park, Jooyoun (2012). "Does Occupational Training by the Trade Adjustment Assistance Program Really Help Reemployment? Success Measured as Occupational Matching," *Review of International Economics*, 20(5), 999–1016.

Pierce, Justin R. and Peter K. Schott (2014). "The Surprisingly Swift Decline of U.S. Manufacturing Employment," CESifo Working Paper, no. 4563.

Schochet, Peter Z., Ronald D'Amico, Jillian Berk, Sarah Dolfin, and Nathan Wozny (2012). *Estimated Impacts for Participants in the Trade Adjustment Assistance (TAA) Program Under the 2002 Amendments*, Washington, DC: Employment and Training Division, Office of Policy Development and Research, U.S. Department of Labor.

Stone, Chad, Danilo Trisi, Arloc Sherman, and Jennifer Beltran (2020). "A Guide to Statistics on Historical Trends in Income Inequality," in *Policy Futures*, Washington, DC: Center on Budget and Policy Priorities,

UNCTAD (2013). "Global Value Chains: Investment and Trade for Development," *World Investment Report 2013*, New York: United Nations Council on Trade and Development, pp. 121–195.

U.S. Census Bureau (2019). *Income and Poverty in the United States: 2018.* Washington, DC: U.S. Census Bureau.

Wasem, Ruth Ellen (2012). *Immigration of Foreign Nationals with Science, Technology, Engineering, and Mathematics (STEM) Degrees*, CRS Report R42530, Washington, DC: Congressional Research Service.

PART II

Sustainability Policy Perspectives

5

CLIMATE CHANGE

Environmental Consciousness

Broad public awareness, such as it may be, of the causes and consequences of climate change has its roots in the environment movement of the past half century or more. Much as publication of *The Jungle* by Lewis Sinclair at the dawn of the twentieth century brought issues of food safety to the forefront of public attention, Rachel Carson's *Silent Spring* in 1962 helped usher in an era of environmental activism. The budding environmental movement was of course part of a much broader, tectonic shift in American popular and political culture during the 1960s. During this transformative period, an assertive generation of Baby Boomers began to critique the precepts taken for granted by a prior generation that had forged its values and beliefs during the post-World War II boom, when America's ascendancy as the world's leading military, economic, and cultural power was unquestioned. Proponents of change during this transformative era also advocated for a more proactive stewardship of the Earth's natural resources, leading to eventual creation of the Environmental Protection Agency (EPA) in 1970, not long after the first Earth Day.

Of course, no one is "against" clean air and water or "in favor" of toxic environments. Instead, pollution generally is understood to be an unwelcome by-product of economic activities that are themselves valued for the benefits they provide. Inevitably, political contestations arise over the degree to which society should trade off environmental quality for economic growth – though this dichotomy should not be overstated, as there can be modes of economic growth ("green growth") that are fully compatible with responsible environmental stewardship. Likewise, debate continues over the appropriate market or regulatory mechanisms for managing such tradeoffs. Issues of social or environmental justice are unavoidable as well, as the most adverse environmental effects of economic growth often fall upon the more marginalized segments of society. These political waters can be further muddied by uncertainty, misinformation, and asymmetric risks. Environmental quality is largely a common property resource, while the incentives that drive environmental degradation are typically rooted in private gain. Markets, in the traditional sense of the term, are ill equipped to manage the externalities intrinsic to environmental quality, so property rights instead assume the form of entitlements within a regulatory realm, with the EPA as a focal point for regulation and enforcement. To the extent that environmental quality is location-specific, such amenities are reflected in land rents, thus further accentuating the divide between the "haves" and the "have-nots." Overlays of economic, environmental, racial, and other socio-economic divides can color public perceptions of environmental justice, power, and wealth.

Many of these same issues are found at a global scale as well. In our current era, characterized by pervasive globalization, it is no surprise that environmental issues also take on a global hue. Poorer countries in the Global South may have fewer environmental protection laws, and those laws that do exist may be weakly enforced. Wealthier nations in the Global North may then, in effect, export pollution as they import goods from their counterparts in the South. This "trading of pollution" is certainly one aspect of the rise of China, and its impact on U.S. environmental policy.[1] The global environmental commons also becomes a source of increasing contention, a problem exacerbated by the lack of effective environmental regulation or oversight at a global or supranational scale. Nowhere is this challenge more evident than in the struggle over climate change, which has taken center stage as the most compelling environmental issue of our time. It is an issue that could or should thrust the United States and China unwittingly into an unlikely odd-couple partnership as chief stewards of the Earth's future.

Climate Change

The Earth basks in the Sun's radiation. A portion of this radiation is reflected back into space by the Earth's atmosphere while a remainder is absorbed and retained for some time. Certain gaseous elements in the Earth's atmosphere, such as carbon dioxide (CO_2) and methane, are more prone to absorb the Sun's radiation. As the quantity of such "greenhouse gases" (GHGs) increases, the Earth's climate becomes warmer.[2] The available scientific evidence marshaled by the Intergovernmental Panel on Climate Change (IPCC) in its *Fifth Assessment Review* (AR5) provides the strongest indication that: (1) the Earth's climate has in fact been warming over the past decades and centuries; (2) this warming trend is directly attributable to the steady accumulation of greenhouse gases in the Earth's atmosphere; and (3) anthropocentric (i.e., human) activities are the principal source of GHG emissions into the atmosphere. The AR5 reports find further that the global warming trend is leading to potentially catastrophic disruptions to human settlements due to rising sea levels, extreme weather events, and other consequences of climate change.

Over the four decades ending in 2010, GHG emissions from anthropogenic activities rose from 27 to 49 gigatons of CO_2 equivalents, with shares from electricity and heat production (25 percent), afforestation and other land use changes (24 percent), industrial activities (21 percent), transport (14 percent), buildings (6.4 percent) and other energy uses (9.6 percent). Over this time span, CO_2 concentrations in the Earth's atmosphere rose from 288 to 395 parts per million (ppm). The gross effect is even more dramatic, as contributing factors – especially burning of fossil fuels – would have brought the total to 540 ppm were it not for the offsetting effect of land and ocean "sinks" that absorbed 145 ppm of CO_2 (IPCC WG III, 2014).

There is a strong correspondence between the magnitude of these GHG emissions and the underlying level of economic activity that generates them. Not surprisingly, therefore, the United States was historically, by a substantial margin, the country with the largest volume of GHG emissions over past decades. That situation changed dramatically in recent years, however, as illustrated in Figure 5.1.[3] Judging from this graphic, China is not the elephant in the room – it is the giraffe! China's rapidly growing economy, coupled with its enormous population, has generated a multiplicative effect that has sent its level of CO_2 emissions soaring beyond anything seen hitherto in history. Indeed,

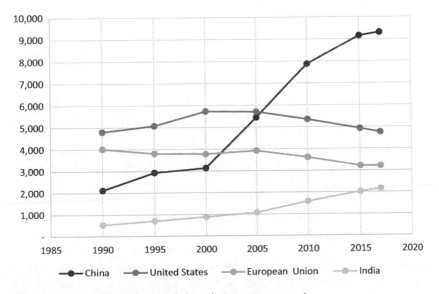

FIGURE 5.1 Comparing CO_2 emissions (megatons per year)

Source: International Energy Agency.

based on current trends, China is poised to generate more CO_2 emissions than the United States and the European Union *combined*. India, meanwhile, could also soon surpass the European Union. The cumulative effect on planet Earth could be devastating, yet these scenarios – as alarming as they are – still entail *per capita* emissions rates in China that are substantially lower than those in the United States.

Data ascribing emission shares between countries are typically formulated on what is termed a *production-based* approach. This method attributes emissions to the country whose territorial boundaries encompass the physical location of the emission's source. Some analysts argue that this method unfairly attributes emissions to producer countries without due consideration of the role of consumer countries on whose behalf such production occurs. An alternative, *consumption-based* approach therefore seeks to draw on trade data to modify emissions assessments accordingly. Misato Sato (2012) reviews the literature on this subject, finding that the methods and estimates vary widely, but the clear consensus is that embodied emissions in trade (EET) "are significant and on a growing trend." The distinction can make an important difference, as Peters et al. (2011, p. 8905) noted that "China is the largest emitter of CO_2 emissions with a territorial-based inventory, with the United States second, but with a consumption-based inventory the United States is first and China second." By now, however, China is likely to be the "winner," regardless of which methodology is applied.

China's Impact on the U.S. Environment

We have already seen that the rise of China is directly correlated with a commensurate rise in its GHG emissions. Although the *sources* of greenhouse gases are localized and specific, the climate change *consequences* are global. As the worldwide concentration of CO_2 particulates exceeds 400 ppm, for example, the environmental impacts on the United States are the same regardless of where those emissions originate. Thus, from a U.S. environmental policy perspective, the problem posed by China's rise is that it makes a serious climate change challenge much more foreboding – both to the U.S. and to the rest of the world, including China. Of course, while we do have concerns for the global implications, adverse *domestic* impacts of climate change are the primary focus of U.S. policy.

The National Climate Assessment (NCA)[4] of the U.S. Global Research Program, undertaken during the Obama Administration, describes the impacts of climate change on the United States. These include extreme climate events as well as a broad range of downstream (literal and figurative) societal impacts. It describes how global warming has manifested itself across the United States, with average temperatures across most of the country in recent decades decidedly higher than those earlier in the twentieth century.[5] Other climate-related changes abound:

Americans are noticing changes all around them. Summers are longer and hotter, and extended periods of unusual heat last longer than any living American has ever experienced. Winters are generally shorter and warmer. Rain comes in heavier downpours.... Residents of some coastal cities see their streets flood more regularly during storms and high tides. Inland cities near large rivers also experience more flooding, especially in the Midwest and Northeast. Insurance rates are rising in some vulnerable locations, and insurance is no longer available in others. Hotter and drier weather and earlier snowmelt mean that wildfires in the West start earlier in the spring, last later into the fall, and burn more acreage. In Arctic Alaska, the summer sea ice that once protected the coasts has receded, and autumn storms now cause more erosion, threatening many communities with relocation.

(NCA, 2014, p. 1)

The National Climate Assessment goes on to assess the implications of climate change on water supplies, energy use and supply, transportation and other infra-structure, agricultural production, forest and other ecosystems, human health outcomes, and human settlements. These impacts vary by region within the United States, but we all get our share, and the rise of China leads to heavier impacts for all. One would be misguided, however, to place the blame for these impacts solely upon China even while recognizing that its GHG emissions are by far the largest on the planet. Climate change is a global phenomenon, and any effective policy response by the United States must be based on a global perspective.

"No, I Insist: After *You* ..."

Climate change is "the ultimate global commons problem" (Tingley and Tomz, 2013). The *policy* challenge, likewise, at a global scale, is one of *collective action*. The global organizational focus for addressing this challenge has been the United Nations Framework Convention on Climate Change (FCCC),[6] which came into force in 1994 and by 2020 had 197 "Parties," or signatory countries (or comparable entities), to the Convention. From the outset, the challenge has been to reach an accord by which (1) global GHG emissions are limited to levels that will contain global warming to within 2.0°C of pre-industrial levels, or to within 1.5°C as per the Paris Agreement of 2016; (2) each individual country develops a strategy for doing its fair share; and (3) full implementation of emissions reductions by all Parties is verified. Each of these three elements presents a substantial challenge, but none more so than item (3) above, because each country has every incentive to be a "free rider" – to have the burden of restraint fall upon others while enjoying the full benefits of reduced emissions by others. Meanwhile, global mean surface temperatures have risen already by

1.0°C relative to pre-industrial levels, and unless dramatic changes are undertaken to control anthropogenic sources of GHG emissions, the erstwhile 1.5°C Paris ceiling is likely to be breached between 2030 and 2052 (IPCC, 2018).

If global warming exceeds 2°C, the predicted effects would be enormously costly and disruptive yet, as Selby (2019, p. 479) observes, "It seems likely that mid- and late twenty-first-century warming will significantly exceed 2°C, even if the Paris pledges are fully implemented.... And, of course, they are not being fully implemented." These challenges were already formidable prior to the election of Donald Trump in 2016, but the symbolic and practical consequences of having a climate change denier in the White House are profoundly troubling, as he nominates other climate change deniers to important positions within his Administration and undermines initiatives and institutions intended to combat climate change, including most notably the Paris Agreement (MacNeil et al., 2020; Selby, 2019). More troubling still is the abandonment of U.S. leadership in what is necessarily and intrinsically a global challenge. Some observers argue, however, that Trump's obstructions should not be attributed to him alone, but are in fact emblematic of trends that have long characterized deep ambivalence and polarization regarding climate change within the American polity (MacNeil et al., 2020; Panno et al., 2019). To the extent that proactive leadership is lacking in the White House, some of the focus for climate change action within the United States shifts to the local level (Landis et al., 2019). This aspect is explored more directly in Chapter 6 (Urban Policy).

A persistent theme in determining fair share burdens is the issue of developing versus developed countries. To the extent that rising GHG emissions are concomitant with economic growth and industrialization, some developing countries in particular view limitations on emissions as a de facto limitation on economic development. These developing countries are asserting their right to enjoy the same privileges of economic growth as those developed countries that have already done so. Accordingly, developing countries such as China and India have couched their pledges in terms of reduced carbon *intensity* (emissions per unit of GDP), rather than in terms of reduced emissions in the aggregate (Bodansky, 2010). The problem is that if developing countries were all to exercise this presumed right, and to move forward along conventional development trajectories, total emissions would quickly overwhelm the agreed upon goals and limitations under the FCCC. This was already a pressing issue at the time of the establishment of the FCCC, but it has become much more acute over recent decades as climate change reaches critical levels and as continuing growth in GHG emissions comes almost entirely from developing countries. Ultimately, the answer must lie in reciprocity, whereby each country makes difficult commitments, knowing that others are prepared to do the same in reasonable measure. Indeed, Tingley and Tomz (2013) find strong public support for such measures based on their survey work of political attitudes across 26 countries, and this is reinforced by the emergence of a next generation of young environmental activists, such as Greta

Thunberg from Sweden. A renewed round of pledges to the Green Climate Fund in 2019 is an encouraging sign that such voices are being heeded, as those pledges totaled $9.8 billion even without U.S. participation (Yeo, 2019).

China and the United States cannot escape the responsibility to provide joint leadership at a global scale through their own examples, individually and in concert with one another. Or, to put it more emphatically, if the U.S. and China cannot get their act together, there is little hope for the rest of the world. It is highly significant that, in addition to being the world's two largest GHG emitters, the United States and China also represent respective sides of the so-called North–South divide. Thus, joint leadership by these two countries has the potential to make definitive progress both at a quantitative level but also qualitatively by helping to shape a North–South accord. Thus, U.S.–China cooperation is a necessary but not sufficient condition for addressing the global challenge of climate change effectively. It may not be easy, though, as some on the U.S. side feel that China is shirking its rightful obligations, while Lieberthal and Sandalow argue:

> many Chinese, including many among the leadership, are deeply suspicious of American motives. They believe that the United States is determined to find some set of measures that will knock China off its current trajectory of rapid economic growth and increasing international influence.
>
> *(2009, p. 37)*

Mutual suspicion undermining potential collaboration on climate change is also evidenced by President Trump's "tweet" insisting that the concept of global warming "was created by and for the Chinese in order to make US manufacturing non-competitive" (Selby, 2019, p. 484).

Such pronouncements are in marked contrast to the "U.S.–China Joint Announcement on Climate Change" issued in November 2014. There, the U.S. announced its intent to reduce GHG emissions

> by 26%–28% below its 2005 level in 2025 and to make best efforts to reduce its emissions by 28% [and for its part] China intends to achieve the peaking of CO_2 emissions around 2030 and to make best efforts to peak early and intends to increase the share of non-fossil fuels in primary energy consumption to around 20% by 2030.
>
> *(White House, 2014)*

For the Obama Administration, this represented a substantial strengthening of its prior commitment to achieve a 17 percent reduction by 2020. Both sides expressed their hope and intent that this agreement would serve as a model for broader agreement within FCCC over the years to come. While this agreement was surely good news – better to have an agreement in place than not – the tough job for both Parties is in its implementation, even in the event that a proponent of climate change action occupies the White House.

For many years, the EPA resisted taking on such direct responsibility for regulating greenhouse gas emissions under the Clean Air Act (CAA). A 2007 Supreme Court case, *Massachusetts* v. *EPA*, changed that (Burtraw et al., 2011), and the Obama Administration proved to be much more proactive in applying the CAA to control GHG emissions. Under the CAA, the EPA has scope and authority to regulate GHG emissions from both mobile and stationary sources. Beginning in 2009, the EPA and Department of Transportation began issuing more stringent regulations on vehicles (Richardson and Fraas, 2013), although Siegel et al. (2012, p. 197) argue that "the transportation sector standards established thus far will not help the U.S. meet even its lackluster Copenhagen commitments, much less drive toward the steeper reductions scientists say are urgently necessary." In any event, stationary sources such as electricity generators must be a central component of any successful effort to reduce GHG emissions. Electricity generators account for roughly one-third of domestic GHG and 40 percent of CO_2 emissions (Burtraw et al., 2014, p. 1). Coal-fired generators are especially problematic, as they produce half of the country's electricity while contributing to 80 percent of GHG emissions from electricity generation (Burtraw et al., 2011, p. 10). Another important practical distinction is that of new generators and other emitting facilities versus older ones, as it is more costly to try to retrofit the latter.

As noted at the outset of this chapter, no one is *in favor of* greenhouse gas emissions per se. Instead, some would argue that the inevitable economic and/or social dislocation costs outweigh the benefits derived from reduced GHG emissions. This is a controversial issue within Congress, to say the least. As stated artfully in a Congressional Research Service report, Members of Congress "continue to be divided in their views on whether climate change risks merit raising current costs to the economy in exchange for benefits that would mostly accrue to future generations …" (Leggett, 2014, p. 1). Or, in another CRS report: "Critics … have accused the agency of reaching beyond the authority given it by Congress and ignoring or underestimating the costs and economic impacts of [EPA] rules" (McCarthy, 2014, p. 21). One way to reconcile this tradeoff, at least in principle, is by establishing a social cost of carbon.

Social Cost of Carbon

CO_2 and other greenhouse gas emissions present a classic case of externalities. The economics literature on this topic is highly evolved, with many of the key principles articulated almost a century ago. Most trained economists, this author included, are naturally inclined to search for pricing solutions to such problems wherever it is practical to do so (Richardson and Fraas, 2013). Indeed, the very term "externality" derives from the fact that decisions about how much to pollute, for example, are made outside the purview of markets. All productive economic activity entails the use of inputs such as labor, capital, or natural resources. Well-functioning markets are a proven albeit imperfect means to allocate scare resources efficiently. Prices, as a measure of value, are key to this process. From this perspective, there is a fundamental and systemic flaw in the way that carbon emissions are "priced" – in fact, the problem is that they are generally not priced at all, so the implicit message is that there is no cost associated with GHG emissions, which is clearly not consistent with the science on climate change as summarized above. The market failure arises because people who are negatively impacted by GHG emissions are not in a position to "purchase" a reduction. There is no market for such a transaction – hence, the externality.

If "zero" is the wrong price, it begs the question of what the right price is. This question was addressed in a rather formal way during the Obama Administration by the *Interagency Working Group on Social Cost of Carbon*, as documented in two reports in 2010 and 2013, respectively. The agencies involved include those shown in Table 5.1.

Their task was, in effect, to "internalize" the externalities attendant to carbon emissions. Or, as they put it:

> The purpose of the 'social cost of carbon' (SCC) estimates [is] to allow agencies to incorporate the social benefits of reducing carbon dioxide (CO_2) emissions into cost-benefit analyses of regulatory actions that impact cumulative global emissions. The SCC is an estimate of the monetized damages associated with an incremental increase in carbon emissions in a given year. It is intended to include (but is not limited to) changes in net agricultural productivity, human health, property damages from increased flood risk, and the value of ecosystem services due to climate change.
>
> *(White House, 2013, p. 2)*

TABLE 5.1 Agencies involved in the Interagency Working Group on Social Cost of Carbon

• Council of Economic Advisors	• Department of Transportation
• Council on Environmental Quality	• Environmental Protection Agency
• Department of Agriculture	• National Economic Council
• Department of Commerce	• Office of Management and Budget
• Department of Energy	• Office of Science and Technology Policy
• Department of Treasury	

The principal finding of their analysis is that the social cost of carbon was approximately \$33 per metric ton of CO_2 in 2010, and that this figure then proceeds to rise steadily by roughly one dollar per year over the next several decades.[7] The steadily rising social cost of carbon reflects the fact that as CO_2 continues to accumulate in the Earth's atmosphere, the cost of additional accumulation becomes even more acute. Incorporating these figures into cost-benefit decisions for projects requiring federal government financial support and/or regulatory approval, this measure can provide a foundation for trading off the benefits of reduced carbon emissions against the benefits of economic activities that give rise to those emissions. It helps to mimic the ideal signaling properties of a market. As explained in more detail below, the rise of China is reflected in a higher social cost of carbon. If China were not rising along its current trajectory, there would be a lower concentration of greenhouse gases in the atmosphere, so the damages from climate change to the United States and the rest of the world would be lessened. Thus, though the impact mechanism is somewhat indirect or latent, the end result is a substantial impact on resource allocation decisions within the United States. A very interesting question in this regard is: *To what extent does the rise of China add to the social cost of carbon?* Of course, a similar question could be asked about the United States or any other country or group of countries. Put another way, what would be the SCC under a scenario whereby China's emissions were to remain flat over time instead of growing as they are projected to do?

Carbon Tax vs. Cap-and-Trade

It is all well and good to calculate a social cost of carbon – indeed, it is of fundamental importance that we understand what that cost is. The next challenge, however, is to incorporate such cost data into the decision-making calculus of a myriad decision-makers whose actions influence emissions levels for better or worse. One way to do this is through regulatory mechanisms, and indeed that is how the SCC is generally used by government agencies, via cost-benefit analysis and other evaluation methods. Another approach, that may be complementary to existing regulatory mechanisms, is to rely on market incentives, of which there are two principal policy instruments. One is a carbon tax while the other is a cap-and-trade market for emissions entitlements. The Appendix to this chapter provides a more detailed discussion of the distinction between these two mechanisms, while what follows here is a more cursory overview.

A *carbon tax* has several advantages. It is a relatively intuitive proposition with direct conceptual links to the social cost of carbon. Setting the tax equal to the social cost of carbon would, in principle, correct for the inherent pollution externality problem. This is a classic Pigovian tax, so-named for the early twentieth-century economist, Alfred Pigou. It would help to correct the misconception that carbon emissions are costless, and would thus recalibrate resource allocation decisions throughout the carbon economy. A carbon tax is also relatively simple to administer, especially if applied to upstream emitters (Richardson and Fraas, 2013). Another compelling advantage of a carbon tax is its potential to generate revenues, especially during a period of chronic public sector deficits. Based on EPA estimates, electricity generation alone produces over 2 billion metric tons of CO_2 emissions annually.[8] At \$33 per metric ton or more – the social cost of carbon figure reported above – this could generate considerable revenue, even after allowing for the hoped-for reductions in emissions in response to such a tax. Taxes are often deeply unpopular, but so too are chronic public sector deficits.

A *cap-and-trade* system, while potentially more complex to administer, also has some distinct advantages. As its name suggests, there are two elements to this approach, the first of which is to set a ceiling or cap on total emissions. This helps link it more directly to emissions targets, which is the focus of most FCCC-related agreements, as well as bilateral agreements between the United States and China. For example, if the U.S. sets an emissions target for 2025 of a 26 percent reduction in GHG emissions relative to the 2005 peak, as pledged in the November 2014 joint announcement by President Obama and President Xi, then a cap set to that level is immediately consistent with the specified goal. In principle, a carbon tax could yield the same result in emissions reductions, but only if the tax were chosen correctly. Choosing the correct level can be a tricky proposition – notwithstanding the valiant efforts of the Interagency Working Group. This is in fact an important distinction between the two market mechanisms for pricing carbon. *With a carbon tax, one in effect fixes the price of carbon and allows the quantity of emissions to adjust accordingly. With a cap-and-trade, one fixes emissions and allows the market to work out the price of carbon.* Unfortunately, it is not generally possible in a market context for regulators to set both the price of carbon and the quantity of emissions.[9]

The "trade" in cap–and–trade is the market mechanism that helps translate a cap on emissions into a price for carbon. By imposing a cap on carbon emissions, regulators create a scarcity for "polluting rights." The right to pollute is an entitlement, and this entitlement is itself an asset. If there is a market to support it, the scarce asset becomes a tradable asset. A key question is *who* will retain the right to emit CO_2. Allocation of the ownership of the *initial* entitlements is a political decision, and is fraught with all of the complications that might entail. Burtraw et al. (2011, p. 21) note that if a cap–and–trade were to emerge under the authority of the existing Clean Air Act, the allocation decision would be the prerogative of the states, but it would likely be a federal prerogative under any new Congressional legislation. A subsequent paper by Burtraw et al. examines a number of plausible options regarding the initial allocation of emissions entitlements, finding that

> producers and consumers together fare much better when the value of assets created by introducing a [price] on carbon is kept within the electricity sector than if the value accrues to government, even though the latter

approach would have lower social cost. [In every scenario] the net benefits of regulation are positive and large.

(2014, p. 11ff.)

As China rises, so too does the social cost of carbon. As a consequence, the
domestic politics in the United States over climate change becomes more
contentious.

Chinese Offsets?

Yet another potential linkage to China in the context of climate change is
through *international offsets*. The challenge for the United States, and likewise for
any other country, is to "pollute efficiently." For any given level of CO_2 emissions, one wishes to obtain as much corresponding economic output as possible.[10] As the U.S. undertakes to reduce its emissions, it makes sense therefore
to prioritize reductions that minimize any consequent loss of economic output.
From this perspective, carbon-intensive activities are "low hanging fruit,"
because a relatively small loss in economic output can be compensated for by a
commensurately large reduction in carbon emissions. For highly carbon-
efficient economies such as those of Japan or some European countries, it is
more costly to achieve additional reductions in carbon emissions because any
readily identifiable opportunities have already been wrung from the system. The
low-hanging fruit has all been picked. By the same token, carbon-inefficient
countries are still ripe with opportunities.

Recall, too, that climate change due to greenhouse gas emissions is an intrinsically global challenge, both in terms of the source of the problem (mitigation)
and in terms of its consequences (adaptation). There may be opportunities for
win–win arrangements, therefore, whereby the United States could earn credits
for emissions reductions by helping China to achieve reductions that might not
otherwise be attained. This is the principle of an overseas "offset." A simple
numerical example can help illustrate the point. Suppose that the most cost-
effective means of reducing carbon emissions by a certain quantity in the U.S.
results in $100 of lost economic output. Suppose further that in China the same
reduction might be achieved for a loss of only $40. By compensating China for
the $40, the United States could earn credit for that quantum of carbon reduc-
tion, while China and the U.S. then might share the $60 efficiency savings. The
Clean Development Mechanism (CDM) is a project-based carbon market
designed for just this purpose, and China is its largest supplier of emissions-
reduction projects. One difficulty with CDM is that of "additionality" – verifying
that actual emissions represent a reduction relative to a default baseline projection
(Zhang and Wang, 2011). Such administrative challenges may be daunting, but
this approach could be worthwhile given the enormity of the reductions required,
and given the substantial cost advantages of "low hanging fruit" in China.

Geoengineering Options for Climate Change Mitigation

Thus far, our discussion of climate change mitigation has focused on reducing greenhouse gas emissions. Bracmort and Lattanzio (2013) provide a nice overview of a full range of additional "geoengineering" technologies that might be applied to climate change mitigation. As the rise of China contributes substantially, along with the U.S. and other countries, to the urgent necessity of climate change mitigation, these are the kinds of policy responses that may be required. One approach is carbon capture and sequestration (CCS) (Folger, 2014). As its name suggests, the technique entails capturing CO_2 emissions at their source and then storing or sequestering them out of harm's way. Folger (2013, p. 1) describes three main steps in an integrated CCS system:

1 Capturing CO_2 and separating it from other gases.
2 Purifying, compressing and transporting the captured CO_2 to the sequestration site.
3 Injecting the CO_2 into subsurface geological reservoirs or storing it in the oceans.

As noted by Bracmort and Lattanzio:

> One of the main challenges to CCS deployment is the lack of a regulatory framework to permit geologic sequestration of CO_2. An integrated structure ... involves identifying who owns the sequestered CO_2, where to sequester the CO_2, defining what constitutes leakage, identifying who will be held liable if the sequestered CO_2 leaks, developing a monitoring and maintenance plan, and developing a robust pipeline infrastructure specifically for CO_2 that will be sequestered.
>
> *(2013, p. 12)*

Another broad category of mitigation response, which we just mention briefly, comprises solar radiation management techniques. These entail means by which some solar radiation is diverted from entering the Earth's atmosphere, thereby reducing the global warming effect to some degree.

Even if this full spate of mitigation measures is applied vigorously, it is likely that the impacts of climate change will be felt with ever more force. This leaves the United States and other countries with no choice but to adapt somehow. Some of the adaptation will be in terms of ecological systems themselves as species migrate or agricultural practices evolve. Much of the adaptation will be felt directly by ordinary Americans in the course of our daily lives. The pace of climate change can be just slow enough that we do not notice its onset, but fast enough that it catches us by surprise. Mitigation measures are costly, but that is the price we must pay if we wish to avoid the impacts of climate change.

Adaptation measures are disruptive, but that is the price we must pay if we do not undertake sufficient mitigation. It is a closed loop system, but the loop is complex and multifaceted, so the tie-ins are not always evident, or are too easy to doubt or deny. The rise of China is the strongest single contributor to the intense discomforts that will be felt increasingly by Americans (and Chinese, and others) as we grapple with the unpalatable choices over mitigation and adaptation. China's role is not so much one of malfeasance as it is one of magnitude. When China belches gigantic quantities of greenhouse gases into the Earth's atmosphere, it is following our lead. Now it is time for us to lead anew and to heed the warning of Siegel et al. (2012, p. 224): "History will not look kindly upon the generation that failed to act on the climate crisis."

Appendix: A Primer on Carbon Tax Versus Cap and Trade

The juxtaposition of Figures 5.2a and 5.2b helps clarify the distinction between a carbon tax versus a cap and trade mechanism, respectively, and the repercussions of each. In both figures, "A" and "B" refer to two firms, each with its own distinctive array of production technologies.[11] Notice that the placement of the two downward sloping curves, denoted A and B respectively, are in precisely the same position in both graphs. This simply reflects the fact that the underlying production technologies are the same, regardless of whether a carbon tax or cap-and-trade mechanism is applied. What does change is how the firms will respond to such policies in either case, as discussed next.

In either figure, the horizontal dimension measures emissions, which increase as one moves from left to right. The vertical dimension indicates the economic product generated from the activities that cause those emissions. Put another way, carbon emissions are an inevitable but unwanted by-product of a full range of economic activities. Not all production processes are the same in this regard, and that is why the production schedules A and B differ from each other. In particular, we can see that the production technology indicated by schedule B lies above and to the right of schedule A, indicating that B is a more emissions-intensive industry or sector than A, relative to the value of their corresponding outputs. Figures 5.2a and 5.2b thus show the tradeoff between emissions and output. For each additional "quantum" of emissions as one moves to the right on the graph, schedule A or B indicates the net value (or "profit") of the corresponding marginal product. In the absence of any external policy intervention, each firm will continue to produce until it has exhausted all of the profit to be derived from that activity. In graphic terms, that point is indicated where schedule A or B intersects the horizontal axis. The corresponding area beneath schedule A or B then represents total profitability.

It is in this context that a carbon tax or cap-and-trade mechanism might be imposed. A simple *carbon tax* is represented in Figure 5.2a by t*, a flat rate tax that yields tax revenues in direct proportion to the volume of emissions. Either

Tax is exogenously determined → Emissions levels are endogenously determined

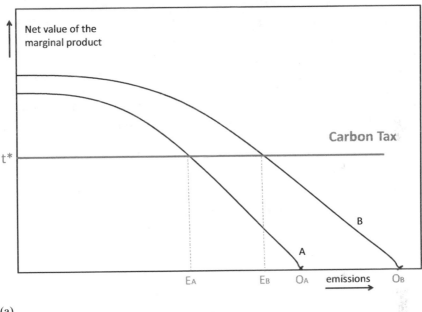

(a)

Cap on emissions set exogenously → Price determined endogenously

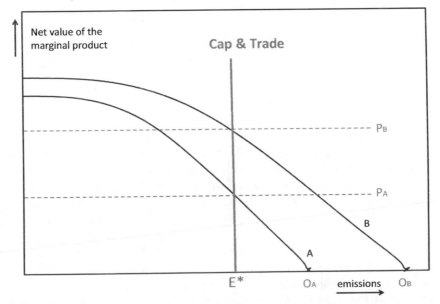

(b)

FIGURE 5.2   (a) Carbon tax; (b) Cap and trade

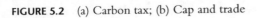

firm will continue to generate emissions up to the point when it is no longer profitable to do so, which now occurs when the carbon tax exceeds any incremental profit. The resulting level of emissions is depicted in Figure 5.2a by E_A for firm A and E_B for firm B. So, as noted in the main text, a carbon tax policy intervention pertains to the price or cost of carbon, with emissions levels adjusting accordingly.

It is useful now to consider the impacts arising from the carbon tax. First, we can see that a carbon tax *should* (in the absence of administrative hurdles, discussed below) lead directly to a reduction in emissions, which is indeed its chief aim. For firm A, the reduction achieved is from the original O_A down to E_A, likewise for firm B emissions are reduced from O_B to E_B. Of course, neither firm will be pleased with this outcome, as total profits will be truncated accordingly. A higher carbon tax results in both reduced emissions AND reduced profits, and that no doubt explains much of the resistance it engenders.

Of course, yet another implication of a carbon tax is that it generates tax revenues as well. In Figure 5.2a, the total carbon tax collected from firm A is represented by the rectangle defined by the carbon tax schedule at E_A, and likewise for firm B at E_B. In principle, these same tax revenues could be used by the government to provide tangible support for the firms. For example, those tax revenues could be earmarked for infrastructure projects that benefit all firms within a particular sector or region. Alternatively, revenues raised by a carbon tax could in principle be used to reduce the level of corporate income tax that would otherwise be raised in the aggregate by those same firms. Of course, in an era of very tight public sector budgets, there will always be a temptation to direct those carbon tax revenues elsewhere, in which case, affected firms are likely to view the carbon tax as an unmitigated loss.

Figure 5.2a also helps us to understand some of the administrative hurdles associated with a carbon tax. One challenge is to set the appropriate carbon tax rate, t^*. If it is set too low, it will result in insufficient emissions reductions. If it is set too high, it will deprive the economy of valuable output in goods and services. Ideally, it should be set to match the social cost of carbon (SCC), as discussed in the text.[12] A related point is that a carbon tax gets at emissions reduction targets *indirectly*. In certain respects, this approach can be preferable, especially if those who are setting the carbon tax have a definitive sense of the social, economic, and environmental costs arising from carbon dioxide emissions. In this case, it may be quite reasonable to set the tax rate t^* to reflect this cost and then allow each firm to adjust accordingly. Indeed, this is the classic approach to taxing externalities, popularized by the early twentieth-century economist Alfred Pigou. In a sense, this "Pigovian" approach is more focused on achieving an appropriate balance between harmful carbon emissions and otherwise beneficial economic productivity, and is content to allow emissions levels to adjust accordingly. To the extent that the imperative to reduce carbon emissions is derived from quota-based international agreements between the

United States, China, and other signatory nations, an approach that targets emissions reductions more directly may be called for.

Cap and trade is one such approach, as illustrated in Figure 5.2b. Here, the underlying production technologies for firms A and B are precisely as depicted in the earlier Figure 5.2a. The "cap" part of cap and trade is an upper bound on the allowable emissions, indicated here by the vertical line at $E^\star$. If this cap is applied effectively in equal measure to all firms, both A and B will have the same level of emissions, but the strain on firm B will be higher. To understand why this is so, suppose that the emissions cap, $E^\star$, were to be eased just a bit, allowing both firms to take "one step" to the right of $E^\star$ in Figure 5.2b. From the graph, we can see that firm B would enjoy an extra increment of profit evaluated at P_B, while firm A would realize a smaller profit gain at P_A. Another way of saying the same thing is that there is a higher opportunity cost for firm B imposed by the $E^\star$ cap compared to firm A. Not only does this raise a fairness issue, it is also inefficient from an economic perspective because it should be possible to achieve the same reduction in aggregate emissions with less loss of economic output. This is where the "trade" part of cap-and-trade comes into play. It sets up a market mechanism by which firm B can purchase emissions entitlements from firm A. If the two firms were to agree to exchange emission entitlements at any intermediate price between P_A and P_B, both firms would be better off as a result of such a trade, while the total emissions level would remain unchanged. Thus, under a cap-and-trade system, the cap targets aggregate emissions level directly while the trade allows market-based adjustments between firms to promote a more efficient and equitable allocation of the imposed cap. Two examples of such cap-and-trade emissions markets are those established through the Regional Greenhouse Gas Initiative (RGGI) and the Western Climate Initiative, respectively (MacNeil and Paterson, 2020).

We are now in a position to view the impacts on the United States arising from the rise of China. From a carbon tax perspective, in Figure 5.2a, the rise of China results first in a higher social cost of carbon, and thus a higher carbon tax than would otherwise be called for. That in turn will prompt firms A and B to reduce their emissions levels further, resulting in an even greater loss of productive output. From a cap-and-trade perspective, in Figure 5.2b, the rise of China means that all countries, including both China and the United States, will be compelled to undertake sharper reductions in emissions than would otherwise be the case. That in turn will increase the scarcity value of emission entitlements.

Discussion Questions

1   President Trump famously tweeted that "the concept of global warming was created by and for the Chinese in order to make US manufacturing non-competitive." Is this plausible? If yes, what line of reasoning might lead to this conclusion? If no, what line of reasoning would refute it?

2   Is it possible for the United States and China to exercise joint leadership in dealing with the global challenge of climate change? Is it necessary – in other words, is there a viable alternative to combatting climate change if the U.S. and China do not cooperate actively and effectively in this area?

3   If you had to choose one or the other, which mechanism would you be in favor of in order to reduce GHG emissions in the United States?: (a) implementing a carbon tax or (b) setting up a cap-and-trade system. For you, what is the deciding factor in making this choice?

Notes

1 As reported below, however, Shapiro and Walker (2014) find that the steady decline over recent decades in pollutants from U.S. manufacturing industries cannot be attributed to a swap of polluting industries to China or other foreign venues. Instead, their careful analysis provides strong evidence that a tougher regulatory posture by EPA is the primary cause of the decline.

2 See www.howglobalwarmingworks.org/400-words.html for a concise explanation of this phenomenon.

3 Note that the data represented in Figure 5.1 are megatons of CO_2 emissions from fuel consumption only. These are indicative of the full range of CO_2 emission sources by country/region.

4 The Third National Climate Assessment, released in May 2014, is available at nca2014. globalchange.gov.

5 More specifically, the map compares average temperatures between one recent period (1991–2012) and an historical baseline reference period (1901–1960).

6 See http://unfccc.int/2860.php.

7 Those figures for the social cost of carbon are all in 2007 constant dollars. Estimates depend upon a range of underlying assumptions, including, critically, the discount rate used to assess future costs and benefits. Those reported here are based on a 3 percent discount rate, which the report identifies as "central."

8 Calculated from data reported in www.epa.gov/climatechange/ghgemissions/gases/co2.html.

9 There are not sufficient "degrees of freedom" in a market context for regulators to specify *both* the quantity of emissions and the price of carbon independently. The reason is that the price–quantity combinations must be consistent with the market demand schedule, which is itself a set of price–quantity combinations indicating how many emissions entitlements market actors are prepared to purchase at a given price. The Appendix to this chapter provides further details.

10 This can be restated in its equivalent "dual" form: For any level of economic output, one wishes to minimize CO_2 emissions.

11 A similar analysis, with appropriate modifications, could apply at the country level, for example, with the United States as country "A" and China as country "B."

12 The desirability of setting $t^* = SCC$ is predicated of course on calculating the latter correctly. This underlines the importance of the work undertaken by the Interagency Working Group on Social Cost of Carbon, as discussed in the text.

References

Bodansky, Daniel (2010). "The Copenhagen Climate Change Conference: A Postmortem," *American Journal of International Law*, 104(2), 230–240.

Bracmort, Kelsi and Richard Lattanzio (2013). *Geoengineering: Governance and Technology Policy*, CRS Report RS41371, Washington, DC: Congressional Research Service.

Burtraw, Dallas, Arthur Fraas, and Nathan Richardson (2011). "Greenhouse Gas Regulation under the Clean Air Act: A Guide for Economists," Discussion Paper RFF DP 11-08, Resources for the Future.

Burtraw, Dallas, Joshua Lin, Karen Palmer, and Anthony Paul (2014). "The Costs and Consequences of Clean Air Act Regulation of CO_2 from Power Plants," Discussion Paper RFF DP 14-01, Resources for the Future.

Folger, Peter (2013). *Carbon Capture and Sequestration (CCS): A Primer*, CRS Report R42532, Washington, DC: Congressional Research Service.

Folger, Peter (2014). *The FutureGen Carbon Capture and Sequestration Project: A Brief History and Issues for Congress*, CRS Report R43028, Washington, DC: Congressional Research Service.

IPCC (2018). "Summary for Policy Makers (SPM)," Special Report on Global Warming of 1.5 °C, Geneva: Intergovernmental Panel on Climate Change.

IPCC WG III (2014). "Summary for Policy Makers (SPM)," *Climate Change 2014: Mitigation of Climate Change*, Working Group III, Fifth Assessment Report (AR5), Geneva: Intergovernmental Panel on Climate Change.

Landis, John, David Hsu, and Erick Guerra (2019). "Intersecting Residential and Transportation CO_2 Emissions: Metropolitan Climate Change Programs in the Age of Trump," *Journal of Planning Education and Research*, 39(2), 206–226.

Leggett, Jane (2014). *President Obama's Climate Action Plan*, CRS Report R43120, Washington, DC: Congressional Research Service.

Lieberthal, Kenneth and David Sandalow (2009). *Overcoming Obstacles to U.S.–China Cooperation on Climate Change*, Monograph Series No. 1, Washington, DC: John L. Thornton China Center, Brookings Institution.

Liu, Runjuan and Daniel Trefler (2008). "Much Ado About Nothing: American Jobs and the Rise of Service Outsourcing to China and India", NBER Working Paper, No. 14061 (June), National Bureau of Economic Research, Cambridge, MA.

MacNeil, Robert and Matthew Paterson (2020). "Trump, US Climate Politics, and the Evolving Pattern of Global Climate Governance," *Global Change, Peace & Security*, 32(1), 1–18.

McCarthy, James (2014). *Clean Air Issues in the 113th Congress: An Overview*, CRS Report R42895, Washington, DC: Congressional Research Service.

McCarthy, James and Claudia Copeland (2014). *EPA Regulations: Too Much, Too Little, or On Track?*, CRS Report R41561, Washington, DC: Congressional Research Service.

NCA (National Climate Assessment) (2014). "Third National Climate Assessment." Available at: www.nca2014.globalchange.gov

Panno, Angelo, Giuseppe Carrus, and Luigi Leone (2019). "Attitudes towards Trump Policies and Climate Change: The Key Roles of Aversion to Wealth Redistribution and Political Interest," *Journal of Social Issues*, 75(1), 153–168.

Peters, Glen, Jan Minx, Christopher Weber, and Ottmar Edenhofer (2011). "Growth in Emission Transfers Via International Trade from 1990 to 2008," *Papers of the National Academy of Science*, 108(21), 8903–8908.

Richardson, Nathan and Arthur Fraas (2013). "Comparing the Clean Air Act and a Carbon Price," Discussion Paper RFF DP 13-13, Resources for the Future.

Sato, Misato (2012). "Embodied Carbon in Trade: A Survey of the Empirical Literature," Working Paper No. 89, Centre for Climate Change and Economic Policy; University of Leeds and London School of Economics and Political Science.

Selby, Jan (2019). "The Trump Presidency, Climate Change, and the Prospect of a Disorderly Energy Transition," *Review of International Studies*, 45(3), 471–490.

Shapiro, Joseph and Reed Walker (2014). "Why Is Pollution from U.S. Manufacturing Declining? The Roles of Trade, Regulation, Productivity, and Preferences." Available at: http://faculty.haas.berkeley.edu/rwalker/research/ShapiroWalkerPollution-ProductivityTrade.pdf.

Siegel, Kassie, Kevin Bundy, and Vera Pardee (2012). "Strong Law, Timid Implementation: How the EPA Can Apply the Full Force of the Clean Air Act to Address the Climate Crisis," *UCLA Journal of Environmental Law and Policy*, 30, 185–225.

Tingley, Dustin and Michael Tomz (2013). "Conditional Cooperation and Climate Change," *Comparative Political Studies*, 47(3), 344–368.

White House (2013). "Technical Update of the Social Cost of Carbon for Regulatory Impact Analysis – Under Executive Order 12866," *Technical Support Document*, Interagency Working Group on Social Cost of Carbon, Washington, DC: U.S. Government.

White House (2014). "U.S.–China Joint Announcement on Climate Change," *Press Release*, 12 November 2014.

Yeo, Sophie (2019). "Green Climate Fund Attracts Record US$9.8 Billion for Developing Nations," *Nature*, November 1. Available at: www.nature.com/articles/d41586-019-03330-9.

Zhang, Junjie and Can Wang (2011). "Co-Benefits and Additionality of the Clean Development Mechanism: An Empirical Analysis," *Journal of Environmental Economics and Management*, 62(2), 140–154.

6

URBAN POLICY

China, U.S. Cities, and Climate Change

Urban policies, both in the United States and in China, provide a natural progression from Chapter 5's focus on climate change. As is true for most developed countries, the United States is predominantly urban and has been so already for many decades. By 2020, as shown in Table 6.1, about five of every six persons in the United States reside in cities, and by 2050 this proportion is expected to reach nine of every ten persons. Therefore, it is largely within cities that most Americans will encounter the challenges posed by climate change. Our urban lifestyles will need to be modified quite radically if we are to do our part in reducing global greenhouse gas (GHG) emissions. And, to the extent that sufficient reductions in emissions are not forthcoming, it is within cities that most Americans will have to learn to cope. Ironically, however, Americans may be even more impacted in terms of climate change by what goes on in Chinese cities. The reason, of course, is that the magnitude of urbanization in China is of consequential significance globally. In just the last three decades alone, China's urban population has risen from 310 million to 875 million. That

TABLE 6.1 Urban population, in thousands (and as percentage of total population)

	1990 (%)	2020 (%)	2050 (%)
United States	190,156 (75.3)	273,975 (82.7)	347,346 (89.2)
China	310,022 (26.4)	875,076 (61.4)	1,091,948 (80.0)
World	2,290,228 (43.0)	4,378,994 (56.2)	6,679,756 (68.4)

Source: United Nations.

net increment to China's urban population over that interval is more than double the entire *existing* urban population of the United States! Thus, the United States and China have a shared interest in ensuring that urbanization in both countries follows a sustainable trajectory. The same is true globally, where a veritable urban tsunami is underway as *each week* the world's urban population increases by 1.3 million.[1]

The Trump Administration's denial of climate change has accelerated a trend toward more active engagement by state and local governments and by non-governmental actors (Landis et al., 2019; MacNeil and Paterson, 2020; Selby, 2019). This includes initiatives such as C40, a global network now comprising more than 90 megacities around the world – including nine in mainland China and 12 in the United States – that are committed to combatting climate change through effective policy action. It also includes regionally based markets for trading emissions entitlements, such as those supported by the Western Climate Initiative and the Regional Greenhouse Gas Initiative (RGGI). The "We Are Still In" coalition is perhaps the most direct response to the Trump Administration's intended withdrawal from the Paris Agreement. Its home page declares emphatically, "President Trump Wants Out – We Are Still In," and avows active participation from thousands of businesses and investors and hundreds of city or county governments.[2] While national-level initiatives are (or should) remain vitally important, the climate change movement is evolving steadily into a more decentralized, multifaceted climate regime complex with local actors energizing global networks (MacNeil and Paterson, 2020).

The IPCC's Working Group III, in its *Fifth Assessment Report* (AR5) finds that urban areas account for between 71 percent and 76 percent of CO_2 emissions from final energy use. It follows that reducing emissions in urban areas is a necessary (but not sufficient) condition for achieving reduction quotas agreed upon through the auspices of the UN's Framework Convention for Climate Change (FCCC). Wringing a substantial reduction in greenhouse gas emissions from U.S. cities may be necessary, but it is a daunting challenge for several reasons. Unlike, for example, an electricity generating plant with a unified ownership structure and a centralized decision-making nexus, cities are agglomerations of millions of largely autonomous residents who make their own decisions (subject to opportunities and constraints, of course) about where to live, where to work, what to drive and a myriad other decisions that – in the aggregate – have an enormous impact on GHG emissions. Moreover, many of these decisions are in fact culturally embedded lifestyle choices that are made at a subconscious level and so are even less subject to policy interventions. For example, in many office settings business attire is expected, so coats and ties are worn even when the weather outdoors may not call for it. Rather than adjusting our clothing to suit the weather, we adjust our indoor climate to "suit the suit." Ironically, this use of climate control at a micro level indoors may result in our losing control of our global climate outdoors.

Things are not much simpler at a jurisdictional level. The National League of Cities[3] reports that there are 19,492 municipal governments in the United States. Each one may have its own set of standards with respect to land use zoning, building codes, speed limits, street layouts, and other factors (including enforcement) that all contribute to lifestyle and behavioral choices of its denizens. These municipal governments are in turn creatures of their respective state governments, of which there are 50. Unlike in China, state governments in the United States are *not* integral units of a national system of governance, nor are municipalities mere sub-units of their respective state governments. Federal agencies do have some leverage through financial and other incentives, and these should not be discounted, but ultimately the decisions that affect urban GHG emissions fall not just to federal government policies, but also to 50 relatively autonomous states, 19,492 municipalities and 274 million urban dwellers.

California is a good example of this, with its 35 million urban dwellers residing in 478 municipalities.[4] It is not just its size that makes California of interest; it has also been on the forefront in responding to climate change. In particular, Assembly Bill (AB) 32 and Senate Bill (SB) 375 have received much attention. AB 32 was adopted in 2006 and called for state-wide reductions in greenhouse gas emissions to 1990 levels by the year 2020. Executive Orders by California governors have gone even further. SB 375 is especially significant, as it is the first example of a U.S. state-level government setting out to achieve targeted reductions in GHG emissions through coordinated land use and transportation policies (Barbour and Deakin, 2012; California Air Resources Board, 2008). This is done through the California Air Resources Board, which in turn has assigned targets to each of the state's 18 Metropolitan Planning Organizations (MPOs).[5] Some of these MPOs are quite large – the Southern California Association of Governments, for example, comprises 191 municipal governments in a region with more than 19 million residents.

Figure 6.1 helps depict what this process entails for a stylized U.S. metropolitan region with multiple jurisdictions. Each individual municipality has primary control over local land use policies, zoning ordinances, building codes, construction permits, design guidelines, and related regulations within its jurisdiction. These policy instruments are intended to help locally elected officials and their professional staffs shape the quantity, quality, and character of the local built environment. Within large metropolitan regions containing numerous municipalities, application of these regulatory tools also helps each municipality to differentiate itself from its neighboring jurisdictions. This in turn prompts households to "vote with their feet" by moving to the jurisdiction that offers the bundle of local public services and other localized characteristics (including attributes of other residents) that best suits the household's budget and preferences. This is analogous in many ways to the method by which individuals may select which club to belong to, based on club location, activities, facilities, prestige, dues, and membership rosters (Heikkila, 1996, 2000).

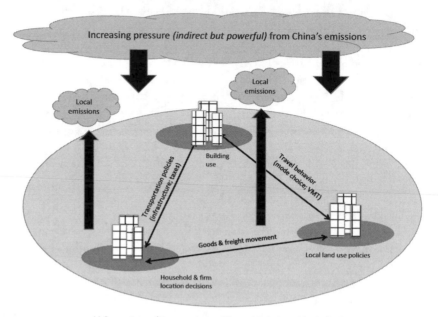

U.S. metropolitan region with multiple local jurisdictions

FIGURE 6.1 Urban regions and climate change
Note: VMT = vehicle miles traveled.

Local regulations as described above set the stage for much of what follows. Local building codes influence the energy efficiency of the buildings within which we live and work. Local regulations also help determine the density of the population and of residential units, offices, or other structures within specified geographic areas. Those in turn become the origin and destination "nodes" within a large matrix of transportation movements of both people and goods. Household decisions about where to live may be based on the cost of housing in different neighborhoods, the quality of schools and amenities, or other such considerations. Meanwhile, decisions about where to work will be based on salary or wage differentials, job specifications relative to qualifications and training, and other considerations, including location. The net result of such decisions helps shape observed travel behaviors, but an additional consideration includes mode choice (automobile versus public transit, for example). Mode choice in turn will be heavily influenced by local, state, and federal transportation policies including gasoline taxes or investments in light rail, roadways, bicycle lanes, buses, or other infrastructure projects. The economic feasibility of those projects in turn depends upon land use density patterns. A similarly complex web of considerations applies to the movement of goods.

This is all a bit unwieldy, with multitudes of autonomous decision makers, but the cumulative impact of those myriad decisions on greenhouse gas emissions is large (Boarnet, 2010). A recent C40 report to the U.N. Secretary-General argues that cities can contribute significantly to bridging the global emissions gap. It shows that collective efforts of the world's cities can partially bridge the gap between the targeted "2°C scenario" and a base case "reference scenario." The former is what would be needed to limit global warming to 2°C while the latter is based on current commitments based on national action plans. The C40 Cities report goes on to say:

> The most significant GHG abatement opportunities for cities (those that comprise at least 10% of the abatement potential) are related to deep building shell energy standards, building energy retrofits, appliance and lighting standards, and mode shift and transit efficiency for personal urban mobility.
>
> *(2014, p. 5)*

Within the United States, and prompted in part by the introduction of California's SB 375, a National Research Council study in 2009 undertook a thorough and systematic review of the nexus between local land use regulations, regional coordination through Metropolitan Planning Organizations, a full range of transportation policies, and greenhouse gas emissions. The NRC report's key findings are echoed and amplified in the *Fifth Assessment Review* by the Intergovernmental Panel on Climate Change (IPCC WG III, 2014).

Landis et al. (2019) undertook a thorough analysis of the potential for local government initiatives to achieve reductions in CO_2 emissions. One set of regulations and initiatives pertains to residential energy conservation mandates through enhanced building codes and other measures. The effectiveness of such measures varies from one metropolitan area to another due to differences in weather, existing building stock, population change, and other considerations. By examining these and other factors across 11 representative metropolitan areas in the United States, they find that on average such measures have the potential to reduce emissions by up to 30 percent by the year 2030. Likewise, using a similar approach, they assess the potential to achieve reduced emissions via stricter emissions standards for automobiles and by shifting travel modes – away from private automobiles in favor of public transit or other more benign travel modes. They estimate a potential for reduced emissions by up to 25 percent by the year 2030. The role of rapidly emerging new technologies further complicates the picture, as the impacts on emissions of ride-hailing apps such as Uber or Lyft (especially as they begin to deploy driverless vehicles) are as yet uncertain (Ward et al., 2019; Wenzel et al., 2019; Young and Farber, 2019).

The discussion thus far has focused on the role of U.S. cities in *mitigating* climate change. That which cannot be mitigated must be adapted to, so climate change *adaptation* is another major pillar of climate change policies. Just as U.S. cities must play a central role in mitigation efforts, they will also bear the brunt of any failure to do so. Heikkila and Huang (2014) outline a framework for selecting from a range of potential adaptation strategies in case of inundation of urban areas. One set of strategies entails modification of the physical geography or topography through construction of berms, levees and other infrastructure projects, and through modifications to dwelling units. Another approach is to restrict land uses in vulnerable areas so as to reduce exposure to potential hazards. Yet another approach is to "self-insure," hope for the best, and then respond after the fact as needed. Each of these adaptation strategies has a distinct cost-benefit calculus, depending on the conditions on the ground, so the best approach will be determined by the particular context on a case-by-case basis. From a political economy perspective, one notes that there is an asymmetry of stakeholder interests in comparing mitigation versus adaptation strategies. Mitigation is inherently a collective global effort, and within the United States it entails a broad effort – even (or especially) during times that federal leadership may be lacking. With adaptation, however, some subsets of the population are clearly more at risk than others, depending upon the disposition of geographical, socio-economic, institutional, or other factors contributing to vulnerability. Those who regard themselves as less vulnerable may be less fulsome in their commitment to costly or inconvenient mitigation measures.

While our focus is on U.S. policy, urban issues loom large in China also and urbanization in China *does* have repercussions for the United States. While one could argue that each country must look after its own climate change accounting, an effective global response will ultimately require a collaborative approach. At the very least, we could and should work with China – to the extent both sides are willing – to help it find ways to ensure that its rapidly evolving cities develop in a manner that is more conducive to climate change mitigation. Urbanization per se is not the problem; it is the quality or character of urbanization that matters. Unfortunately, and ironically, China appears to have adopted an auto-dependent urbanization paradigm inspired by the U.S. model. Nonetheless, the United States could play a positive and influential role in fostering a global awareness of urbanization options for countries such as China that are home to most of the world's new urban dwellers. This could be done through bilateral agreements and exchanges of practitioners and scholars, as well as through multilateral efforts such as the World Urban Forum.[6]

By Land, by Sea, and by Air

The rise of China impacts our cities not only through climate change. As discussed in Chapter 4 (*Employment and Income*), China's rise reshapes the U.S. employment landscape, thereby directly impacting the communities in which varying jobs are gained or lost. And as we shall see here, the physical movement of people and of traded goods to and from China also impacts American communities. An obvious example of this is the metropolitan region encompassing

Los Angeles and much of southern California, which is home to the largest seaport complex in the nation. As the flow of cargo from China grows, its effect on these port and related transport facilities is akin to a boa constrictor swallowing large prey — it can be done, but it has an enormous distending effect on the entire system. The physical dimensions of this enterprise are conveniently measured in TEUs (twenty-foot equivalent unit), where the term refers to a standardized cargo container unit.[7] In 1995, the combined ports complex of Los Angeles (POLA)/Long Beach (POLB) handled a total of 5.4 million TEUs, including both loaded and unloaded containers, inbound and outbound.[8] Just five years later, in 2000, this total had jumped to 9.5 million, and then to 14.2 million TEUs by the year 2005. Subsequently, those throughput volumes have held fairly steady, rising to 17.0 million TEUs in 2019.

The Los Angeles region is attractive to cargo handlers because it also offers powerful economies of scale derived from the country's largest manufacturing area. (Monios and Lambert, 2013). Consequently, each day, between 40 and 50 trains[9] carry freight from the ports through the Los Angeles metropolitan region, with negative impacts on traffic flows, noise, and air pollution. Many of these adverse impacts fall disproportionately on communities with low incomes and high proportions of ethnic minority populations, thus raising environmental justice concerns. To help alleviate the burden of these impacts, the cities of Los Angeles and Long Beach formed a joint powers authority, the Alameda Corridor Transportation Authority, which undertook to invest $2.43 billion in major transportation improvements that facilitate the movement of freight from the ports complex to transcontinental rail links and to interstate freeway routes (ibid.). This corridor upgrading is now being extended further, with the Alameda Corridor East project.

These impacts are clearly evident also at a national scale, as increasing volumes of freight are funneled through and then beyond American seaports. It is important to note the distinction between international *overland* trade and international *overseas* trade. The eastern Great Lakes area is a highly developed industrial region that integrates Canadian and U.S. goods producers in cross-border overland trade. While it is international freight in the strict sense of the term, it is also largely intra-regional trade that is based on close proximity and joint production in one highly integrated Great Lakes regional industrial complex. Likewise, overland freight routes north from Mexico have been consolidated over past recent decades within the framework of the North American Free Trade Agreement (NAFTA), and its successor, the United States-Mexico-Canada Agreement (USMCA). By far the largest volume of *overseas* cargo originates in China and elsewhere in East Asia, and the way it enters and moves through the United States impacts many port cities in the United States on the Pacific, Atlantic, and Gulf coasts.

Figure 6.2 shows a persistent shift over the past 20 years whereby an increasing proportion of cargo from China and elsewhere in East Asia is being shipped directly to U.S. Atlantic and Gulf ports. While, as we have seen, the cargo volumes flowing through the combined Port of Los Angeles/Port of Long Beach complex have been holding steady or growing modestly in recent years, the *share* of cargo from China being directed through U.S. West Coast ports is steadily declining. In short, the POLA/POLB complex is handling a smaller share of a larger volume. Two factors are at play, both of which are in turn propelled by the rise in cargo volumes from China. One, as already noted, is that U.S. West Coast ports and the surrounding metropolitan regions are becoming highly congested (Fan et al., 2012). A related factor is that the shipping industry, driven by economies of scale, has been opting for larger and larger container ships. These, in turn, have been facilitated by the major expansion of the Panama Canal and the Suez Canal, which are key bottlenecks in global shipping routes. Expansion of the Panama Canal, completed in 2016, has been termed a "game changer" by the U.S. Army Corps of Engineers (Hricko, 2012), ushering in "a new era in container shipping" (Cope et al., 2014). Until recently, the Panama Canal could only accommodate ships carrying a maximum of 5,000 TEUs (ibid.). The largest ships conforming to this upper bound are termed "Panamax," while those that exceeded the limit have been called "Post-Panamax." Following the $5.25 billion expansion of the capacity of the Panama Canal, it now accommodates ships of up to 13,000 TEU (Autoridad de Canal de Panamá, 2012). This is helping to drive the partial shift of China trade port calls from the U.S. West Coast to the East Coast. As a result, in just three years following the Panama Canal expansion, the deployment of a Neo Panamax class of ship (10,000–13,300 TEUs) has increased by 40.1 percent (Rodrigue, 2019).[10]

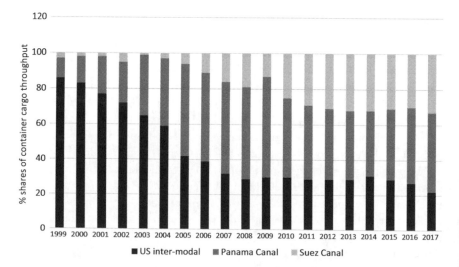

FIGURE 6.2   Cargo container route shares, NE Asia to US East Coast

Source: Rodrigue (2019); Autoridad de Canal de Panamá (2012).

The Port of Virginia at Hampton Roads expects to be the prime beneficiary of this shift. The Port Authority of New York and New Jersey, the Port of Jacksonville, Florida; the Port of Savannah, Georgia; the Port of Baltimore, Maryland; the Port of Miami, Florida, and various U.S. Gulf Coast ports are all keen to get their shares as well (Hricko, 2012; Monios and Lambert, 2013; Rodrigue, 2019). The extent to which China trade cargo enters the United States through East Coast ports will depend upon the ability of U.S. East Coast port authorities to work with other stakeholders to make the requisite investments to expand their own throughput capacities while addressing the adverse impacts associated with such large cargo movements. Drawing lessons in part from the Alameda Corridor projects in the Los Angeles area, East Coast port authorities are pulling together consortia to develop their own corridors, including two (the "Heartland Corridor" and the "National Gateway") projects that will facilitate freight movement from Virginia through Ohio and into Chicago. The latter, for historical and geographic reasons, is a junction point for six of the country's seven Class I railway networks (Monios and Lambert, 2013). A parallel effort is a "Marine Highway," which seeks to shelter the already congested Interstate I-95 from the adverse impacts of China trade cargo entering U.S. East Coast ports by shuttling smaller cargo ships up and down the coast to carry cargo to and from the larger post-Panamax ships calling at major ports. (ibid.). These impacts will be geographically differentiated by a number of factors including linked markets, commodity types and infrastructure capacity (Martinez et al., 2019; Park et al., 2020).

These developments, driven ultimately by our trade with China and others, will contribute to the ongoing transformation of the land use – transportation nexus at a national scale, stimulating growth in some regions more than others. All of this will play out at the day-to-day scale of where Americans live and work. The increasing complexity of the nation's intermodal transportation system, with its many moving parts and diverse constituent and stakeholders, has led some to call for a national transportation strategy. Of course, the same elements of complexity that might justify or necessitate such a strategy may also present formidable obstacles to implementing it. Over the years, Congress has passed significant legislation impacting the U.S. intermodal transportation system, as summarized by Monios and Lambert (2013). Many of these are significant in their own right, but they do not in themselves or in the aggregate constitute a national transportation strategy. Without that, it is likely that the whole of such legislative actions will remain less than the sum of its parts.

In addition to cargo movements, transportation systems have also been shuttling *people* back and forth between China and the United States in increasing numbers. Chinese arrivals to the United States were 249,000 in 2000, jumped to 802,000 in 2010, and then peaked at 3,174,000 in 2017.[11] The subsequent decline that began in 2018, no doubt due in part to trade tensions was of course further accelerated by the U.S. travel ban imposed in early 2020 on visitors from

China due to the coronavirus COVID-19 epidemic. Until recently, U.S. visits to China have been of a similar order of magnitude, in part due to relaxed visa requirements.[12] The air travel industry is not covered in WTO agreements; instead, the U.S. Department of Transportation normally negotiates Air Service Agreements (ASA) with different countries on a bilateral basis. China and the United States have amended their ASA five times since 1980, each time allowing for an expansion in service, as measured by number of flights, airlines, and destinations served (Ke and Windle, 2014). Thus far, liberalization of the terms of the China–U.S. Air Service Agreement has favored U.S. air carriers disproportionately (ibid.), but this may begin to even out as Chinese carriers upgrade their service standards, and once Chinese nationals resume traveling in large numbers again.

There Goes/Here Comes the Neighborhood

Another direct impact of China's rise on urban policies in the United States is through Chinese purchases of U.S. housing and other real estate assets that can transform the character of local neighborhoods. Although per capita income and wealth in China are still low relative to the United States, its enormous size and considerable aggregate wealth ensure that there are many households in China with both the incentive and the means to purchase real estate in the U.S. In 2019, according to a study by the National Association of Realtors (Yun and Cororaton, 2019). China had 4.4 million millionaires, more than any other country except the United States, with its 18.6 million millionaires (Credit Suisse, 2019). China also had 18,130 "ultra-high-net-worth" (UHNW > $50 million) households, which is far behind the United States, with 80,510 UHNW individuals, but well ahead of any other country. Looking ahead, the same study predicts that by 2024, China's total wealth will increase by $23 trillion (or 34 percent).

The newfound wealth of Chinese households has been finding its way into America's real estate markets. Until 2013, Canada had consistently been the leading source of foreign purchases of U.S. residential real estate, which is readily explained by its geographic proximity to the United States and its relative affluence. Canadian winters also appear to be a factor, as the bulk of Canadian purchases are in the sunny climes of Florida, Arizona, and California. Figure 6.3 shows that China's share then mushroomed quickly, and, by 2016, China's share was triple that of Canada's. After peaking at $31.7 billion in 2017, however, Chinese purchases of U.S. residential real estate fell precipitously. While this decline was a general trend across the board, perhaps reflecting changing circumstances in the United States, China's share had further to fall. U.S.–China trade tensions may be a contributing factor to this recent decline in Chinese purchases of U.S. residential real estate, no doubt exacerbated further by the COVID-19 epidemic. The *median* price of a Chinese purchased home in

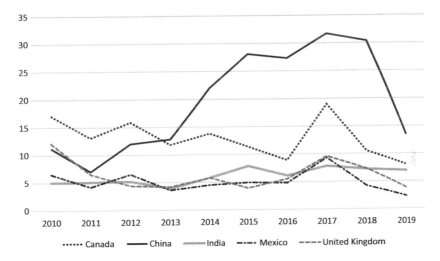

FIGURE 6.3   Foreign purchases of U.S. residential real estate ($ billions)

Source: Yun and Cororaton (2019).

the United States in 2018–2019 was $454,900, compared to $268,200 for Canadian purchases.[13] The latter closely resembles the median sale price of $259,600 (Yun and Cororaton, 2019) for all U.S. residential sales. The much greater geographic distance of China from the United States, together with other transactional barriers, no doubt poses a greater hurdle for Chinese, thereby setting a higher minimum wealth threshold. Canadians, in contrast, can manage such transactions with relative ease due to geographic proximity and similar institutional and cultural norms, so less wealth is required to enter the game. Another differentiating factor is that Chinese purchases of U.S. real estate are concentrated in relatively high-priced metropolitan markets.

Szto (2014, p. 177) cites three principal reasons that Chinese households are inclined to purchase U.S. residential real estate: (1) it is seen as a safe financial investment; (2) it is a hedge against potential political instability at home and elsewhere; and (3) a home in the U.S. can be used by Chinese children studying in the U.S. As mentioned in Chapter 2 (Fiscal *Policy and Deficits*), Chinese households have much higher savings rates than their American counterparts, but Chinese financial institutions offer scant opportunities for channeling those savings into assets yielding high returns. Chinese real estate has thus absorbed much of the savings, causing housing prices there to soar in many localities. The Chinese government has taken steps to dampen speculation in real estate, so overseas investments appear all the more attractive to those Chinese households who have sufficient means at their disposal. The United States, for all its own political and economic woes, is still regarded by many as a relatively safe investment, both financially and politically. Political risk in China includes anti-corruption campaigns that can and do target the accumulated wealth of those who come under investigation, whether they be government officials or business people who may be suspected of collusion. One hedge against such political risk is to move valuable assets abroad.

The most precious asset of all, of course, is one's own progeny. Szto stresses the traditional Confucian linkages between housing, prosperity and education. While bearing in mind the potential pitfalls of stereotypes, one might posit a contrast between a prototypical U.S. view of education and a traditional Chinese view. The former may be represented by a neoclassical economic model of human capital formation (popularized by Becker, 1962), where an autonomous individual invests in higher education based on a calculation of long-run returns to human capital in the labor market as weighed against the upfront cost of education. The time horizon for such decisions is typically a single lifespan. In contrast, the traditional Chinese perspective is based on a multigenerational "dynastical" view, and extended Chinese clans have historically maintained strong internal linkages even as they disperse geographically. In the contemporary context, a foreign education for one's offspring is a crucial part of the family's long-term accumulation strategy (Ong, 1999; Waters, 2005).

The United States is still regarded by Chinese as the "gold standard" for higher education, and this is reflected in the data. Over a ten-year interval ending in 2019, the number of international students jumped over 60 percent, from 677,000 to 1,095,000, where Chinese students comprised over one-third of that latter total.[14] Business and tourist visas can now be issued for ten years, while student visas will be good for five years. Previously, Chinese visitors required visa renewals annually. The conditions are now ripe for more extended stays, and that calculus will likely strengthen Chinese demand for U.S. residential real estate (Rapoza, 2014). Not surprisingly, the influx of Chinese students to the United States tends to concentrate in the same metropolitan areas that also attract the highest concentrations of Chinese purchases of U.S. residential real estate. Even within these high-attraction metropolitan areas, there is a high degree of concentration, leading to outsized impacts in those localities.

A case in point is the suburban community of Monterey Park, together with neighboring cities situated in the West San Gabriel Valley in the Los Angeles metropolitan region. This area has been a magnet for ethnic Chinese immigration, and makes for a useful case study of the kinds of socio-economic impacts engendered by such population inflows. In 1970, Monterey Park was a suburban community that was predominantly White with a substantial Latino minority as well, but with very few Asians. In just two short decades, there was an almost complete reversal, whereby Monterey Park became the first majority Asian American city in the continental United States (Cheng, 2013, p. 23), with Latinos the second largest grouping in Monterey Park and Whites a distant third. A similar transformation extended geographically, so that Asians and Asian Americans comprise a majority throughout the West San Gabriel Valley as a whole, including the cities of Monterey Park, Alhambra, San Gabriel, Rosemead, and the unincorporated community of South San Gabriel (ibid., p. 16).

The causes and consequences of such transformations have received considerable attention in the scholarly literature in ethnic studies, urban planning, sociology, and related fields. Much of this work refers to the notion of "ethnoburbs," a term introduced by Wei Li (2006):

> An ethnoburb is a suburban ethnic cluster of residential areas and business districts in a large metropolitan area. It is a multiracial, multiethnic, and multicultural community in which one ethnic minority group has a significant concentration but does not necessarily comprise a majority of the total population.
>
> *(Ibid., p. 12)*

We have already examined many of the driving factors behind this rapid growth in Chinese investments in U.S. residential real estate. The underlying factors contributing to its concentration in specific ethnoburbs is a mix of historical and institutional causes. Ethnographic studies of Monterey Park's transformation, for example, consistently point to early exclusionary land use practices that discouraged Asian families from settling in suburban communities that were predominantly White.[15] After a highly publicized 1960s case in which Monterey Park earned a reputation as a community that welcomed minority families, the influx began to grow rapidly, with ethnic Chinese being the most numerous of the newcomers. Momentum grew, as restaurants, banks, travel agencies, accountant offices, and other professional services sprang up to service the new arrivals. This process began to feed on itself, as well as on the food served there, as more Chinese-oriented business establishments prompted additional new arrivals, further strengthening the market for such services. This did result in considerable backlash as some long-standing White residents felt increasingly alienated in their own neighborhoods. Fong (1994, p. 64) quotes residents expressing sentiments such as "I feel like I'm in another country" or "I don't feel at home anymore." Such sentiments no doubt contributed to the "White flight" that ensued. The flip side of feeling drawn to Chinese-language services by those who speak it can be a feeling of alienation and estrangement by many of those who do not.

A similar phenomenon arises regarding the size, shape, and appearance of the built form of neighborhoods. A case in point is the City of Alhambra, a municipality abutting Monterey Park. Lawrence-Zuniga (2014) describes how design guidelines, historic preservation initiatives, and other regulatory tools are used by long-standing residents to preserve the character of, existing neighborhoods. As she describes it:

> Municipal design review processes are a form of 'aesthetic governmentality' ... a legal framework that empowers the state to exercise specific controls over individual expressivity in order to protect [property values].... The codes obscure the cultural biases embedded in the landscapes by emphasizing Western traditions and aesthetic principles.

Similar issues swept through Vancouver, Canada, at the height of large-scale migration there from Hong Kong, with vocal concerns about "monster houses" transforming quaint English Tudor "Old Charm" neighborhoods into an alien "Hongcouver".

In many ways, this is the classic American story told over and over again. The history of American cities is largely one of successive waves of English, Dutch, French, Irish, Finns, Italian German, Polish, Mexican, Swedish, Japanese, Philippine, Armenian, Korean, and any number of other immigrant groups that have settled in clusters with their strange languages and customs as they strove to find their way in this exciting but formidable new land. At the urban scale, this process was recognized by sociologists Robert Park and Ernest Burgess in the early twentieth century, in their landmark study that spawned the so-called "Chicago School" of urban ecology. Now, it is a wave of immigrants from a rising China that is disrupting the prior set of sensibilities. *Plus ça change, plus ça reste la même chose.* 万变不离其宗. While it can be unsettling to see foreign symbols – linguistic, architectural, or cultural – inserted abruptly where one is unaccustomed to them, we should not underestimate our capacity to adapt and thrive.

In a very tangible way, the dynamic and cosmopolitan nature of American cities gives the United States an important edge in engaging with the rest of the world effectively. A collection of case studies in Heikkila and Pizarro (2002) examines the nexus between Los Angeles (LA) and the world beyond our borders in terms of three key ideas: (1) LA as a microcosm of the world; (2) LA as a significant node in a networked world; and (3) the iconic representation of LA as projected throughout the world. The same is true for many other urban areas in the United States that are being transformed by globalization. From a U.S. policy perspective, the challenge is to maximize the potential benefits from such homegrown hybridity while managing and containing the disruptive effects. Although many of the issues (such as land use zoning or local building ordinances) discussed in this chapter are under local jurisdiction, there is an intrinsic and essential global element to them as well. This creates an opening for us to introduce a broader perspective at the state and federal level while taking care not to intrude upon local prerogatives.

Discussion Questions

1   If you were elected mayor of the city you reside in, what steps could you take to substantially reduce GHG emissions there? What do you see as the

chief political obstacles you would encounter, and how would you respond?

2   Many cities in the United States, Houston and New Orleans being prominent examples, have been compelled to adapt to major flooding and other disasters emanating from climate change. These adverse impacts typically hit the poor and other marginalized persons disproportionately, yet they are often the least able to cope. Continuing in your role as mayor, as in question 1, what steps would you take to ensure that those who are most vulnerable are adequately protected? What are the political dimensions of that challenge?

3   Some long-standing residents of a community feel threatened by a lost sense of place, or of neighborhood, or of home, when there is a major influx of Chinese or other ethnic minorities with their foreign languages and mores. Is this a legitimate concern? How can it be reconciled with the right of all residents in the United States to choose where and how to live? What is the appropriate role of land use regulations, building codes, business licenses, and other aspects of local governance in such contexts?

Notes

1   IPCC WG III (2014, p. 6).
2   See www.wearestillin.com.
3   See   www.nlc.org/build-skills-and-networks/resources/cities-101/city-structures/number-of-municipal-governments-and-population-distribution.
4   Although California has 13.7 percent of the country's urban population, its 478 municipalities comprise a mere 2.4 percent of the 19,492 municipalities in the country. California has fewer municipalities than Arkansas, but of course the average population size of California's municipalities is much larger.
5   See www.arb.ca.gov/cc/cc.htm.
6   See http://unhabitat.org/habitat-iii/.
7   The term TEU refers to a "twenty-foot equivalent unit," based on a standard cargo container with length and width dimensions of 20 feet and 8 feet, respectively.
8   These annual TEU counts are reported on the respective websites of the Port of Los Angeles and the Port of Long Beach.
9   Train counts from Alameda Corridor Transportation Authority website: www.acta.org. Monios and Lambert (2013, p. 15) state that the capacity of the corridor is 150 trains per day.
10   Notable increases are also seen in the deployment of the largest new class of megaships, with capacity above 18,000 TEUs (Rodrigue, 2019).
11   Chinese visitor counts from a Market Profile of China undertaken by the National Travel and Tourism Office of the International Trade Administration, U.S. Department of Commerce.
12   Visitation data from ITA (2018) and from www.china.org.cn.
13   Median prices are for the 12-month interval through March 2019 (Yun and Cororaton, 2019).
14   Data on international students in the United States are from the Open Doors Fast Facts compiled by the Institute of International Education.
15   Fong (1994, p. 18), for example, documents that in the 1920s, "To sustain the growth trend, real estate agents and civic leaders were determined to make the city

a racially restricted community," where one prominent suburban estate had "a rigid racial restriction policy that would 'exclude those whose blood is not wholly of the Caucasian race'."

References

Autoridad de Canal de Panamá (2012). Available at: www.pancanal.com/common/maritime/advisories/2012/a-16-2012.pdf

Barbour, Elisa and Elizabeth Deakin (2012). "Smart Growth Planning for Climate Protection: Evaluating California's Senate Bill 375," *Journal of the American Planning Association*, 78(1), 71–86.

Becker, Gary S. (1962). "Investment in Human Capital: A Theoretical Analysis," *Journal of Political Economy*, 70(5), 9–49.

Boarnet, Marlon (2010). "Planning, Climate Change, and Transportation: Thoughts on Policy Analysis," *Transportation Research Part A*, 44, 587–595.

C40 Cities (2014). "Advancing Climate Ambition: Cities as Partners in Global Climate Action," A report to the UN Secretary-General from the UN Secretary General's Special Envoy for Cities and Climate Change, in partnership with the C40 Cities Climate Leadership Group.

California Air Resources Board (2008). Available at: ww2.arb.ca.gov/homepage

Cheng, Wendy (2013). "The Changs Next Door to the Diazes: Suburban Racial Formation in Los Angeles's San Gabriel Valley," *Journal of Urban History*, 39(1), 15–35.

Cope, Robert, Rachelle Cope, and John Woosley (2014). "Evaluating Container Ship Routes: A Case for Choosing Between the Panama Canal and the U.S. Land Bridge," *International Journal of Research in Business and Technology*, 4(2), 395–401.

Credit Suisse (2019). *Global Wealth Report 2019*. Zürich: Credit Suisse.

DOT (2018). *Freight Facts & Figures*, Department of Transportation. Available at: www.freight.dot.gov.

Fan, Lei, William Wilson, and Bruce Dahl (2012). "Congestions, port expansion and spatial competition for US container ports." *Transportation Research Part E*, vol. 48, 1121–1136.

Fong, Timothy P. (1994). *The First Suburban Chinatown: The Remaking of Monterey Park, California*, Philadelphia, PA: Temple University Press.

Heikkila, Eric J. (1996). "Are Municipalities Tieboutian Clubs?," *Regional Science and Urban Economics*, 26, 203–226.

Heikkila, Eric J. (2000). *The Economics of Planning*, New Brunswick, NJ: CUPR Press, Rutgers University.

Heikkila, Eric J. and Mylinh Ngo Huang (2014). "Adaptation to Flooding in Urban Areas: An Economic Primer," *Public Works Management & Policy*, 19(1), 11–36.

Heikkila, Eric J. and Rafael Pizarro (2002). *Southern California and the World*, New York: Praeger Press.

Hricko, Andrea (2012). "Progress & Pollution: Port Cities Prepare for the Panama Canal Expansion," *Environmental Health Perspectives*, 120(12), A470–A473.

IPCC WG III (2014). "Human Settlements, Infrastructure and Spatial Planning," in *Climate Change 2014: Mitigation of Climate Change*, Working Group III, Fifth Assessment Report (AR5), Geneva: Intergovernmental Panel on Climate Change.

ITA (2018). "Fast Facts: United States Travel and Tourism Industry," Washington, DC: International Trade Administration.

Ke, Jian-yu and Robert Windle (2014). "The Ongoing Impact of the US–China Air Services Agreements (ASAs) on Air Passenger Markets," *Transportation Journal*, 53(3), 274–304.

Landis, John, David Hsu, and Erick Guerra (2019). "Intersecting Residential and Transportation CO_2 Emissions: Metropolitan Climate Change Programs in the Age of Trump," *Journal of Planning Education and Research*, 39(2), 206–226.

Lawrence-Zuniga, Denise (2014). "Bungalows and Mansions: White Suburbs, Immigrant Aspirations, and Aesthetic Governmentality," *Anthropological Quarterly*, 87(3), 819–854.

Li, Wei (Ed.) (2006). *From Urban Enclave to Ethnic Suburb: New Asian Communities in Pacific Rim Countries*, Honolulu: University of Hawaii Press.

Macneil, Robert and Matthew Paterson (2020). "Trump, US Climate Politics, and the Evolving Pattern of Global Climate Governance," *Global Change, Peace & Security*, 32(1), 1–18.

Martinez, Camil, Adams Steven, and Martin Dresner (2019). "East Coast vs. West Coast: The Impact of the Panama Canal's Expansion on the Routing of Asian Imports into the United States," *Transportation Research Part E*, 91, 274–289.

Monios, Jason and Bruce Lambert (2013). "Intermodal Freight Corridor Development in the United States," in R. Bergqvist, G. Wilmsmeier, and K. Cullinane (Eds.), *Dry Ports: A Global Perspective*, Farnham: Ashgate, pp. 197–218.

Ong, Paul (1999). *Flexible Citizenship: The Cultural Logics of Transnationality*, Durham, NC: Duke University Press.

Park Changkeun, Harry W. Richardson, and Jiyoung Park (2020). "Widening the Panama Canal and U.S. Ports: Historical and Economic Impact Analyses," *Maritime Policy & Management*, DOI:10.1080/03088839.2020.1721583.

Rapoza, Kenneth (2014). "Obama's New Visa Law Seen Helping Chinese Buy U.S. Real Estate," *Forbes*, 14 November 2014.

Rodrigue, Jean-Paul (2019). "The Expanded Panama Canal: Initial Impacts on North American Ports," Ontario: Transport Canada.

Selby, Jan (2019). "The Trump Presidency, Climate Change, and the Prospect of a Disorderly Energy Transition," *Review of International Studies*, 45(3), 471–490.

Smart and Smart (1996). **Reference required???**

Szto, Mary (2014). "Representing Chinese Real Estate Investors in the United States," *Minnesota Journal of International Law*, 23(2), 173–211.

Ward, Jacob, Jeremy Michalek, Ines Azevedo, Constantine Samaras, and Pedro Ferreira (2019). "Effects of On-Demand Ridesourcing on Vehicle Ownership, Fuel Consumption, Vehicle Miles Traveled, and Emissions Per Capita in U.S. States," *Transportation Research Part C: Emerging Technologies*, 108, 289–301.

Waters, Johanna (2005). "Transnational Family Strategies and Education The Contemporary Chinese Diaspora," *Global Networks*, 5(4), 359–377.

Wenzel, T., Rames, C., Kontou, E., and Henao, A. (2019). "Travel and Energy Implications of Ridesourcing Service in Austin, Texas," *Transportation Research Part D: Transport and Environment*, 70, 18–34.

Young, Mischa and Steven Farber (2019). "The Who, Why, and When of Uber and Other Ride-Hailing Trips: An Examination of a Large Sample Household Travel Survey," *Transportation Research Part A*, 119, 383–392.

Yun, Lawrence and Gary Cororaton (2019). *Profile of International Transactions in U.S. Residential Real Estate 2019*, Chicago: National Association of Realtors.

7

ENERGY POLICY

An Energetic Overview

Although it was written three decades ago, Daniel Yergin's (1991) Pulitzer Prize-winning book, *The Prize*, still reads with a freshness and verve that vividly recount the manic history of the oil industry over the past century and a half. Oil – and by extension, other energy products – is not just another commodity like canned peas or trousers.[1] It is an essential lubricant to modern life as it cools and heats living spaces, mobilizes transport, provides muscle for manufacturing, empowers warfare, and hums away behind everything else we do. As such, the scramble to identify, locate, secure, extract, and deliver energy supplies has consistently entailed high stakes drama among nation-states, multinational conglomerates, and outsized entrepreneurs. The role of technology has also been instrumental to this history, as technological innovations may drive sudden shifts in energy demand or energy supply, with attendant spikes or troughs in energy prices.

It was one of these episodic twists and turns that presaged the creation of the U.S. Department of Energy. Just as the Department of Labor had its roots in the Great Depression and the Department of Homeland Security was a response to 9/11, the oil crisis induced by the Organization of the Petroleum Exporting Countries (OPEC) prompted the Energy Organization Act of 1977 which established the Department of Energy. That also marked the beginning of a widespread recognition that U.S. energy supplies and prices were determined in a global context, and that U.S. energy security was vulnerable to economic and geopolitical events well beyond our borders. Most of this geopolitical focus has understandably been on the Middle East with its abundant petroleum resources, fragile states, sectarian animosities, and unremitting wars. Nonetheless, the rise of China is also altering the global energy picture, with important implications for U.S. energy demand, energy supply, energy prices, environmental quality, science & technology policy, and energy security. In many ways, as we shall see, energy has the potential be an important component of any constructive approach to the U.S.–China relationship. Although both countries view energy supply as a strategic commodity, and in this sense, there is perhaps an inevitable rivalry, we nonetheless have a shared interest in promoting fuel efficiency, in expanding alternative energy sources, and in reducing fuel consumption.

Energy Prices

Energy comes bundled in many forms, but petroleum is a good place to begin our investigation, as it was the OPEC-led oil embargo in the 1970s that brought energy policy issues into sharp focus in the United States. Figure 7.1 tracks imported crude oil prices over the past five decades. Two large price spikes dominate this graph. The one induced by OPEC begins its rise in the 1970s and then it peaks and falls abruptly in the early 1980s. The more recent price spike begins its climb as the new millennium approaches, starts to falter around 2009, and then falls more decisively a few years later.

Although the story is a complicated one at many levels, the fundamental principles of supply and demand do also apply. Prices will tend to increase whenever the relevant supply curve shifts up and to the left or when the corresponding demand curve shifts up and to the right, as illustrated in Figure 7.2. The OPEC oil embargo was a clear case of the former, as those petroleum-exporting countries insisted on higher prices for any quantity supplied.[2] The reasons for the embargo were strongly linked to Middle East politics and war, but American consumers felt the economic impacts acutely here at home as gas prices rose sharply while long queues formed at filling stations. Ironically, the dizzying rise in oil prices sowed the seeds of subsequent price declines, both economically and politically. Much higher oil prices prompted increased

FIGURE 7.1   Crude oil prices, 1968–2019 (in constant 2010 $)

Source: U.S. Energy Information Administration.

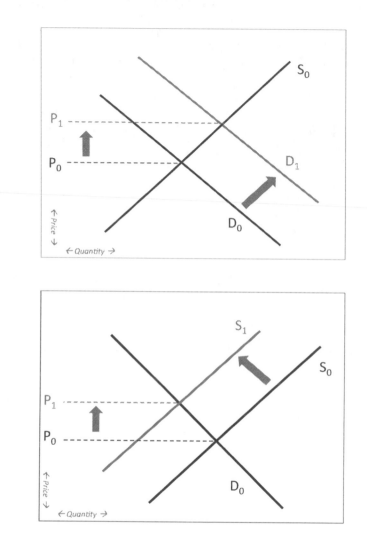

(a)

(b)

FIGURE 7.2   (a) Price increase induced by shift of demand curve; (b) Price increase induced by shift of supply curve

domestic supply that would not have been economically viable at lower prices.[3] There was also "leakage" from the cartel, as some producing countries were prepared to lower prices to gain market share. Politically, consumer outrage in the U.S. over higher gasoline prices prompted producer-friendly changes in regulations that might have otherwise restricted supply.

The second notable price peak shown in Figure 7.1 had a different dynamic. In his analysis of this event, Hamilton (2009, p. 216) concludes that, "Whereas previous oil price shocks were primarily caused by physical disruptions of supply, the price run-up of 2007–08 was caused by strong demand confronting world production." In terms of our discussion, this represents what is shown in Figure 7.2b, with an outward shift of the demand curve driving up prices. As Hamilton (ibid., p. 228) observes, China was "particularly noteworthy" in driving the strong growth in the global demand for oil during this period. As with so many facets of the rise of China, the numbers are staggering. In ten years, China's imports leapt from 4.1 million barrels per day in 2009 to 10.2 million in 2019.[4] Meanwhile, its own crude oil production hovered at about 4 million barrels per day throughout this same period. The fall in energy prices beginning in 2009 had two primary causes. One was a recession-induced reduction in demand prompted by the global financial crisis. On the supply side, the emergence of hydraulic fracturing ("fracking") helped shift the supply curve outwards. Saudi Arabia's decision to keep prices low, based on strategic market and geopolitical considerations, also boosted supply. In effect, the notable price peak of 2007–2008 was undone by a *reversal* of the demand and supply curve shifts depicted in Figure 7.2a.

Not all that burns is petroleum. In comparing effective energy prices across different fuel types, one should consider as well the application at hand. It is not enough just to know that, for example, fuel oil is $4.02 per gallon, electricity is 12 cents per gallon, and anthracite coal is $200 per ton.[5] In effect, this presents an apples-and-oranges problem, so each must be converted to some common energy measure. The British thermal unit (Btu) is the standard measure of the heat content of fuel products, and the effective cost varies by fuel type. The effective price variation is considerable, with electricity, kerosene, and propane costing more than four times as much as coal, on an equivalent Btu basis. What matters ultimately is the full effect of the fuel product, and this must be taken into consideration when undertaking comparisons. For example, although fuel oil is relatively expensive in terms of its intrinsic Btu content, its combustive properties are better suited to powering an automobile than wood, coal or corn. Other considerations include pollution, bulk, delivery, safety, reliability, or storage. Each fuel type rates differently along such dimensions, and so the effective price must be evaluated accordingly.

We have seen that energy prices vary over time and by fuel type. They also vary by country, and these price variations primarily reflect differences in policy rather than differences in underlying fuel costs. Compared to most countries, the price at the pump in the United States is relatively low, averaging just $2.91 per gallon at the end of 2019. Comparable prices in Japan ($5.08), the United Kingdom ($6.17) and Norway ($7.32), for example, are much higher. In China ($3.96), too, the average price of gasoline at the pump is significantly higher than in the U.S. Those countries – and many more like them – apply much higher fuel taxes in an effort to discourage fuel consumption, promote clean energy alternatives, and generate tax revenues. Of course, some countries take a very different approach, with Venezuela ($0.01) being a prime example, where gasoline is almost given away as a matter of public policy. To recapitulate briefly, one must be cautious in speaking of "the price of energy," because the latter varies by country, over time, and by fuel type. We have seen, however, that fundamentals of supply and demand can be important determinants of larger trends. We now examine these fundamentals in more detail, with a view to understanding how the rise of China fuels U.S. energy policy issues.

Energy Demand

The history of energy consumption in the United States is clearly demarcated by three distinct energy eras. For centuries, through the late nineteenth century, wood was the dominant fuel. Then, during first half of the twentieth century, it was coal. More recently, petroleum and natural gas have reigned supreme, although the consumption of coal in the U.S. continued to grow until just this past decade. During recent decades nuclear energy also grew quite noticeably, but still comprises a relatively small share of the total. These distinct energy eras correspond closely (and causally) to developmental phases of the U.S. economy as it progressed from pre-industrial, to early industrial, and then to modern industrial stages. Other countries have followed similar progressions, depending upon their stage of industrial development and other factors.

Ultimately the demand for oil is normally a global demand, notwithstanding segmented markets, geographical complexities, and other considerations. Again, Yergin's (1991) gripping historical account makes clear that petroleum and other energy products can and do find their way to all corners of the world through an increasingly integrated yet multifaceted supply chain. On the demand side, therefore, each country's demand for petroleum or other energy products at any given price is added cumulatively to total global demand. Looking forward, the base case scenario of the U.S. Energy Information Agency forecasts that global energy consumption will increase by about one-half over the next 30 years, from just over 600 quadrillion Btu in 2020 to more than 900 quadrillion Btu by the year 2050. Total U.S. energy consumption is expected to remain fairly constant (at roughly 100 quadrillion Btu) throughout this forecast period, with conservation measures offsetting increases in consumption that might otherwise accrue due to continuing economic growth. A similar story holds for the rest of the OECD countries. Non-OECD countries, however, are forecast to account for the lion's share of net increases in global consumption. China, in particular, has been moving through a phase of accelerated energy consumption, much like the U.S. evinced in earlier decades. It recently surpassed the United States as the largest energy-consuming nation on Earth, so the United States and China are roughly on a par now. Within just 20 years, however, China is forecast to double its energy consumption, reaching roughly 200 quadrillion Btu by the year 2040. These developments are of course in parallel with global trends in greenhouse gas emissions, as we saw in Chapter 5 (Climate Change), and indeed they are two aspects of the same phenomenon.

These forecasts are broadly consistent with an S-shaped trajectory, such as the one depicted in Figure 7.3, describing the long-run growth in energy consumption over time for countries moving through their respective development phases. During earlier phases of development, the demand for energy increases only modestly in response to growth in income levels, i.e., the demand is relatively inelastic.[6] During the intermediate stages of development, this income elasticity increases markedly, so that the demand for energy rises sharply in response to income growth. Eventually, an inflexion point is reached, after which one finds diminishing demand responses to income growth. Wolfram et al. (2012) characterize this S-shaped relationship between energy demand and income as a "pervasive" one that applies consistently across countries and times. Because China and other developing countries are still in the relatively early stages of development, their demand for energy is likely to continue to rise steadily for "many more years" (Fouquet, 2014).

An important contributing factor to this rapid increase in China's energy demand is the acquisition of automobiles and a range of energy-consuming appliances as more and more households in China emerge from poverty. (Wolfram et al., 2012). Demand for these items, too, follows an S-shaped pattern as documented by Wu et al. (2014), as they forecast that the inflexion point for automobile ownership will not be reached until the year 2030. To put this into perspective, consider that in the United States there are currently about 838 cars for every 1,000 people, compared to 181 cars per 1,000 people in

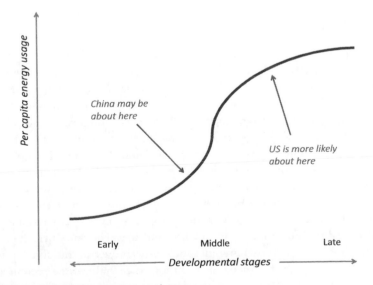

FIGURE 7.3 S-shaped energy use trajectory

China.[7] And of course, China has four times the population of the U.S., so if China's S-shaped trajectory mimics that of the United States, or even of Europe or Japan, in the years ahead, the impacts on global energy demand will be enormous. One might hope that energy-efficiency technologies would alleviate the burden somewhat, but research by Fouquet (2014) and others suggests otherwise. He finds evidence of substantial "rebound effects," first identified by William Stanley Jevons in the nineteenth century, whereby increases in energy efficiency might actually stimulate *increased* use of energy products. From an economic perspective, the effect of energy-efficient technologies is to lower the effective cost of energy services (heating, transportation, etc.). As the price of a factor input such as energy (or labor, or land, or machinery) is lowered, one tends to use more of that factor in lieu of possible substitutes. If the price elasticity is sufficiently high, this may even result in an increase in the use of energy products as the energy efficiency of automobiles or energy-consuming appliances is enhanced.

Whatever the details, the overall trend is clear – China's demand for energy is already on par with that of the United States, and it can only be expected to increase substantially over the years ahead, continuing to outpace domestic production in China. Because of China's enormous size, these net additions to global energy demand will impact the United States and every other country. Referring once again to Figure 7.2a, the rise of China translates into an outward shift of the demand curve for energy, as indicated in the lower part of Figure 7.2b. This will translate into higher energy costs for all. The magnitude of those price impacts will depend in large measure on global energy supply responses, so we turn next to that subject.

Energy Supply

Several aspects of global energy supply will shape the overall market response to China's growing demand for energy. One is the price elasticity of supply. If the supply is highly inelastic (i.e., if the supply curve depicted in Figure 7.2a is relatively vertical), then we may expect the price of energy to rise relatively sharply in response to outward expansion of demand. In effect, this would be a repeat of the demand-driven price spike experienced around 2010. If, on the other hand, the supply curve is highly elastic (more horizontal in disposition), then the market response would be felt less through an increase in prices, and more in terms of quantity of energy products supplied. These two alternative scenarios have very different implications for U.S. consumers and industries, so which is it? Baumeister and Peersman (2013) investigate this question rather carefully for the case of crude oil supplies, and they conclude that the supply curve has become decidedly more inelastic (vertical) over recent decades. Interestingly, they find that the global demand for crude oil has also become more inelastic over that same period, so the demand curve is also relatively vertical.

They point to this dual phenomenon as a primary reason for the increasing volatility in the price of crude oil over their study period, contrasted with a decline in the volatility of quantities supplied. Again, reference to Figure 7.2 helps to visualize this phenomenon, where if one imagines both the supply (S) and demand (D) curves to be relatively vertical, then the price responses to shifts in either S or D will be rather sharp.

Baumeister and Peersman (ibid.) speculate that the increasingly inelastic supply and demand for crude oil may have its roots in the growth of oil trading via futures markets. Futures markets are designed to allow both buyers and sellers to "hedge" or manage the risks inherent in volatile crude oil prices. For example, airlines often need to set airfares well in advance, but it is risky to do so if they do not know what their fuel costs will be. They can reduce this risk (on both the upside and the downside) by purchasing their fuel in advance through the futures markets. As this practice has flourished, both buyers and sellers of crude oil have become commensurately less sensitive or responsive to short-term changes in prices because they have hedged themselves against such changes. This lack of responsiveness to price changes translates into the increasing inelasticity of both supply and demand. Ironically, this creates a reinforcing feedback mechanism, whereby: [*increased price volatility*] begets [*increased use of futures markets*], which begets [*increased inelasticity of S & D*], which feeds back to [*increased price volatility*].

To recapitulate briefly, China is at a stage in its economic growth and transformation where energy use is expected to increase rapidly, i.e., approaching the inflexion point of the S-shaped curve in Figure 7.3. Because the market for oil and related energy products is global, and because China's thirst for fuel is so enormous, the result of China's rise is an outward shift in global demand, as depicted in Figure 7.2b. The extent to which this demand shift translates into higher global energy prices depends upon the supply response. The more inelastic (vertical) the supply curve, the larger the rise in the global price for oil. Recent research strongly suggests that the global supply curve is indeed highly inelastic, so the rise of China translates fairly directly into higher prices for energy consumers everywhere: the United States, China, and the rest of the world. There may be variations on this baseline, but, in the long run, fundamental economic principles will assert themselves one way or the other.

China is not just a "burden" on the demand side of the global energy equation; it also contributes to the global supply. China's oil production has increased somewhat in past years. Unfortunately, these accretions to supply have not kept pace with China's growing demand, so China continues to loom large as a net importer of oil and gas, with resulting upward pressure on energy prices. Although any consumer would rightly prefer to pay less rather than more, an increase in the price of energy is not necessarily a bad thing, given the underlying circumstances. The fact is that energy is in finite supply, so price adjustments are in fact a useful signal to potential users that energy is a precious commodity that ought to be used wisely. Admonitions to that effect may help, but out-of-pocket reminders can provide effective reinforcement of that message. We shall return to these pricing issues later in this chapter.

What the Frack ...?

Another important aspect of the supply curve for oil or related energy products is its placement, left or right, in Figure 7.2b. An outward shift of the supply curve represents an increased quantity supplied at any given price.[8] Such a shift may occur, for example, due to technological advances, newly discovered or newly accessible oil deposits, a less stringent regulatory environment, or other such enabling factors. One very important example of this is the recent dramatic rise in hydrological fracturing, or "fracking," as a technological advance in drilling for oil and natural gas. It has long been known that substantial oil and gas deposits were trapped in tight impermeable formations such as shale, but until recently these remained largely unexploited due to the forbidding costs of production. Hydrological fracturing is a technique by which the powerful injection of water, sand, and chemicals fractures the shale formations containing the oil or natural gas deposits so that they can be accessed and recovered (Spence, 2013). Fracking techniques (including directional drilling) were initially developed to exploit shale gas formations but were subsequently applied to oil as well (Ratner and Tiemann, 2014).

The speed at which this new technology has altered the energy supply balance in the United States is breath-taking, leading to a "renaissance" of production, with new production records set almost every year thus far this century (CRS, 2018; Greenley, 2019). For example, the Energy Information Administration did not even begin compiling statistics on shale gas production until 2007, when it comprised 7 percent of U.S. natural gas production. Just six years later, that share had jumped to almost 40 percent (Ratner and Tiemann, 2014). Domestic consumption of natural gas has not grown nearly as rapidly. As a result, in just a very few years, the United States suddenly became a major net *exporter* of energy products. This remarkable transition is illustrated in Figure 7.4. As a direct consequence of this new energy production technology, the United States now produces more oil than any other country: 18 percent of global production, compared to 12 percent for Saudi Arabia and 11 percent for Russia.[9] As summed up by a recent Congressional Research Service report:

> The United States is the largest producer of natural gas (NG), is the largest consumer of natural gas, has the most natural gas storage capacity, and has the biggest and most expansive pipeline network. Production from shale formations has transformed the United States from a growing importer of natural gas to an increasing exporter, with some of the lowest prices in the world.
>
> *(Ratner, 2019, p. 1)*

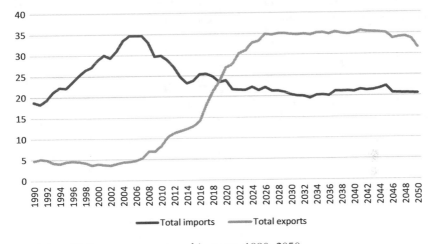

FIGURE 7.4 U.S. energy exports and imports, 1990–2050

Source: U.S. Energy Information Administration.

Here again, the global and strategic dimensions of energy production come into play. In the mid-2010s, Saudi Arabia began to flood the market with oil. The volumes supplied were sufficient to send the price of a barrel of crude oil plummeting from above $100 per barrel in June 2014 to below $60 per barrel just half a year later (Yacobucci, 2014). Saudi Arabia's motives were no doubt based on a combustive mixture of economic and geopolitical considerations. Higher energy prices were a spur to the increased use of fracking methods; conversely, lower energy prices would undermine the profitability of this competing source of oil.[10] Thus, by flooding the market with cheaper oil, Saudi Arabia sought to retain its dominant position as a supplier. Nor has it gone unnoticed that the drop in crude oil prices has been most upsetting for rival oil-exporting countries such as Russia, Iran, and Venezuela – regimes that are friendly towards neither Saudi Arabia nor the United States.[11]

This Saudi supply response provides yet another perspective on the question of the global elasticity of supply of petroleum-related products. By making clear that it stands ready to expand supply indefinitely at a given price, the Saudis were in effect inscribing a perfectly elastic supply curve. This would appear to reverse the findings of Baumeister and Peersman (2013), who, of course, were working with data for the period that precedes this dramatic Saudi intervention. Recall that in their case, they attributed strengthening *in*elasticities to the introduction of futures markets for oil products, while subsequent geopolitical considerations appear to have contributed to *more elastic* supply conditions. A lesson to be learned from this is that the impacts of China's rise on global energy prices depend not only on market considerations, but also upon broader institutional considerations such as producer cartels, futures contracts, and geopolitics. This increases the inherent uncertainty within which the "energy game" is played, thereby heightening the potential risks and rewards.

Energy and the Environment

Another element of risk associated with energy is environmental degradation. The BP Deepwater Horizon oil spill in the Gulf of Mexico in 2010 is an example of how massive such damage can be, as described in the U.S. federal government court complaint:

> As a result of the uncontrolled well event, uncontrolled blowout, multiple explosions, and fires, millions of barrels of oil were discharged into and upon waters of the Gulf of Mexico and adjoining shorelines of the United States … resources and resource services that have been injured, destroyed, or lost include, but are not limited to, hundreds of miles of coastal habitats, including salt marshes, sandy beaches, and mangroves; a variety of wildlife, including birds, sea turtles, and marine mammals; lost human-use opportunities associated with various natural resources in the Gulf region, including but, not limited to fishing, swimming, beach-going, and viewing of birds and wildlife; and waters of the Gulf of Mexico, including various biota, benthic communities, marine organisms, coral, fish, and water-column habitat.[12]

The subsequent $18.7 billion settlement in 2015 was the largest civil settlement against a single entity in the nation's history.[13] Nor are oil spills confined to marine environments. A Congressional Research Service study (Parfomak et al., 2015) reports high volumes of oil leakages from pipeline and rail transport as well. The advent of hydraulic fracturing has also ushered in a host of environmental concerns, including contamination of ground waters. Moreover, Carter (2013) states that onshore oil and gas wells in the U.S. generate in the order of 2.3 billion gallons of wastewater daily, and the energy sector in general is an intensive user of precious water resources.

Although the environmental costs associated with energy use are real, one must take care not to double-count them. To the extent that oil prices already factor in risk premiums, it may suggest that large energy companies essentially self-insure. If settlement costs arising from such court cases do indeed represent the underlying damages, and if the risk premiums generate sufficient funds to pay those settlements, then the oil prices may be said to incorporate the possibilities for such environmental costs indirectly.

Nuclear energy does have certain advantages from an environmental perspective, but the Fukushima disaster in Japan was a grim reminder of the potentially devastating downside risks. There are 103 nuclear energy plants in the United States, comprising roughly 20 percent of total U.S. electricity production

(RFF and NEPI, 2010). Public concern over the potential for nuclear hazards has hampered the construction of more nuclear facilities in the United States, as the last plant came into service in 1996, with construction beginning in 1973 (CRS, 2018; RFF and NEPI, 2010). A host of federal government programs seeks to promote the use of environmentally friendly, renewable energy resources, but the challenge is more difficult when conventional energy prices are relatively low.[14] A related challenge is the so-called "energy paradox," a phenomenon whereby businesses and consumers appear disinclined to invest in energy-saving appliances, equipment and related technologies even where the expected savings (return on investment) over the life of the investment are demonstrably high (RFF and NEPI, 2010).

Energy Security

Energy security has been a central pillar of U.S. energy policy for the past several decades, so energy supply and demand have an intrinsic geopolitical dimension to them.[15] The good news, as reported in the first-ever *Quadrennial Energy Report* (QER, 2015, pp. 4–2) is that "U.S. energy security is stronger than it has been for over half a century." That same report also advises, however, that energy security has many facets, and the way we conceive of energy security must evolve to reflect the times. Important factors "include U.S. oil demand; the level of oil imports; the adequacy of emergency response systems; fuel inventory levels; fuel substitution capacity; energy system resilience; and the flexibility, transparency, and competitiveness of global energy markets" (ibid., pp. 4–2). A second installment of this report, referred to as "QER 1.2," released early in January 2017, focused more specifically on strategic considerations pertaining to the nation's electricity system and its aging infrastructure (QER, 2017; CRS, 2018).

The salient characteristics of global energy markets bear further consideration. The analysis of the supply and demand graphs in Figures 7.2a and 7.2b were in fact predicated upon an assumption of the "flexibility, transparency and competitiveness of global energy markets." It was this assumption that enabled us to represent growth in China's demand for energy through an equivalent horizontal shift in the placement of the global demand curve. As an example of this outward shift of the global demand curve, Asian importers (including but not only China) by 2017 absorbed 72 percent of globally traded liquified natural gas (LNG), with Asia's share of global demand rising from 29 to 43 percent (Vivoda, 2019). Likewise, similar assumptions might apply on the supply side, so that the advent of hydraulic fracturing in the United States, for example, would shift the global supply curve to the right. If global energy markets were indeed perfectly integrated and dependable in this way, the notion of energy self-sufficiency for any single country would be moot. Global self-sufficiency would benefit all countries in more or less equal measure. This vision comes undone, however, in light of the essential and strategic nature of energy. As mentioned at the outset of this chapter, energy is not just another commodity like canned peas or trousers. It is the essential lubricant of the social, economic and military machinery of modern nation-states – similar to the role that information is playing in the digital world, as discussed in Chapter 8 (Homeland Security).[16] Both the United States and China therefore have incentives to define national energy security as central to their respective core interests. As the two largest consumers of energy by far, and as the two most powerful nation-states on Earth, they are each bound to cast a wary eye upon the other as they contemplate worst-case scenarios in energy security.

Striving for national self-sufficiency is essential in this case, because it is the means by which any nation-state can limit its vulnerability and exposure to external threats against energy supply. This was clearly the thinking behind the establishment of the U.S. Strategic Petroleum Reserve, which was established after the Arab oil embargoes (Yacobucci, 2015) and the Energy Independence and Security Act of 2007 (ibid.). Likewise, the Energy Policy and Conservation Act of 1975 restricted the export of domestically produced crude oil from the U.S. to global markets (Alquist and Guenette, 2013; QER, 2015). So, in terms of our previous analysis, accretions to U.S. supply may *not* be allowed to shift the global supply curve to the right. As each country acts accordingly, trading blocs emerge. Within these blocs, energy products flow freely in response to routine market and other protocols. In contrast, energy products are much less likely to transgress these trading bloc delimiters. Vivoda (2019) points to evidence of this, with three distinct regions for trading natural gas, with prices in the Pacific region notably higher than either the Atlantic or North American regions.

If a powerful nation-state such as China or the United States can be energy self-sufficient entirely unto itself, that is all for the best, as far as their own energy security is concerned. As noted already, and illustrated in Figure 7.4, the United States is now attaining energy self-sufficiency, due in large measure to the growth of hydraulic fracturing, increased use of renewable energy sources, fuel efficiency gains, and conservation measures on the demand side. China is a different story, as it is ever more reliant on energy imports. Moreover, more than 85 percent of its oil imports are transported via potentially vulnerable shipping lanes, such as the Straits of Malacca or the Gulf of Aden (Wrobel, 2014). This situation no doubt helped prompt the formation in 2010 of China's National Energy Commission, whose "members include the heads of ten government ministries, several quasi-ministries and regulatory commissions, the governor of the Central Bank, a deputy chief of the People's Liberation Army" and other powerful actors (Campbell, 2014, p. 3). This organization parallels the coordinated effort in the United States to assess energy matters comprehensively and strategically, where the *Quadrennial Energy Review* is the most tangible expression of that effort. The QER task force is co-chaired by the Director of the Office of Science and Technology Policy and the Director of the Domestic Policy Council, and the task force includes the heads of a host of other federal departments or agencies.

Another expression of China's energy security concerns is the establishment in 2001 of the Shanghai Cooperation Organization (SCO) with six founding members: China, Russia, Kazakhstan, Kyrgyzstan, Tajikistan, and Uzbekistan, with China as the prime initiator. The SCO was established primarily in response to collective security concerns but has increasingly become an important platform for energy agreements (Zhao, 2013). Already, Kazakhstan has become one of China's primary oil suppliers (Wrobel, 2014), and in 2015 Russia became China's top source of crude oil, as China's imports of Russian crude oil sextupled over the past decade (Downs, 2019). Russia's natural gas exports are also set to rise dramatically, following a major agreement between Russia's Gazprom and the China National Petroleum Corporation, and with the Power of Siberia pipeline delivering large quantities of natural gas to China (ibid.). As explained by Wrobel:

> China has turned to Central Asia for its energy resources for two main reasons: first, Central Asia provides stable access to closer sources of energy, circumventing the bottleneck of the Strait of Malacca; and second, the development of close ties with Central Asia through an energy nexus will help China to avoid the threat of separatism in the Xinjiang Uyghur Autonomous Region by more regional cooperation.
>
> *(2014, p. 34)*

China addresses its energy security issues through a variety of market initiatives as well. It is now the world's largest hydropower producer, the world's leader in photovoltaic panel production, and the world's leader in installed wind power capacity (Campbell, 2014). There are still some growing pains in these areas, however. For example, nearly a third of the wind power capacity remains unconnected to the energy grid (ibid.), and "overzealous" pursuit of the photovoltaic industry has led to "massive" overcapacity (Zhang et al., 2014, p. 911) in that sector. Likewise, China has 1.1 trillion cubic feet of shale gas resources, the world's largest, but these are not readily accessible due to "[companies with insufficient capacity], difficult geological features, lack of water resources, technical constraints, a lack of sufficient transport capacity to ship the gas to demand centres, an underdeveloped pipeline network, and an uncertain regulatory framework" (IEA, 2014, p. 11).

China has three national oil companies (NOC): China National Petroleum Corporation (CNPC), China Petroleum and Chemical Corporation (Sinopec Group), and National Offshore Oil Corporation (CNOOC). Their missions are tied to China's energy security objectives in myriad ways. The International Energy Agency observes:

China's NOCs have emerged to become international operators, with activities spreading across more than 40 countries and producing 2.5 million barrels of oil equivalent per day (mboe/d) of oil and gas overseas in 2013.... Between 2011 and 2013, NOCs invested record amounts of capital totalling USD 73 billion in upstream mergers and acquisitions, and USD 29 billion in long-term loan-for-oil and gas deals with Russia and Turkmenistan to bring additional oil and gas supplies to China.

(Ibid., p. 6)

That same IEA report goes on to conclude that there is "no evidence to suggest that the Chinese government imposes a quota on the NOCs regarding the amount of their overseas oil that they must ship to China." Instead, the observed behavior of Chinese NOCs is, in its opinion, consistent with normal market operations of other international oil companies, with whom China's NOCs are beginning to compete on roughly equal terms.

Although well more than a decade has passed since CNOOC withdrew its 2005 bid to acquire the U.S. energy company, Unocal, China was no doubt stung by the vociferous opposition to the deal from Members of Congress and the public at large. It sent a message, intended or otherwise, to China that normal market rules do not apply in the case of strategic energy and related resources, and that China is viewed as outside the U.S. energy "bloc." This message, which in some ways presaged the Huawei ban imposed by the Trump Administration, as discussed in Chapter 8 (Homeland Security), would have heightened China's sense of energy insecurity and may explain in part its subsequent efforts to foster enhanced energy security through the Shanghai Cooperation Organization and from other sources in Africa, the Middle East, and elsewhere. The latter includes North America, as CNOOC signed a landmark $15.1 billion deal in 2013 to acquire the Canadian company, Nexen, which also required U.S. approval because of Nexen's ownership of energy assets in the Gulf of Mexico.[17] The inability of backers in 2015 to win necessary support for the proposed Keystone XL Pipeline likely enhanced the potential for more energy trade between China and Canada. In a CRS report written shortly after CNOOC's failed Unocal bid, Nanto et al. provided a succinct summary of the key issues that it prompted:

The policy debate centered on whether a company that is majority owned by China – a country some view as a potential military threat – should be allowed to acquire American assets that include vital energy supplies, dual use technology, or access to sensitive geographical locations.

(2006, p. i)

How U.S. policy-makers choose to respond to that question will do much to set the tone of U.S.–China relations not just in energy, but across the entire policy spectrum.

Energy as a Lynchpin

Energy policy is an essential factor to be considered in formulating U.S. policies on economics, finance, science and technology, the environment, urban development, transportation, climate change, nuclear proliferation, homeland security, defense, and international diplomacy. No other single policy focus exhibits such centrality. For this reason, energy policy can and should be a lynchpin for U.S. policy toward China. The United States and China have held regular Strategic Dialogue talks on two parallel tracks, led by the Secretaries of Treasury and of Defense, but this vital middle piece has been missing. This could be framed as a Strategic Dialogue on Sustainable Development, which in turn dovetails nicely with the broader global conversation on the Sustainable Development Goals as discussed in Chapter 5 (Climate Change). Energy policy, including energy security, would inevitably be a core component of this strategic dialogue. Its strong horizontal linkages to so many other policy domains enhances its strategic importance, and framing it in terms of climate change and other aspects of sustainable development puts it on a relatively cooperative footing where win–win outcomes trump zero–sum gains.

A comprehensive approach to a constructive U.S.–China energy relationship should be based on a mutual and frank recognition that both countries are at once rivals and collaborators. The most promising place to begin is by finding ways to reintegrate both countries into a relatively seamless global supply and demand energy economy as represented in Figures 7.2a and 7.2b. That implies a reduction in the institutional and other barriers that lead to market segmentation, the formation of rival energy blocs, and a scramble for national energy security while undermining global security. Such a task should not be approached naïvely by either side, and the narrower pursuit of national self-reliance in energy should be an ever-present default option that is viable but inferior. That effectively challenges both parties to explore mutually agreed upon arrangements that are viable but superior.

For example, as we have seen, China has over 1.1 trillion cubic feet of territorial shale gas reserves, but has difficulty accessing them under current conditions. This presents all kinds of opportunities for mutually beneficial collaboration tempered on both sides by an ever-present predilection for national self-interest. From a U.S. trade perspective, this opens up the potential for enhanced exports to China – not only of advanced hydrological fracturing technologies, but also of the many highly specialized business services that accompany such activities. From a U.S. fiscal policy perspective, this activity would be a welcome counterweight to the chronic balance of trade deficits we have run with China, and from an employment perspective, it means *jobs* for U.S. workers. From a climate change perspective, helping China's shift from coal to natural gas eases the global burden of greenhouse gas emissions, which in turn lessens the demands on the United States for GHG emission reductions.

That, in turn eases the burden on U.S. transportation and urban development planners, who will be less constrained in their scope. And of course, from a U.S. energy policy perspective, any additions to global energy supply are most welcomed. Enhanced energy security for China also eases geopolitical tensions. Tankers, pipelines, rail transport, and other facets of global energy supply lines become less fragile and thus less susceptible to terrorist acts if global energy supplies are relatively abundant. Likewise, geopolitical pressures ease as potential energy vulnerabilities are mitigated through additional global supplies. All of these mutual gains may be consolidated through international protocols based on mutual accommodations. With this context in mind, the next suite of chapters addresses the geopolitical aspects of U.S. policy toward China.

Discussion Questions

1   In recent decades, China has grown increasingly dependent upon energy imports to fuel its economic growth. Meanwhile, due in large measure to the wide-scale introduction of "fracking," the United States in very short order has switched from being a major net importer of petroleum and other energy supplies to being a major exporter. How might U.S. energy policies build upon these rapidly evolving circumstances?

2   Energy prices have historically been quite volatile, due to unanticipated "shocks," up or down, in global energy demand and supply. With this in mind, how do you think energy prices ten years from now will compare to today? To what extent does your answer to this question depend upon China's future trajectory?

3   Especially in an era of increasing rivalry between the United States and China, is energy security a zero sum game? In other words, does increased energy security for either country necessarily come at the expense of energy security for the other? What win-win arrangements might work to the mutual benefit of both countries regarding energy security?

Notes

1   France's Prime Minister Georges Clemenceau referred to petroleum as the "blood of the earth," while one of the founding forces behind OPEC, Venezuela's Pérez Alfonzo, later called it "the excrement of the devil" (Yergin, 1991).

2   Or, equivalently, OPEC countries supplied lower quantities at any given price, thus shifting the supply curve up and to the left as depicted in Figure 7.2a.

3   The increased domestic supply of oil and other energy products in this case represents an upward movement *along* the domestic supply curve, rather than a shift, as higher prices prompted increased domestic supply. Producer-friendly changes in regulatory policies, however, represented an outward *shift* of the domestic supply curve, as producers could deliver more supply at any given price.

4   China's crude oil imports and production data are taken from www.ceicdata.com.

5 The fuel type prices used here are taken from the Energy Information Agency's "Heating Fuel Comparison Calculator," version HEAT-CALC-Vsn-D_1-09.xls. See www.eia.gov/tools/faqs/heatcalc.xls.

6 From an energy demand modeling perspective, it is useful to distinguish between the demand for *energy* and the demand for *energy services*. As consumers, it is the latter that matters; we do not buy fuel for its own sake, but for the services it provides in terms of space heating or transportation mobility. This distinction becomes important in the context of technological change, whereby a given amount of energy may yield higher levels of energy services. See Fouquet (2014) for additional explanation.

7 Cars per capita figures (China vs. United States) from https://en.wikipedia.org/wiki/List_of_countries_by_vehicles_per_capita.

8 An outward *shift* of the supply curve is very different from a movement *along* the supply curve, but (confusingly) both are often referred to in common parlance as an "increase in supply." As explained in the text, the crucial difference is that an outward shift of the supply curve normally is associated with a decrease in prices while an outward movement along the supply curve implies an increase in prices.

9 Oil production data for the U.S. and other countries taken from EIA, see www.eia.gov/tools/faqs/faq.php?id=709&t=6.

10 Alquist and Guenette (2013, p. 2) state that "a precondition for the commercial viability of the extraction of tight oil from shale is a price level above $50 per barrel."

11 See, for example, Wolf (2014).

12 See www2.epa.gov/sites/production/files/2013-10/documents/deepwater-cp121510.pdf.

13 See *New York Times* (2015).

14 During a recent period of relatively high energy prices, from 2008 to 2014, electricity generation from wind and from solar power in the U.S. grew 3.3-fold and 20-fold, respectively (QER, 2015).

15 Yacobucci (2015) identifies to three pillars of U.S. energy policy since the Arab oil embargo of the 1970s: (1) to ensure energy security; (2) to keep energy affordable; and (3) to protect the environment.

16 Moreover, as *QER 1.2* points out, electricity is the essential underpinning of the Internet of Things, so the link between energy supply and the digital realm is real, not virtual (QER, 2017).

17 See Reuters (2013).

References

Alquist, Ron and Justin-Damien Guenette (2013). "A Blessing in Disguise: The Implications of High Global Oil Prices for the North American Market," Working Paper 2013–23, Bank of Canada, Ottawa.

Baumeister, Christiane and Gert Peersman (2013). "The Role of Time-Varying Price Elasticities in Accounting for Volatility Changes in the Crude Oil Market," *Journal of Applied Econometrics*, 28(7), 1087–1109.

Campbell, Nicole (2014). *China and the United States: A Comparison of Green Energy Programs and Policies*, CRS Report R41748, Washington, DC: Congressional Research Service.

Carter, Richard (2013). *Energy-Water Nexus: The Energy Sector's Water Use*, CRS Report R43199, Washington, DC: Congressional Research Service.

CRS (2018). *21st Century U.S. Energy Sources: A Primer*, CRS Report R44854, Washington, DC: Congressional Research Service.

Downs, Erica (2019). "China-Russia Energy Relations," testimony before the U.S.–China Economic and Security Review Commission, 21 March 2019.

Fouquet, Roger (2014). "Long-Run Demand for Energy Services: Income and Price Elasticities over Two Hundred Years," *Review of Environmental Economics and Policy*, 8(2), 186–207.

Greenley, Heather (2019). *The World Oil Market and U.S. Policy: Background and Select Issues for Congress*, CRS Report R45493, Washington, DC: Congressional Research Service.

Hamilton, James (2009). "Causes and Consequences of the Oil Shock of 2007–08," *Brookings Papers on Economic Activity*, Spring, 215–261.

IEA (2014). *Update on Overseas Investments by China's National Oil Companies: Achievements and Challenges since 2011*, Washington, DC: International Energy Agency.

Nanto, Dick, James Jackson, and Wayne Morrison (2006). *China and the CNOOC Bid for Unocal: Issues for Congress*, CRS Report RL33093, Washington, DC: Congressional Research Service.

New York Times (2015). "BP to Pay $18.7 Billion for Deepwater Horizon Oil Spill," July 2.

Parfomak, Paul, Linda Luther, Richard K. Lattanzio, et al. (2015). *Keystone XL Pipeline: Overview and Recent Developments*, CRS Report R43787, Washington, DC: Congressional Research Service.

QER (2015). *Quadrennial Energy Review: Energy Transmission, Storage, and Distribution Infrastructure*, Washington, DC: U.S. Department of Energy.

QER (2017). *Quadrennial Energy Review: Transforming the Nation's Electricity System*, Washington, DC: U.S. Department of Energy.

Ratner, Michael (2019). *U.S. Natural Gas: Becoming Dominant*, CRS Report R45988, Washington, DC: Congressional Research Service.

Ratner, Michael and Mary Tiemann (2014). *An Overview of Unconventional Oil and Natural Gas: Resources and Federal Actions*, CRS Report R43148, Washington, DC: Congressional Research Service.

Reuters (2013). "CNOOC-Nexen Deal Wins U.S. Approval, Its Last Hurdle," February 12, 2013. Available at: www.reuters.com/article/2013/02/12/us-nexen-cnooc-idUSBRE91B0SU20130212

RFF and NEPI (2010). *Toward a New National Energy Policy: Assessing the Options*, Washington, DC: Resources for the Future.

Spence, David B. (2013). "Backyard Politics, National Policies: Understanding the Opportunity Costs of National Fracking Bans," *Yale Journal on Regulation*, 30, 30–38.

Vivoda, Vlado (2019). "LNG Import Diversification and Energy Security in Asia," *Energy Policy*, 129, 967–974.

Wolf, Martin (2014). "Two Cheers for the Sharp Fall in Oil Prices," *Financial Times*, December 2, 2014. Available at: www.fundamenta.adm.br/arquivos/artigos/Two_cheers_for_the_sharp_falls_in_oil_prices.pdf.

Wolfram, Catherine, Orie Shelef, and Paul Gertler (2012). "How Will Energy Demand Develop in the Developing World?," *Journal of Economic Perspectives*, 26 (Winter), 119–138.

Wrobel, Ralph (2014). "China's New Energy Geopolitics: The Shanghai Cooperation Organization and Central Asia," *ASIAN*, 133 (October), 24–51.

Wu, Tian, Hongmei Zhao, and Xunming Ou (2014). "Vehicle Ownership Analysis Based on GDP per Capita in China, 1963–2050," *Sustainability*, 6, 4877–4899.

Yacobucci, Brent (2015). *Energy Policy: 114th Congress Issues*, CRS Report R42756, Washington, DC: Congressional Research Service.

Yergin, Daniel (1991). *The Prize: The Epic Quest for Oil, Money and Power*, New York: Free Press.

Zhang, Sufang, Philip Andrews-Speed, and Meiyun Ji (2014). "The Erratic Path of the Low-Carbon Transition in China: Evolution of Solar PV Policy," *Energy Policy*, 67, 903–912.

Zhao, Huasheng (2013). "China's View of and Expectations from the Shanghai Cooperation Organization," *Asian Survey*, 53(3), 436–460.

PART III

Geopolitical Policy Perspectives

8

HOMELAND SECURITY

Borderline Vigilance

In its recent review of threats faced by the United States, the Department of Defense concluded grimly that "It is now undeniable that the *homeland is no longer a sanctuary*" (DOD 2018, p. 3). 9/11, as the tragically momentous events of September 11, 2001, will forever be known, first focused the nation's attention on the potentially lethal consequences of unwelcome non-military intrusions across our nation's borders. In direct response, the Homeland Security Act of 2002 established the Department of Homeland Security (DHS), which was cobbled together from parts of 22 different government agencies when it began official operations the next year (Painter, 2019). In its first *Quadrennial Homeland Security Report*, DHS observed that the nation's security challenges are increasingly borderless and unconventional, so an effective policy response must also be prepared to cut across traditional boundaries and introduce new approaches (DHS, 2010). Moreover, the threat to homeland security is multifaceted, and this too is reflected in the mandate of DHS, which ranges from terrorism concerns to global pandemics, natural hazards, immigration & borderland security, critical infrastructure, community resiliency and more. An overview of DHS's implementation strategy for addressing these challenges is set out in its second *Quadrennial Report* (2014).

Some aspects of the Homeland Security mandate, such as community resilience in the face of natural hazards, although very important in their own right, are not directly impacted by the rise of China. For our purposes therefore, with a China focus in mind, we shall emphasize certain aspects of homeland security pertaining to "borderline vigilance,"[1] specifically, a concern with the potential intrusion of harmful elements across the U.S. border. These may include food products, pharmaceuticals, pathogens, computer viruses, and threats to critical infrastructure. This suggests a spectrum of cumulative concerns as illustrated in Figure 8.1, beginning with imports of *food and pharmaceuticals*, many of which do indeed originate in China. One can delineate food products and pharmaceuticals from other consumer products because the former category is specifically intended for ingestion by consumers. As such, those items are the specific and primary concern of the Food & Drug Administration (FDA), an agency within the U.S. Department of Health & Human Services (HHS). FDA collaborates actively with other government agencies, including the Department of Homeland Security, with a view to ensuring that food products and pharmaceuticals imported to the United States, whether from China or elsewhere, are not contaminated.

Another agency within HHS that liaises closely with DHS is the Centers for Disease Control and Prevention (CDC). The CDC also works with FDA, for example, in cases involving foodborne pathogens. As indicated in Figure 8.1, combatting outbreaks of *communicable diseases* entails many of the same pathogen-related issues arising from food product safety concerns, but with the additional complexity of *infectiousness*. As we shall, see, the rise of China is again an important factor here because it is a significant breeding ground for infectious diseases such as SARS, H1N1, H5N1 and, most recently and devastatingly, COVID-19. When

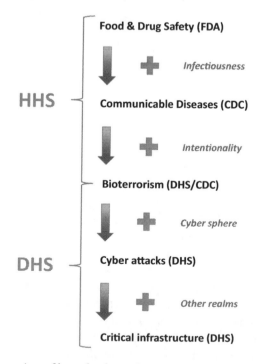

FIGURE 8.1   Progression of homeland security concerns

such outbreaks do occur in China, the risk to U.S. national health security is magnified through relatively high levels of physical interaction between Chinese and American denizens, as well as others throughout the world.

Referring again to Figure 8.1: If one adds yet another element of complexity, *intentionality*, then what were previously communicable disease issues take on the even darker specter of *bioterrorism*, where the specific intent of terrorists is to bring harm to the American public through deliberate propagation of infectious diseases. Although the CDC remains involved in such cases, DHS becomes the lead agency in coordinating a national-level response. Bioterrorism has not been a significant issue from a U.S.–China perspective to date, but it is useful here to acknowledge bioterrorism as a kind of "missing link" between the primarily health-related policy concerns of the FDA and the CDC, on the one hand, and the traditional homeland security issues addressed by DHS, on the other. The next successive wrinkle illustrated in Figure 8.1 moves from *biological* viruses to *computer* viruses in the realm of the cyber sphere. *Cyber attacks* are a major area of concern for U.S.–China policy. Finally, extending beyond the cyber sphere to other realms, one may address *critical infrastructure* concerns more broadly, especially as the rollout of fifth generation (5G) internet technologies gets underway, ushering in an extensive Internet-of-Things (IoT).

For the purposes of this chapter, the FDA and CDC will be treated as integral components of the Homeland Security mission. Taken together, they may be thought of as "DHS+." In fact, this is largely consistent with the premise of the *Implementation Plan for the National Health Security Strategy* prepared by the Department of Health & Human Services, wherein the term "DHS" appears almost two hundred times. This premise is reinforced by the spectrum of homeland security issues depicted in Figure 8.1, where elements of HHS and DHS both provide partial but complementary and essential responses to a range of homeland security threats. Figure 8.1 also serves as a rough schematic for the remainder of this chapter.

Food for Thought

The term "consumer" in a routine or generic economic sense refers to an individual who purchases a product or service. That designation is all the more apt when the act of consumption actually entails physical ingestion of the item in question, such as a food and beverage or pharmaceutical product, or the bodily insertion or application of a medical device. In such cases, there is an immediate potential link to the physical health of the end user. This is indeed a genuine public policy concern, as "each year, 48 million Americans get sick, 128,000 are hospitalized, and 3,000 die from foodborne diseases."[2] Foodborne diseases are not new, but the nature of the phenomenon reflects the underlying characteristics of food production and distribution. By the early twentieth century, the food economy of the United States was increasingly one of mechanized production, wide-scale distribution, and product commodification. As a result, the typical consumer is increasingly removed or alienated from the entire process by which the end product arrived. This in turn led to gaps in oversight, making the *caveat emptor* edict ineffectual. It is difficult for the buyer to beware when the buyer is rendered unaware.

Enactment of the *Food Safety Modernization Act* (*FSMA*) in 2011was prompted by a number of factors, including the greatly increased globalization in recent decades of food and drug production chains. Imports of FDA-regulated products *tripled* during the first decade of the millennium, notwithstanding stagnant or even shrinking FDA budgets (Czarnezki et al., 2013; Liu, 2010). Ensuring that regulated products are subject to proper scrutiny becomes a daunting task under such conditions. The FDA (2011, p. 8) identifies a host of challenges posed by globalization:

- increasing volume of imported products;
- greater complexity in imported products;
- more foreign facilities supplying the U.S.;
- incomplete regulatory information about supply chains;
- patchwork of foreign, federal, and state oversight of product safety;
- greater opportunities for economic adulteration and intentional fraud;
- national security threats;
- enforcement tools that do not reflect today's commercial practices;
- corporations lacking accountability;
- current import regulatory system, an honor system.

The FDA has been compelled to respond to these global trends. Maintaining the regulatory status quo operationally would help contain costs but would surely erode safety levels over time, resulting in potentially severe downside risks of regulatory failure. In light of the many emerging challenges enumerated above, maintaining the desired levels of quality control could be prohibitively expensive if tackled with obsolete procedures. Thus, the only viable option is to adapt operational methods to suit evolving circumstances.

In this regard, Liu (2010) observes that there are two fundamental approaches to enforcement: an *outcome-based* approach and a *production-based* approach. The former emphasizes inspection of regulated products after production but just prior to distribution, delivery, and consumption. The latter approach, in contrast, extends the active purview of the regulating agency to include the production process. In a perfect world, these two approaches would be mutually redundant: If every step of the production process were fully scrutinized and found to be flawless, one could rest assured that the output was also up to standard. Likewise, if the inspection of final products were thorough and complete, there would be no need to go back and examine the chain of production from which those products were derived. In reality, of course, neither approach is flawless, so each can serve as a partial check on and backstop for the other.

Ultimately, judging from the nature of global production, a "secure pipeline" approach may be the more viable approach. Indeed, this pipeline approach has been implemented on a selective basis. According to Liu (ibid., p. 281), our agreement with China exceeds the rights ceded to either Canada or Mexico, two of America's closest trade allies.[3] This is not to understate, however, the challenges of regulating food production in China, with its 170,000 food processing firms, the vast majority of which have fewer than ten employees (ibid.). Regulatory responsibility for food safety is similarly fragmented, as China's *Food Safety Law* of 2009 holds subordinate jurisdictions accountable, down to the county level (ibid.). Chinese consumers themselves have had serious concerns about the safety and reliability of domestic food products, as evidenced in part by the high demand for milk powder and other items regularly brought across the border from Hong Kong. According to Czarnezki et al. (2013), recent food incidents in China fall into three broad categories: (1) environmental degradation in farms; (2) excessive use of chemicals in agricultural production; and (3) food fraud, the economic adulteration of food products (Spink and Moyer, 2010). Or, as described by Lin (2017, p. 33): "Melamine-tainted milk, rat meat sold as lamb, recycled 'gutter oil' for cooking, and most recently, juice made from rotten fruit, there have been a considerable number of Chinese food producers involved in various scandals of contamination and economic adulteration."

From a U.S. policy perspective, what is of specific concern is not the overall quality of food produced in China; rather, it is the specific quality of food imported to the United States from China. As Lin (ibid.) points out, however, tightly woven global supply chains make it likely that regulatory shortcomings in one nation can lead to health repercussions in others. This brings us back to the concept of a special and secure pipeline. In fact, this concept is not so alien to China either. According to Liu (2010), a dedicated supply system was put in place during the initial decade of the People's Republic so that high-level government officials were assured of high-quality food. In a rather ironic twist, the aforementioned agreement between the U.S. and China may be seen as a modern-day replication of the former "*tegong*" (特工) system, but geared now to the U.S. and other overseas importers. Note that this arrangement need not be viewed as China kowtowing to the U.S. There is good reason to believe that a trustworthy certification process of domestic production adds value for China as well. For example, Ortega et al. (2011), using detailed consumer choice simulations, find that Chinese consumers are prepared to pay more for reliable food assurance programs. Likewise, Mangelsdorf et al. (2012) link trade data on Chinese exports to detailed information on international standards for food products, such as those set by the Codex Alimentarius Commission.[4] They provide strong evidence showing that conformance to (or "harmonization with") international standards has a positive effect on Chinese exports.

This also may help to address the flip side of the regulatory challenges of the safety of food items imported from China – that of stagnant or even declining budget allocations, notwithstanding the formidable regulator challenges posed by globalization. A kind of virtuous cycle may ensue whereby the regulatory process provides assurances that have a discernible value added in the marketplace. That value added in turn may provide "room" for both extra returns to producers and tax or excise revenues to support a continuation of the assurance programs. A similar logic applies to other regulated import products such as pharmaceuticals and medical devices. A helpful overview of those challenges can be found in Marucheck et al. (2011). However, it is not only through consumption of imported food or drug products that Americans put their health at potential risk from foreign exposures. Another major potential health threat for Americans is through exposure to communicable diseases from abroad, including from China.

When China Goes Viral ...

The United States is linked to China not just through trade; we are linked physiologically and biologically as well. At no time was this more evident than during the Coronavirus epidemic that began quietly, at first, in Wuhan at the very close of 2019, but then flared into prominence in early 2020, spreading quickly and virulently throughout the world. Within months, the COVID-19 disease spawned by the coronavirus had led to millions of confirmed cases and hundreds of thousands of deaths, prompting the World Health Organization (WHO) to declare a Public Health Emergency of International Concern (PHEIC).[5] In addition to its devastating health impacts, the economic and social impacts were also pervasive. This coronavirus – or, more specifically, fears and anxieties pertaining to its persistent yet uncertain progression – caused stock market gyrations, major disruptions in air travel, paralysis of global supply chains, widespread cancellations of public events, and changes in monetary and fiscal policies, including of course the emergency allocation of substantial funding to combat the disease.

On a social level, widespread quarantines and other social distancing measures impacted the daily lives of people throughout the world, with people scrambling to adjust to school closures and panic buying of food and other staple supplies. Although COVID-19 set a grim new benchmark for such disruptive pandemics originating in China, foreboding precedents had already been set by the SARS pandemic beginning in 2003, and subsequently with the H1N1 "swine" flu virus.[6] On a less spectacular level, but of concern nonetheless, China is also a potentially major source for contagion of tuberculosis (TB). The latter is not a problem unique to China, as the U.S. Congressional Research Service reports that an estimated two billion people worldwide are infected with the bacterium that causes TB – nine million of whom have transmissible TB disease (Wasem, 2014, p. 4). Tuberculosis has been, however, a persistent problem within China, and is "probably the most important communicable disease that China has struggled to control" (Hipgrave, 2011, p. 231).

China is a significant global health factor from a U.S. public health perspective for several reasons. As Bogich et al. (2012, p. 1) note, "[the] process leading to spillover, localized emergence, and finally pandemic spread is complex, but is generally driven by underlying ecological, political, or socioeconomic changes." In China's case, its immense size, diversity, and dynamic characteristics are such that it stands a good chance of being a breeding ground for pathogens. It has one-sixth of the world's population and thus, *prima facie*, a comparable share of people who might unwittingly host deadly pathogens. Moreover, notwithstanding China's rapid urbanization, much of its population still resides in rural or peri-urban settings where poultry and livestock are found routinely in close proximity to human dwellings, marketplaces, or other venues where sanitary conditions can be quite primitive, as was the case in Wuhan at the outset of the COVID-19 pandemic. Once the initial human infections occur, China's high population densities in many regions offer ample opportunities for additional exposures through close human interactions. This tendency is further exacerbated by China's dynamic society and economy, characterized in part by substantial rural-urban migration, personal and business travel, and other significant population movements that lessen the prospects for containing outbreaks to a single region within the country.

More to the point from an American public health perspective, China as a country is increasingly open to the world beyond its borders, including the United States. Visitations to the U.S. from China have trended skywards, literally and figuratively: from 320,000 total arrivals in 2006 to 1.8 million in 2013, and 3.0 million in 2018. While this is all very good for any number of reasons, it does pose the potential for further transmission of communicable diseases through interpersonal contacts. American visitations to China are of comparable levels, thereby doubling the prospects.[7] Global trends in travel reinforce this pattern of interaction from afar. During the past decade, the number of unique city-pairs connected by regular air service has roughly doubled, and China and the United States are the two leading sources for growth in passenger journeys (IATA, 2019). Many of those travelers will have China and/or the United States as either a destination or origin, and so the potential pathogen pathways expand.

SARS served as an initial wakeup call for China (Nuttall and Dye, 2013), prompting a concerted effort to revamp its public health capabilities for communicable diseases, although evidently not enough to deter the subsequent advent of COVID-19. In addition to a steep increase in CDC funding, China introduced mandatory reporting of certain notifiable conditions and established an electronic reporting system, which in turn drew hospitals more squarely into the effort (Hipgrave, 2011). In some respects, China has come full circle from almost a century ago, when a survey "conducted in 1929–1931 [found that] more than half of all deaths were caused by infectious diseases" (ibid., p. 225). Following the establishment of the People's Republic of China in 1949, the famed barefoot doctors had a huge positive impact on public health conditions in what was then a predominantly rural China where their purview included "environmental sanitation, health education, disease screening, surveillance and control, basic clinical care or referral and family planning" (ibid., p. 227). This all changed with the introduction of market reforms, whereupon "village doctors have ever since relied on generation of income from fees and the sale of drugs, resulting in abandonment of public health work and major problems with over-prescribing of drugs and inappropriate use of parenteral preparations" (ibid., p. 229).

In the post-SARS era, some balance was restored to this public health effort within China. As Bogich et al. observe:

> The connection between H5N1 and backyard poultry production in particular has led to significant interest and support in a "systems approach" to combating avian influenza as a development agenda driven by agricultural, cultural, poverty, and equity constraints, rather than a purely human health issue.
>
> *(2012, p. 2)*

Additionally, Hipgrave notes:

> The response to the ongoing highly-pathogenic H5N1 and 2009 H1N1 influenza outbreaks, despite accusations of under-reporting and heavy-handed quarantine of travelers, demonstrate China's increased capacity and intention to act quickly, decisively and in unison across national, provincial and county levels on CDC when population health is threatened.
>
> *(2011, p. 234)*

Although China has made impressive inroads in its public health provisions, Feng et al. (2011) argued that gaps remained in China's ability to put together disparate clues to spot trends in emerging pathogens, and this could lead to crucial delays in targeting responses effectively. Their prediction proved correct, as evidenced by gaps in early enforcement that enabled COVID-19 to establish a lethal foothold in China before extreme measures were undertaken to contain its spread. The lack of a prompt, proactive response in Wuhan as COVID-19 first began to emerge is attributed by some observers as a reflection of China's increasingly centralized control, which can stifle local initiative. On the flip side, once the central authorities did act, they imposed sweeping quarantines and other mitigation measures that might not be feasible in other countries.

The emergence of COVID-19 in China, and its subsequent and rapid spread to other parts of the world, including the United States, underline the public goods nature of efforts to identify, contain, and treat globally rampant communicable diseases. As with the case of climate change, discussed in Chapter 5 (Climate Change), the intrinsically global dimensions of COVID-19 would *normally* compel the United States to work effectively with a diverse set of partners around the world. Our seeming inability to do so in 2020 is a woeful example of the consequences of undermining crucial international institutions. There are, in effect, strong pecuniary externalities to be derived for the United States from China's efforts to strengthen its public health capabilities. Not to put too fine a point on it: It is in our interest, even narrowly defined, for China not to host contagious diseases, because their spread will almost surely be far-reaching. It is from an explicit recognition of this fact that in the past the U.S. CDC maintained a presence in China.[8] Knowledge spillovers also work in both directions. Asymmetries in U.S. and China public health systems reflect underlying political, economic, institutional, environmental. and social differences in our societies. One example pertains to quarantine and isolation measures.[9] Schwartz and Schwartz (2010) point out that China is able to move much more swiftly to place such measures into effect, whereas in the United States there is a stronger public aversion to any governmental restriction on individual liberties. A jaw-dropping example of this is China's decision – after an initial slow start to recognize, acknowledge, and respond to the COVID-19 outbreak – to quarantine Wuhan and its entire surrounding province of Hubei. It is almost impossible to imagine that the United States government would or could in effect quarantine a city-region the size of, say, Chicago or Houston. Yet, these seemingly draconian actions did appear to yield a positive result. Just a few short months after the COVID-19 outbreak, the infection rate in China outside of Hubei Province was minimal, even compared to the rates of infection in the United States, and elsewhere in the world, where the per capita infection rates far exceeded those for China as a whole. The seemingly draconian *cordon sanitaire* clearly had an effect.

Another example of difference between the U.S. and China is in the realm of mandatory vaccination programs. Similar distinctions apply in terms of public messaging through popular media, where open skepticism of government is viewed by many in the U.S. as a "healthy" attitude. In an era of global pandemics, the public health relationship linking the U.S. and China is not strictly dyadic. By far the most severe pandemic of the twentieth century was the Spanish influenza of 1918 that killed 3 percent of the entire world's population. There is potential for an even more devastating and swift-moving pandemic now, in an age where global air travel is increasingly commonplace and where formerly remote corners of the world are readily accessible. This underlines the imperative for the United States to work closely with China and other partners around the world – a pandemic that begins *anywhere* is a homeland security threat at home. Bobashev et al. (2011) demonstrate that collaboration of this kind may be supported in some measure without depending on altruistic motives. Again, the core argument hinges on the intrinsically global nature of pandemics. Using a Global Epidemiological Model that is calibrated to current data on travel patterns, demographics, and other key variables, they conclude:

> In a world in which low-income countries are unlikely to hold stockpiles of antiviral drugs, it may be in the self-interest of wealthy countries to (collectively) fund the purchase and distribution of antivirals to low-income countries, even without any altruistic or humanitarian motivations.
>
> *(Ibid., p. 41)*

The essential question is whether it is more cost-effective to try to eradicate pathogens in those source environments, or instead, whether it is better to focus on preventive measures in our homelands. A key consideration is the soundness of the public health infrastructures in place in the source countries.

Bioterrorism

Recall from Figure 8.1 that the element of *intentionality* delineates bioterrorism from other outbreaks of disease. More specifically, the U.S. Model State Emergency Health Powers Act defines bioterrorism as

> the intentional use of any naturally occurring microorganism, virus, infectious substance, or biological product, or any bioengineered component of any such [thing], to cause death, disease, or other biological malfunction in a human, an animal, a plant or another living organism in order to influence the conduct of government, or to intimidate or coerce a civilian population.[10]

While there is general agreement regarding the gravity of potential bioterrorism attacks, there is less agreement on the appropriate policy response. Some would argue that overblown pronouncements about the risks of and potential damage from bioterrorism may lead to a misallocation of scarce government resources.

A recent RAND study supports this view, based on a portfolio analysis of research projects funded by the National Institute of Health and other U.S. government civilian agencies. The RAND study found that a disproportionate number of funded research projects addressed bioterrorist threats, thereby depriving other scholars of funding for research projects that could have addressed other, equally valid, national health security threats (Shoshana et al., 2012). Likewise, Gottron and Shea, in their Congressional Research Service report, gently suggest:

> Congress might mandate the augmentation of government-wide planning documents, such as the *National Response Framework*, or the

development of a forward-looking planning document, similar to the *Quadrennial Homeland Security Review* or the *National Strategy for Pandemic Influenza* and its implementation guide, for cross-agency federal bio-defense activities.

(2011, p. 6)

In other words, appropriate responses to threats of bioterrorism should be formulated and calibrated within a more comprehensive risk assessment framework.

Unlike concerns of food product and pharmaceutical safety, or communicable diseases, or cyber-attacks or other threats to U.S. critical infrastructure, there are few if any indications at this point that China itself poses an overt bioterrorism threat to the United States. Instead, bioterrorism serves as a kind of "hidden bridge" here, linking FDA and CDC concerns with broader homeland security concerns:

[biological pandemics] → [biological virus attacks] → [computer virus attacks]

Having traversed that bridge, we now move on to threats to homeland security emanating from computer viruses and other forms of cyberattacks.

Cyber Dragons

After depicting a range of cyberattacks around the world, Richard Clarke and Robert Knake (2010, p. 21) conclude with five sobering observations:

1. Cyber war is real.
2. Cyber war happens at the speed of light.
3. Cyber war is global.
4. Cyber war skips the battlefield.
5. Cyber war has begun.

According to recent intelligence community testimony to Congress, "China remains the most active strategic competitor responsible for cyber espionage against the US Government, corporations, and allies" (quoted in Lawrence, 2019, p. 23). As fifth generation (5G) internet technology lays the foundation for an emerging Internet-of-Things (IoT), the same open structure that makes the internet so powerfully ubiquitous also underscores its vulnerability to sabotage. In a very real sense, it is the cyber-analogue to the inherent vulnerability of an open society to infiltration. A recent Congressional Research Service report surveying a range of cybersecurity issues facing the United States observed:

The interconnectivity of IoT devices may also provide entry points through which hackers can access other parts of a network. Control of a set of smart objects could permit hackers to use their computing power in malicious networks called botnets to perform various kinds of cyberattacks.

(CRS, 2018)

5G technologies are also supporting new and emerging military applications in the realm of autonomous vehicles, command and control, logistics, smart warehousing and intelligence, reconnaissance and surveillance systems. For example, networked autonomous vehicles can be programmed to conduct "swarming" maneuvers (Hoehn and Saylor, 2020). A ubiquitous Internet-of-Things also raises the grim prospect of a "surveillance web" blanketing much of the planet (Kaska et al., 2019).

The advanced technological standing of the United States magnifies this vulnerability. Increasingly, the appliances we use routinely – be they automobiles, elevators, or photocopiers – are linked back to dealerships, manufacturers and/or service providers via wireless transmissions. "The designers of the copier never thought anyone would make it a weapon, so they never wrote their software in a manner that would make that difficult or impossible to do" (Clarke and Knake, 2010, p. 39). Similar vulnerabilities apply to a whole host of infrastructural services upon which myriad civilian or governmental entities rely: Photocopiers are networked computers linked to cameras. Elevators are networked computers suspended on cables. Telephones are networked computers linked to audial equipment. Automobiles are networked computers on wheels. Trains are networked computers on rails. Airplanes are networked computers with wings. Satellites are networked computers in orbit. Heaters are networked computers attached to fuel supply lines. Refrigeration units are networked computers in which we store our perishables. Medical devices are networked computers that probe our bodies. Personal devices are networked computers that track our movements. Who is running those computers? Who is controlling the networks that strap them all together, and how vulnerable are they to infiltration?

A Congressional Research Service report catalogues a variety of commonly recognized cyber-aggressors, where the targets, methods, and motivations may vary accordingly:

Cyberterrorists are state-sponsored and non-state actors who engage in cyberattacks as a form of terrorism …

Cyberspies are individuals who steal classified or proprietary information used by governments or private corporations to gain a competitive strategic, security, financial, or political advantage …

Cyberthieves are individuals who engage in illegal cyber-attacks for monetary gain …

Cyberwarriors are agents or quasi-agents of nation-states who develop capabilities and undertake cyberattacks in support of a country's strategic objectives ...

Cyberactivists are individuals who perform cyberattacks for pleasure, philosophical, or other nonmonetary reasons.

(Painter, 2013, pp. 11–12)

All indications are that China is well represented across this spectrum. According to Kaska et al. (2019, p. 10), "China has a notorious reputation for persistent industrial espionage, and in particular for the close collaboration between government and Chinese industry in targeting academia, industry and government facilities for the purpose of amassing technological secrets." A report by Mandiant, a cybersecurity-consulting firm, made quite a public splash upon its release in early 2013 for its detailed documentation of an Advanced Persistent Threat, Level 1 (APT-1) emanating from an identifiable organizational unit of the People's Liberation Army (Mandiant, 2013). By spying on the spies, Mandiant was able to produce a dizzying array of evidence – including sample code and even video recordings of attacks underway – to present a prosecution-like case setting out the motive, means, and methods by which China's military command infiltrates and compromises the integrity of the computer networks underpinning essential functions of major U.S. corporations. China is not alone in this realm. As Clarke and Knake (2010, p. 34) wryly observed, "U.S. intelligence officials do not ... rate China as the biggest threat to the U.S. in cyberspace. 'The Russians are definitely better, almost as good as we are,' said one."

Huawei and Critical Infrastructure

A core focus of Homeland Security's efforts is the protection of critical infrastructure, defined as "the machinery, facilities, and information that enable vital functions of governance, public health, and the economy" (Humphreys, 2019). The mounting importance of this mission is reflected in the establishment by Congress in 2018 of the Cybersecurity and Infrastructure Security Agency (CISA). Table 8.1 sets out the 16 critical infrastructure sectors identified by the Department of Homeland Security. What Table 8.1 does not show is how intertwined these sectors are, so a failure in any one critical infrastructure sector can lead to cascading negative effects on the others. Just to identify and inventory critical assets is a formidable task; to put in place an effective operational strategy for protecting them is much more so. These complications are magnified significantly because many critical assets are in the private sector, and this poses additional challenges of coordination. Likewise, some sectors depend in part on global supply chains that are further removed from direct oversight by DHS or allied federal agencies. A related issue of concern is the list of rare earth

TABLE 8.1 Critical infrastructure sectors

Chemical	Commercial Facilities	Communications	Critical Manufacturing
Dams	Defense Industrial Base	Emergency Services	Energy
Financial Services	Food and Agriculture	Government Facilities	Healthcare and Public Health
Information Technology	Nuclear Reactors, Materials, and Waste	Transportation Systems	Water and Wastewater Systems

Source: U.S. Department of Homeland Security, *NIPP 2013: Partnership for Critical Infrastructure Security and Resilience*; Humphreys (2019).

elements and other critical minerals that can only be found in significant quantities outside the United States. Humphries reports:

> China ranked as the lead global producer of 16 minerals and metals listed as critical. Although there are no single monopoly producers in China, as a nation, China is a dominant or near-monopoly producer of yttrium (99%), gallium (94%), magnesium metal (87%), tungsten (82%), bismuth (80%), and rare earth elements (80%).
>
> *(2019, p. 1)*

Digital infrastructure is of ever-increasing strategic importance in this landscape. Not only is it central to the information technology sector, but to the other 15 critical infrastructure sectors in Table 8.1 as well. This applies, for example, to industrial control system (ICS) networks that are key to managing the nation's electric grid (CRS, 2018). Similar vulnerabilities apply in other sectors. Artificial Intelligence (AI) is now being employed routinely by hostile actors to enhance the effectiveness of malware design and deployment. A Congressional Research Service report gives the example of adversaries using AI methods to systematically feed disinformation to a surveillance system, thereby creating "an unwitting automated double agent." The human factor, however, is still considered by many to be the weakest link in cybersecurity (ibid.).[11] More broadly, as catalogued in another CRS report, the nation's information technology infrastructure can be damaged through denial of service, ransomware, data breaches and undermining data and system integrity (ibid.). China has actively exploited U.S. vulnerabilities. In 2011, Chinese security forces breached the CIA's network to identify and eliminate, sometimes ruthlessly, U.S. espionage sources in China. In another egregious example, hackers from China's Ministry of State Security in 2014 obtained confidential files on 21.5 million Americans, including many U.S. government employees, from the U.S. Office of Personnel Management (Hvistendahl, 2020).

As noted earlier, the emerging Internet-of-Things is an increasingly core part of the nation's critical infrastructure, as its disparate "Things" (devices) become vital points of entry and egress for information flows. The 5G internet technology that supports IoT is increasingly dominated by a single Chinese company, Huawei, and this has raised concerns about the potential exposure and vulnerability that this may pose from a U.S. national security standpoint. Although other prominent Chinese technology-related companies may also pose significant potential national security risks,[12] Kaska et al. (2019, p. 4) find that Huawei "is currently the only company that can produce 'at scale and cost' all the elements of a 5G network, with its closest competitors Nokia and Ericsson not yet able to offer a viable alternative." One advantage that Huawei and other Chinese internet technology companies have is a huge and protected domestic market in China that provides the necessary scale to make their 5G technologies economically viable. Many observers point to China's national cybersecurity law of 2016 as a serious additional and related concern:

> [It] imposes several restrictions on internet firms including requiring operators of critical information infrastructure (defined as sectors such as telecommunications, energy, and finance) to store certain data in China, and requiring companies to assist Chinese police and national security agencies. The law's security reviews may force companies to disclose source code, a concern of many U.S. firms who are hesitant to reveal proprietary information about their business intellectual property that could potentially expose them to further cyberattacks.
>
> *(CRS, 2018, p. 17)*

A policy issue for the United States and its allies is to what degree Huawei and other Chinese companies should be precluded from participating in the buildout of critical 5G infrastructure. This question in turn depends on technological, economic, and diplomatic factors. The responses of western democracies have varied, with the United States and Australia taking a hard line relative to others that leave the door open to Huawei under certain conditions.[13] A novel approach was adapted by the United Kingdom, which set up a special oversight mechanism, the Huawei Cyber Security Evaluation Centre, to ensure transparency and accountability (Kaska et al., 2019). In the longer term, however, if the United States does not want to expose its critical IT infrastructure to potential threats from Chinese firms that may be compelled to comply with directives issued by China's national security agencies, it will be important to find viable alternatives to Huawei. This, in turn, means working with like-minded partners to foster such alternates by creating a consistent set of guidelines and criteria to support potential competitors such as Nokia or Ericsson. As noted earlier, China's massive and relatively unified domestic market gives Huawei a strong advantage. The contrast with the U.S.

and Europe's fragmented markets and lack of consistent public sector support underlines, yet again, the importance for the United States of maintaining strong alliances based on enduring mutual trust and accommodation. It also echoes the call, in Chapters 3 (Trade Policy), 5 (Climate Change) and 10 (Foreign Relations), for a club theoretical framework to guide the United States in formulating its approach to such alliances.

Cyber Defense

A review of the literature affirms a consensus regarding the strong offensive cyberwar capabilities of the United States. The same does not apply, however, regarding U.S. defensive capabilities. According to Clarke and Knake, two former NSA heads agree:

> All the offensive cyber capability the U.S. can muster won't matter if no one is defending the nation from cyber-attack ... Cyber Command's mission is to defend DoD and maybe some other government agencies, but there are no plans or capabilities for it to defend the civilian infrastructure.... Homeland has no current ability to defend the corporate cyberspace that makes most of the country work.
>
> *(2010, p. 26)*

Likewise, former Defense Secretary Leon Panetta has been quoted as saying that the U.S. faces "an impending cyber-Pearl Harbor that would be capable of crippling the nation's critical infrastructure."[14] A special task force on critical infrastructure concluded that our defensive posture was too "brittle," and narrowly focused on preventing intrusions, and was not sufficiently proactive in ensuring resilience in the face of attacks (Humphreys, 2019).

These concerns are heightened by the prospects of a first-strike capability by potential aggressors. The *National Military Strategy for Cyber Operations* (NMSCO) notes:

> If you wait for the other side to attack you in cyberspace, you may find that the opponent has, simultaneously with their attack, removed your logic bombs or disconnected the targets from the network paths you expected to use to access them.[15]

Clarke and Knake observe that, notwithstanding the word "Strategy" in its title,

> [The NMSCO] is not really a strategy, but more of an appreciation. To the extent that it provides guidance, it seems to argue for initiating combat in cyberspace before the other side does, and for doing all that may be needed to dominate in cyberspace, because to do otherwise would

put other kinds of American dominance at risk.... The strategy does not discuss the problems associated with going first or the pressure to do so.

(2010, pp. 26–27)

This situation is somewhat unsettling. There is a certain flawed but beguiling logic that avers that because we might be unable to mount a proper cyber defense, we should take the cyber offensive and strike first. That might hold true if cyberwar were looming and inevitable, but its own assertion precludes altogether even the possibility of cyber peace. Instead, it becomes a self-fulfilling prophecy of cyberwar. Some would argue that the best defense is a good offense; but it may be that the best chance for something akin to peaceful cyber co-existence is a strong and reliable cyber defense. Thus, a crucial policy question centers on the prospects for securing such.

There are several challenges in this regard. One concerns the multiplicity of actors that must necessarily be fully engaged in putting together and maintaining a strong collective cyber defense. Even within the federal government, each federal agency has responsibility for its own cybersecurity systems, but with myriad cross-agency responsibilities superimposed (Fischer, 2013). And, as noted above, there are separate agencies with responsibility for cybersecurity in the realms of national security (NSA), defense (U.S. Cyber Command), and the civil sector. Beyond this, there is also need for coordination between federal, state, and local authorities. More daunting yet are the challenges of coordination with myriad private sector entities that in the aggregate own and control much of the nation's officially designated critical infrastructure. Such private sector operators have two primary concerns in this regard. One is what they regard as the potential for overly intrusive federal regulation of private sector rights and prerogatives. A related concern of the private sector focuses on information sharing requirements that might be imposed upon them. All this illuminates the challenges of developing and implementing a viable and coordinated (if not integrated) cybersecurity strategy to protect the nation's critical yet disparate infrastructure. The rise of China further heightens the stakes of that challenge.

Discussion Questions

1   In retrospect, what could the United States have done differently to minimize negative impacts emanating from the COVID-19 epidemic?

2   Do you think that Huawei should be banned from providing 5G internet technologies for U.S. digital infrastructure? If yes, and if countries in Europe choose not to follow suit, is there a danger of the United States isolating itself digitally? If no, what steps can the U.S. take to ensure that its national security interests are not compromised?

3   As the Internet-of-Things begins to reach into all realms of daily life in the United States and elsewhere, with "Things" provided by a wide array of

people and institutions, how can the U.S. federal government best coordinate Homeland Security policies among all stakeholders?

Notes

1 The inherent ambiguity or *double entendre* of the term "borderline vigilance" is noted.
2 From the HHS website: www.hhs.gov.
3 *Agreement Between the Department of Health and Human Services of the United States of America and the General Administration of Quality Supervision, Inspection and Quarantine of the People's Republic of China on the Safety of Food and Feed.* Available at; www.fda.gov/ InternationalPrograms/Agreements/MemorandaofUnderstanding/ucm107557.htm.
4 Codex Alimentarius is a Commission established by the World Health Organization and the Food and Agriculture Organization of the United Nations. Its purpose is to work with counterpart organizations (such as the FDA) in member countries to help set and maintain international standards for food products. See www.codexalimentarius. org/codex-home/en/.
5 The WHO official declaration on January 30, 2020, of a Public Health Emergency of International Concern (PHEIC) was no doubt dismissed in some quarters as "PHEIC news."
6 See www.flu.gov.
7 Visitation data from ITA (2018) and from www.china.org.cn.
8 See "CDC in China Factsheet," Center for Global Health, Centers for Disease Control and Prevention. Available at: www.cdc.gov/globalhealth/countries/china/pdf/china.pdf.
9 Swendiman and Jones (2009, p. 10) clarify the technical distinction between these terms:

> Although [they] are often used interchangeably, quarantine and isolation are two distinct concepts. Quarantine typically refers to the "(s)eparation of individuals who have been exposed to an infection but are not yet ill from others who have not been exposed to the transmissible infection."

Isolation refers to the "(s)eparation of infected individuals from those who are not infected."

10 Quote taken from Cieplak (2013, p. 5). See also, www.aclu.org/other/text-msehpa.
11 A former IT director at my institution informed me that the most common problem his team dealt with routinely was termed "DEU," for defective end user.
12 Kaska et al. (2019) identify other Chinese communications and video surveillance technology manufacturers – primarily ZTE, but also Hytera Communications Corporation, Hangzhou Hikvision, and Dahua Technology – all of whose technology has been banned from use in government networks under U.S. law.
13 See "Huawei 5G in Europe and Beyond" at the Carnegie Endowment for International Peace website, https://carnegieendowment.org/publications/interactive/huawei-timeline.
14 Panetta quote taken from Gomez (2013, p. 1).
15 NMSCO quote from Clarke and Knake (2010, p. 26).

References

Bobashev, Georgiy, Maureen Cropper, Joshua Epstein, et al. (2011). "Policy Response to Pandemic Influenza: The Value of Collective Action," Discussion Paper, RFF DP 11–41, Resources for the Future.

Bogich, Tiffany, Rumi Chunara, David Scales, et al. (2012). "Preventing Pandemics Via International Development: A Systems Approach," *Policy Forum*, 9(12), December, PLOS Medicine. Available at: www.plosmedicine.org.

Cieplak, Mary Victoria (2013). "Bioterrorism Policy Reform and Implementation in the United States: The Impact of the 2001 Anthrax Attacks," e-theses repository, University of Birmingham Research Archive.

Clarke, Richard A. and Robert K. Knake (2010). *The Next Threat to National Security and What to Do About It*, HarperCollins e-books.

CRS (2018). *Cybersecurity: Selected Issues for the 115th Congress*, CRS Report R45127, Washington, DC: Congressional Research Service.

Czarnezki, Jason, Yanmei Lin, and Cameron Field (2013). "Global Environmental Law: Food Safety & China," *The Georgetown International Environmental Law Review*, 25, 261–287.

DHS (2010). *The Quadrennial Homeland Security Review Report: A Strategic Framework for a Secure Homeland*, Washington, DC: U.S. Department of Homeland Security, February.

DHS (2014). *The Quadrennial Homeland Security*, Washington, DC: U.S. Department of Homeland Security, June.

DOD (2018). *Summary of the 2018 National Defense Strategy*, Washington, DC: Department of Defense.

FDA (2011). *Strategic Priorities 2011–2015*, Washington, DC: U.S. Food and Drug Administration.

Feng, Zijian, Wenkai Li, and Jay K. Varma (2011). "Gaps Remain in China's Ability to Detect Emerging Infectious Diseases Despite Advances Since the Onset of SARS and Avian Flu," *Health Affairs*, 30(1), 127–135.

Fischer, Eric (2013). *Federal Laws Relating to Cybersecurity: Overview and Discussion of Proposed Revisions*, CRS Report R42114, Washington, DC: Congressional Research Service.

Gomez, Miguel (2013). "Awaken the Cyber Dragon: China's Cyber Strategy and its Impact on ASEAN," paper presented to the Second International Conference on Cyber Security, Cyber Warfare and Digital Forensics.

Gottron, Frank and Dana A. Shea (2011). *Federal Efforts to Address the Threat of Bioterrorism: Selected Issues and Options for Congress*, CRS Report R41123, Washington, DC: Congressional Research Service.

Hipgrave, David (2011). "Communicable Disease Control in China: From Mao to Now," *Journal of Global Health*, 1(2), 224–238.

Hoehn, John and Kelley Sayler (2019). "National Security Implications of Fifth Generation (5G) Mobile Technologies," *In Focus* IF 11251, Washington, DC: Congressional Research Service.

Humphreys, Brian (2019). *Critical Infrastructure: Emerging Trends and Policy Considerations for Congress*, CRS Report R45809, Washington, DC: Congressional Research Service.

Humphries, Marc (2019). *Critical Minerals and U.S. Public Policy*, CRS Report R45810, Washington, DC: Congressional Research Service.

Hvistendahl, Mara (2020). *The Scientist and the Spy*, New York: Riverhead Books.

IATA (2019). *WATS: World Air Travel Statistics*, Geneva: International Air Transport Association.

ITA (2018). "Fast Facts: United States Travel and Tourism Industry," Washington, DC: International Trade Administration.

Kaska, Kadri, Henrik Beckvard, and Tomas Minarik (2019). "Huawei, 5G and China as a Security Threat," Tallinn, Estonia: NATO Cooperative Cyber Defence Centre of Excellence.

Lawrence, Susan (2019). *U.S.–China Relations*, CRS Report R45898, Washington, DC: Congressional Research Service.

Lin, Ching-Fu (2017). "Outsource Power, Import Safety: Challenges and Opportunities of the U.S.–China Food Safety Regulatory Cooperation," *Food and Drug Law Journal*, 72(1), 32–52.

Liu, Chenglin (2010). "The Obstacles of Outsourcing Imported Food Safety to China," *Cornell International Law Journal*, 43, 249–305.

Mandiant (2013). *APT1: Exposing One of China's Cyber Espionage Units*. Available at: www.mandiant.com

Mangelsdorf, Axel, Alberto Portugal-Perez, and John Wilson (2012). "Food Standards and Exports: Evidence from China," *World Trade Review*, 11(3), 507–526.

Marucheck, Ann, Noel Greis, and Carlos Mena (2011). "Product Safety and Security in the Global Supply Chain: Issues, Challenges and Research Opportunities," *Journal of Operations Management*, 29(7–8), 707–720.

Nuttall, Isabelle and Christopher Dye (2013). "The SARS Wake-Up Call," *Science*, 339, 1287–1288.

Ortega, David, Holly Wang, Laping Wu, and Nicole Olynk (2011). "Modeling Heterogeneity in Consumer Preferences for Select Food Safety Attributes in China," *Food Policy*, 36, 318–324.

Painter, William L. (2013). *Issues in Homeland Security Policy for the 113th Congress*, CRS Report R45701, Washington, DC: Congressional Research Service.

Painter, William L. (2019). *Selected Homeland Security Issues in the 116th Congress*, CRS Report R42985, Washington, DC: Congressional Research Service.

Schwartz, Rachel D. and Jonathan Schwartz (2010). "Confronting Global Pandemics: Lessons from China and the U.S.," *Global Health Governance*, III(2), Spring.

Shoshana, Shelton, Kathryn Connor, Lori Uscher-Pines, et al. (2012). "Bioterrorism and Biological Threats Dominate Federal Health Security Research; Other Priorities Get Scant Attention," *Health Affairs*, 31(12), 2755–2763.

Spink, John and Douglas C. Moyer (2010). "Defining the Public Health Threat of Food Fraud," *Journal of Food Science*, 76(9), R157–R163.

Swendiman, Kathleen and Nancy Lee Jones (2009). *The 2009 Influenza Pandemic: Selected Legal Issues*, CRS Report R40560, Washington, DC: Congressional Research Service.

U.S. Department of Homeland Security (2013). *NIPP 2013: Partnership for Critical Infrastructure Security and Resilience*. Available at: www.cisa.gov/publication/nipp-2013-partnering-critical-infrastructure-security

Wasem, Ruth Ellen (2014). *Immigration Policies and Issues on Health-Related Grounds for Exclusion*, CRS Report R40570, Washington, DC: Congressional Research Service.

9

DEFENSE POLICY

Historical and Global Context of the U.S. Military

As is the case with many other countries, the United States of America was founded through war, and the country's historical narrative has a strong military baseline. America's position in the world, and its own internal view of itself, can be traced through major military milestones. The War of Independence against the world's leading colonial power established the United States as a new model of sovereignty and governance of the people, by the people, and for the people. It also laid the foundations for the creation of the country's Department of War, predecessor to the Department of Defense. The wrenching, bloody Civil War in the next century was a violent eruption of deeply rooted internal contradictions that seemingly could not be resolved otherwise. The magnitude of this trauma is evident by the fact that U.S. military deaths in the Civil War outnumbered all other wars combined, and at a time when the country's population was still relatively small. It also established the effective primacy of the federal government relative to state and local governments.

Subsequent war efforts reflected America's evolving position and role in global affairs beyond its own borders, beginning with the first expressions of colonial expansion exhibited through the Spanish–American War near the turn of the nineteenth/twentieth century. American primacy was confirmed emphatically during World War II, a truly massive global conflagration that reshaped the world order. A new U.S. military command structure also emerged in the immediate post-WWII years, with the formation of a Department of Defense and a globally oriented, geographically based Unified Command Plan (Drea et al., 2013). It was from this time forward that the U.S. military posture straddled the world both literally and figuratively.

The post-WWII years also ushered in the rise of a bipolar world order and a long Cold War between the United States and the Soviet Union. This era marked a break from the past in several important respects. First, it was the advent of the nuclear era and of an arms race that saw U.S. and Russian (Soviet) military expenditures skyrocketing for three decades. The "Cold" nature of the war was also a reflection of the times, as the realization set in that outright full-scale military confrontation between the two major global powers would be MADness – mutually assured destruction. This was also the first ideologically riven (cold) war fought by the United States, and this in turn gave shape to the internal politics of the country, epitomized most dramatically by the "red scare." This anti-communist ideological framing also provided the rationale for U.S. involvement in the Korean and Vietnam Wars, where opposing sides in those conflicts were seen as local proxies for the world's superpowers. It was during the Vietnam War that the ideological foundations supporting the war effort began to fray seriously, as anti-war sentiments were a core component of a much broader counter-culture movement of the late 1960s and early 1970s in the United States.

The policy of containment that guided U.S. military doctrine throughout the Cold War era seemed to be vindicated with the sudden implosion of the Soviet Union in 1991, as Russian military expenditures fell off dramatically, and the United States was suddenly left alone as the world's sole superpower. These events gave rise to academic and political discourses about the emergence of a unipolar global order centered on the economic, political, and military might of the United States (CRS, 2017b). In many ways, this status remains today as current U.S. defense expenditures are comparable in scale to those of the next 15 largest countries combined, where many of those are also U.S. allies (IISS, 2017).

Posen, in an influential paper, ascribed the military dominance of the United States to its command of the commons:

> The "commons," in the case of the sea and space, are areas that belong to no one state and that provide access to much of the globe.... Command of the commons is the key military enabler of the U.S. global power position. It allows the United States to exploit more fully other sources of power, including its own economic and military might as well as the economic and military might of its allies.
>
> *(2003, pp. 8ff.)*

This command of the commons is a qualitative distinction that further amplifies the already commanding quantitative edge that the United States has in terms of military expenditures. This quantitative edge is reinforced by the qualitative advantages that the U.S. military has in terms of precision-guided munitions, Artificial Intelligence, robotics, big data, and next generation technologies (Symonds, 2018).

Brooks and Wohlforth (2015) build on this concept further to develop a set of metrics allowing for a direct comparison of the relative capacities of the world's six major powers. They show that the United States does indeed have a commanding advantage over any other potential military rivals. Here again, however, static comparisons only go so far as they do not, for example, address the potential vulnerability of orbiting U.S. satellites that follow very predictable trajectories. If high cost advantages can be neutralized by relatively low-cost means, the military edge over potential adversaries may be more apparent than real. That is the fundamental premise of anti-access/area denial (A2/AD) defense strategies, as discussed in more detail below.

From [1+X] to [1+X+Y]

In recent years, the presumed primacy of the United States as the world's sole superpower has been increasingly called into question. In part, this is a recognition that even the United States could be stretched too thin. As a superpower, it may be obliged to take on super-burdens. Extended wars in Afghanistan and Iraq imposed heavy costs on the U.S. military even though its adversaries were by no means global powers in their own right. Moreover, military command of the commons does not automatically translate into command over contested zones that may lie closer to an adversary's hearth. Quoting again from Posen:

> the real problems [are] presented once U.S. forces get close to the adversary. Below 15,000 feet, within several hundred kilometers of the shore, and on the land, a contested zone awaits them. The U.S. military hopes that it can achieve the same degree of dominance in this zone as it has in the commons, though this is unlikely to happen.
>
> *(2003, p. 22)*

These intrinsic limitations faced by the U.S. military are further compounded by sequestration and other budget constraints. Military expenditures in the United States have declined steadily over past decades, both as a share of GDP and as a share of all federal government spending. One hard lesson from the demise of the Soviet Union is that maintaining superpower military status is inherently expensive, and thus not easy to sustain economically. This lesson certainly was not lost on China, nor is it lost on American planners who seek to retain U.S. military dominance. As starkly worded in the 2017 White House *National Security Strategy* report, "The United States must retain overmatch ... to ensure that America's sons and daughters will never be in a fair fight" (2017, p. 28).

But beyond the problems of the U.S. military being stretched too thin, beyond the challenges of contested zones proximate to enemy domains, and beyond the budgetary trials of sequestration lies a more direct challenge to the erstwhile supremacy that the U.S. might hope to enjoy over a unipolar world –

that challenge is embodied by the resurgence of Russia and the rise of China. As summarized in a recent report to Congress:

> World events in recent years – including Chinese actions in the East and South China Seas and Russia's seizure and annexation of Crimea in March 2014 – have led observers, particularly since late 2013, to conclude that the international security environment in recent years has undergone a shift from the post-Cold War era that began in the late 1980s and early 1990s ... to a new and different situation that features, among other things, renewed great power competition with China and Russia and challenges by these two countries and others to elements of the U.S.-led international order that has operated since World War II.
>
> *(CRS, 2017a, p. 2)*

Following the demise of the Soviet Union, Russia's defense expenditures plunged from about $246 billion in 1988 to $14 billion in 1994. This may have emboldened the U.S.-led NATO alliance, which – much to the consternation of Russia – bombed Yugoslavia in 1999 and invaded Iraq in 2003 (Trenin, 2016). Expansion of the NATO alliance at about the same time saw the induction of a sizeable group of former Warsaw Pact member-states that expanded its geographic extent eastward and southward in a manner that Russia no doubt found problematic.[1] Beginning in 2008, Putin's Russia began to reinvest heavily in its military, and as seen in Table 9.1 currently spends about 3.9 percent of its GDP on defense, compared to 3.2 percent for the United States and 1.9 percent for China. Because the Russian economy is small relative to its U.S. and China counterparts, it cannot hope to reassume superpower status. It can, however, focus its military resources on areas of strategic importance, such as the NATO

TABLE 9.1 Defense expenditures by country, 2018

	Defense expenditures ($ billion)	% of top ten	% of world	% of GDP
United States	648.8	48.2	36.4	3.2
China	250.0	18.6	14.0	1.9
Saudi Arabia	67.6	5.0	3.8	8.8
India	66.5	4.9	3.7	2.4
France	63.8	4.7	3.6	2.3
Russia	61.4	4.6	3.4	3.9
Britain	50.0	3.7	2.8	1.8
Germany	49.5	3.7	2.8	1.2
Japan	46.6	3.5	2.6	0.9
South Korea	43.1	3.2	2.4	2.6

Source: World Bank; Stockholm Peace Research Institute (SIPRI).

front and in the Middle East. With its invasion of Crimea and its kinetic support of Syria, Russia has reasserted itself militarily. As Trenin (ibid., p. 26) observes, "The year 2014 was when European security again became bipolar."

Meanwhile, as described in more detail below, China's military has also posed more direct challenges to the United States in its own contested zones, especially those strategic maritime areas that are deemed to be of vital interest by China. While China devotes a smaller percentage of its GDP to military expenses than either the U.S. or Russia, its large and relatively fast-growing economy has supported a steady and commensurate increase in military expenditures over recent decades. Taken together, the increased assertiveness of both Russia and China has prompted observers to suggest that a new world order is emerging. (CRS, 2017a; Brooks and Wohlforth, 2015; Posen, 2012). This trend is also evident in the growing share of China and Russia in global military expenditures, in contrast to the declining U.S. share.

Brooks and Wohlforth (2015) extend a terminology introduced by Buzan (2004) to describe this phenomenon. The latter had postulated a "1 + X" terminology to signify that during the unipolar era the United States stood in a category of its own, and that while there were a host of other great powers, the addition of one more (or one less) did not alter the fundamental balance of power on a global scale. Brooks and Wohlforth argue that this terminology is no longer sufficient to describe the emerging new world order whereby Russia and China are increasingly assertive:

> It is necessary to carefully differentiate between great powers that are not in a position to bid for superpower status and those that are. We need to be open to the possibility of a 1 + Y + X system, in which one or more Y powers have the potential to rise to superpower status or are moving in this direction and thus need to be differentiated from the other great powers.
>
> *(2015, pp. 14ff.)*

The question for the United States thus becomes one of how best to respond to this gradual but steady evolution in the world order. The CRS (2017a) report cited earlier points to the "ambiguous" or "hybrid" warfare methods of Russia in the Crimea and the "salami slicing" tactics of China in the South and East China Sea as indicative of the kinds of challenges that the U.S. military will be increasingly confronted with. Such measures may not in themselves comprise full-scale war, but they can lead to a steady attrition of any military advantages that the U.S. might otherwise enjoy. As described in the *National Security Strategy* issued by the White House in 2017, "China and Russia … are contesting our geopolitical advantages and trying to change the international order in their favor" (2017, p. 27).

This begs the question of what counter-measures the U.S. might take, short of war. The CRS report advocates for a fresh examination of U.S. military strategic priorities in this context. Such a "bottom–up review" would be comparable to one undertaken in 1993 shortly after the dissolution of the Soviet Union, and would address a whole range of military issues, including defense funding levels and budget priorities, re-examination of the NATO alliance, military technology requirements, defense acquisition policies and related concerns, including trade policies designed to ensure supply chains in times of military conflict. It is with this backdrop in mind that we turn now to a more focused examination of the rise of China from a U.S. defense policy perspective.

China's Evolving Military Strategy

The profound changes that have extended throughout all aspects of China over the past several decades have also transformed its military. At the behest of the Communist Party of China to which it is immediately subordinate, the People's Liberation Army (PLA) is steadily transforming itself from a large, low-tech, land-based, personnel-heavy army to a much leaner and more modernized fighting force prepared to engage potential adversaries across a full spectrum of combat venues. PLA personnel numbers have been drastically *reduced* from 19.1 million in 1990 to 3.5 million in 2014, with the bulk of those reductions in paramilitary and reserves personnel (Cordesman, 2014). There have been equally marked qualitative changes as well, with the PLA being compelled to shed itself of many side businesses that had provided lucrative sources of income but were seen to be a distraction from the PLA's primary mission.

That mission, and the strategic thinking behind it, are perhaps best described by a 2015 White Paper on "China's Military Strategy" issued by the State Council of the People's Republic of China (State Council, 2015). That document begins with an overview of the national security situation from China's perspective, noting at the outset the same trends described above of the movement from a unipolar to a multipolar global order, and alluding to "profound changes" across economic, geostrategic, technological, scientific, and military fields. China is no doubt also anxiously aware that it shares borders with 15 other Asian countries,[2] including several that pose significant security concerns (Cordesman, 2014). The White Paper declares forthrightly that "The Chinese Dream is to make the country strong." It goes on to outline its strategic military doctrine of "active defense" that includes a proactive stance toward any perceived threats. And in a clear message to a potential adversary, it emphasizes a flexible approach based on whatever comparative advantages it might find, stating frankly that "you fight your way and I fight my way." It emphasizes the need for technological prowess in an era of what it refers to as the "informationization" of war, a term that one can only hope sounds better when expressed in Mandarin. Meanwhile, the U.S. Department of Defense, in its *Summary of the 2018 National Defense Strategy*, gave its view of the challenge posed by China in the Indo–Pacific region:

China is leveraging military modernization, influence operations, and predatory economics to coerce neighboring countries to reorder the Indo-Pacific region to their advantage. As China continues its economic and military ascendance, asserting power through an all-of-nation long-term strategy, it will continue to pursue a military modernization program that seeks Indo-Pacific regional hegemony in the near-term and displacement of the United States to achieve global preeminence in the future.

(DOD, 2018, p. 2)

"A2/AD," referring to *antiaccess/area denial*, is an acronym often used by U.S. commentators to describe China's military posture and general strategy to defend against a stronger adversary's encroachment upon China's near seas. As described by Beckley:

China may be able to destroy U.S. ships, aircraft, and bases within 500 miles of China's territory and disrupt the satellite and computer networks that underpin U.S. military power throughout East Asia. Many American analysts fear that China could use these [A2/AD] capabilities to hold the U.S. military at bay while enforcing its expansive territorial claims, which include most of the East and South China Seas.

(2017, p. 28)

This dovetails with our earlier discussion of contested zones that lie away from the commons, where U.S. dominance is well established, and closer to (in this case) China's own periphery. A general rule of thumb is that power-projection is an order of magnitude or even 50 times more resource-intensive than a corresponding measure of A2/AD defense (ibid., pp. 81, 110).

There can be little doubt that China views the United States as a potential obstacle to realizing the China Dream. This view was no doubt reinforced by the Department of Defense's 2014 *Quadrennial Defense Review* that set out a "rebalancing" plan whereby 60 percent of U.S. Navy assets were being stationed in the Pacific (DOD, 2014, p. 34). In terms of conventional geostrategic considerations, China seeks to break out of the confines of a near-sea defense. The first and second island chains in the western Pacific Ocean are the geographic embodiment of this aspiration and of the related obstacles that China perceives. The *first island chain* embraces the eastern waters of the Yellow Sea, the East China Sea, and the South China Sea. Beginning with the southern portion of the Korean peninsula and Japan's home islands in the north, it follows a dotted line of islands extending to the island of Taiwan, which is widely regarded as the central anchor to the first island chain and thus of strategic *geographic* importance in a broader military context. The first island chain then continues south along portions of the coastlines of the Philippines, Brunei, and Malaysia before curling back west and northward along the coastlines of

Indonesia and Vietnam. The *second island chain* runs roughly parallel to the first, but further to the east, extending from Japan through Guam and Palau southward to eastern Indonesia.

This geography figures prominently in China's defense strategy, which seeks to move progressively from control of waters within the first island chain, then to those within the second island chain, and that would finally put an end to U.S. dominance of the open seas beyond (Cordesman, 2014, p. 141). As Brooks and Wohlforth (2015, p. 50) point out, however, the A2/AD strategy works both ways, as the island chains can be used to curtail China's ability to mount a successful attack on Taiwan or on key strategic waterways. Accordingly, the island chains have been a major focus for military planning by both China and the United States (Erickson and Wuthnow, 2016).

Goldstein (2017) provides a systematic overview and assessment of the US–China naval balance in the Western Pacific. He ascribes an edge to the United States in terms of maritime domain awareness and surveillance. Likewise, he sees substantial advantages for the U.S. in the realm of undersea warfare, with a decisive edge to American submarines, "known for speed, quieting and their formidable mix of weapons" (ibid., p. 919). For a variety of reasons, neither the United States nor China have a clear advantage in missile surface warfare, and much may depend upon first strike considerations. According to Goldstein, "evolving naval warfare is almost certain to be inhospitable to *any* surface ships, American or Chinese ... the outcome of a major US–China clash of arms at sea will be very much determined by the aerial and undersea campaigns" (ibid., p. 913). Due in large measure to China's more immediate proximity to any field of engagement with the United States in the western Pacific, Goldstein sees advantages for China in terms of Coast Guard operations and other forms of maritime law enforcement. Noting that China has been described as a "cruise missile sponge," due to its ability to absorb or mitigate the impacts of any U.S. missile strikes, Goldstein sees China's own growing missile strike capacity as a potential threat to U.S. operational capacity in the region. He describes mine warfare as a relatively inexpensive means by which China could neutralize U.S. advantages, noting that "Sea mines are a good fit with Chinese strategic culture given the asymmetric warfare characteristics of their employment ..." (ibid., p. 920).

Indeed, asymmetry is a general theme in many descriptions of potential U.S.–China military confrontations, particularly in the context of the western Pacific. A Congressional Research Service report ponders China's "salami-slicing" or "gray-zone" tactics in these areas (CRS, 2017a, p. 12).[3] Likewise, the White House *National Security Strategy* observes: "adversaries and competitors became adept at operating below the threshold of open military conflict and at the edges of international law" and that such actions "are calculated to achieve maximum effect without provoking a direct military response from the United States." Seeming to echo the quote noted earlier, taken from China's own White Paper on military strategy, the White House cautions that "Our adversaries will not fight us on our own terms" (White House, 2017, pp. 27–28). A much-cited Rand Corporation analysis concludes:

> The PLA is not close to catching up to the U.S. military in terms of aggregate capabilities, but it does not need to catch up to the United States to dominate its immediate periphery. The advantages conferred by proximity severely complicate U.S. military tasks while providing major advantages to the PLA.
>
> *(Heginbotham, 2015, p. xxx)*

A related "x-factor" in favor of China is the extra motivation that comes from fighting nearer to one's own turf. Both Goldstein (2017) and Chase et al. (2017) quote a statement attributed to Chinese Rear Admiral Yin Zhou, who reportedly said: "If in the future, there is US–China conflict, then it will likely take place on China's doorstep. Speaking bluntly, fighting on our doorstep, we fear no one."

Three Potential Hot Spots in the Western Pacific Region

Within this broader geographic context of the western Pacific, there are three potential hotspots that provide distinct foci for Chinese and American military planners: North-east Asia, the South China Sea, and Taiwan. While the United States and China are the two dominant powers in this region, several other countries figure in as well in important ways. Thomas (2017) outlines a progression of combined operations of U.S. military alliances in the region. At the low end are "deconflicted" operations, where allied forces are friendly but not effective partners due to lack of familiarity or large differences in capacities. As an example, he cites U.S. military operations with the Philippines Navy and Coast Guard. "Coordinated" operations, which characterize the U.S. military alliances with the South Korea and with Thailand, entail shared aims and an effective working familiarity. Thomas assesses the U.S. military alliances with Japan and with Australia at an "interoperable" level, where shared objectives and close coordination are enhanced through more comparable capabilities and technologies. Other countries in the western Pacific region such as Vietnam, Malaysia, and Singapore, observe a careful neutrality (Cordesman, 2014).

North-east Asia

A small, uninhabited crop of islands north-east of Taiwan provides a focal point for conflicting territorial claims by China and Japan. As Beckley notes:

> [The] eight islets, which the Japanese call the Senkakus and the Chinese call the Diaoyutai … are the symbolic epicenter of a broader struggle

between China and Japan for control of the East China Sea.... This conflict is rooted in geography. China and Japan are two great powers packed into a small space and sit astride each other's vital sea-lanes.

(2017, p. 95)

These contentious claims have their roots in history but they have important implications for future military planning purposes. The Japanese see "their" Senkakus as a natural geographic extension of the nearby Ryukyus, a chain of more than 100 islands stretching from Japan's home islands to within 70 miles of Taiwan (ibid., p. 96). Viewed in the aggregate, these islands constitute an important part of the first island chain described earlier, and constitute potential "choke points" for China's maritime access to the open seas of the Pacific.

Another reason that the tiny Diayutai/Senkakus have an outsized importance is that the United States recognizes that they are effectively administered by Japan. The Department of Defense therefore maintains that Article 5 of the U.S. Japan Mutual Security Treaty applies to them, and so the United States is obliged by international treaty to come to the aid of Japan in the event of hostilities. Article 5 reads, in part, as follows:

> Each Party recognizes that an armed attack against either Party in the territories under the administration of Japan would be dangerous to its own peace and safety and declares that it would act to meet the common danger in accordance with its constitutional provisions and processes.[4]

From a military perspective, the balance of naval tonnage has been steadily shifting in China's favor but, due in large measure to Japan's excellent antisubmarine warfare capabilities, Japan has enduring geographic and technological advantages that can effectively deny China sea and air control in the East China Sea (Beckley, 2017, p. 97).

These considerations have not stopped China from asserting its claims in less direct ways. Most notably, in 2013 China announced the creation of a new airdefence identification zone (ADIZ) in the East China Sea, extending more than 500 kilometers from its coastline and covering a large area that includes the disputed islands. An ADIZ in and of itself need not be contentious. As noted by Bitzinger (2013), such zones are declared unilaterally, do not constitute territorial claims, and have no basis in international law. Nonetheless, they typically are adhered to by other nations. In China's case, its ADIZ overlaps with those already established by Japan, South Korea, and Taiwan and, unusually, it requires civilian aircraft entering the zone to identify themselves and file a flight plan with Chinese authorities even if they have no intention of entering Chinese national airspace (Cordesman, 2014). Ironically, the contentious nature of China's ADIZ has united sentiment against it by its neighbors, and the United States pointedly does not recognize it. Another indirect means by which

China advances its claims to the disputed islands is through the use of its Coast Guard and fishing vessels, with naval vessels as an implicit backup support (Rinehart, 2016).

One would be remiss in assessing the military balance in North-east Asia without addressing the problem of North Korea. Indeed, China's own White Paper observes: "The Korean Peninsula and Northeast Asia are shrouded in instability and uncertainty." The United States is treaty-bound to come to the aid of South Korea in case of military aggression against it, presumably from North Korea, with which it remains technically at war. The East China Sea is a vital passageway to the Korean Peninsula from the U.S. naval base at Guam, which is one of the anchors of the second island chain in the western Pacific. The continuous drama on the Korean peninsula between dueling regimes in the North and South is vitally important in its own right, but it also has direct implications for U.S.–China military relations, with the potential for missteps on either side to escalate quickly to dangerous levels.

A brief examination of the recent THAAD controversy helps to illuminate the many dimensions to this complex interplay. Because North Korean missile launchers are so close to Seoul and other potentially vulnerable locations in the South, it is essential for the U.S. and its ally to have accurate and timely information about any hostile launches immediately upon the outset of hostilities. This imperative is magnified by the increasingly threatening nuclear capabilities, flaunted by the North, that pose a direct threat to the U.S. military installation at Guam. It is in this context that the United States has sought to deploy a Terminal High Altitude Area Defense (THAAD) radar in South Korea. China believes that this powerful radar system is actually designed to peer deep into China and thus undermine China's nuclear deterrent (Swaine, 2017; Wu, 2016). China has made it clear, and U.S. military analysts confirm, that the Chinese military strictly adheres to a no first strike nuclear doctrine. China does, however, seek to ensure that if it were the target of a first strike that it would retain the capability of launching a devastating retaliatory strike. The introduction of THAAD to South Korea could undermine that deterrent effect, which in turn could lead to a more jittery response by China to unexpected developments on the Korean peninsula. More generally, any implosion of the North Korean regime or other catastrophic events on the Korean peninsula could bring U.S. and Chinese military forces into close, unwelcome proximity to one another in a volatile and unpredictable setting.

South China Sea

The South China Sea is increasingly seen as a contentious maritime zone with potential for military conflict involving China and possibly the United States. It is an area rife with directly overlapping maritime claims from China, the Philippines, Brunei, Indonesia, Malaysia, and Vietnam – in addition to broader claims regarding freedom of passage asserted by the United States and other countries. These contestations are made all the more intense by the imperative of energy supply. China is heavily dependent on imported oil; in 2016, 64 percent of its oil needs were met through imports, and this is projected to rise to 80 percent by 2035 (DOD, 2017, p. 43). This same dependency extends throughout North-east Asia, as more than 80 percent of the crude oil delivered to China, Japan, South Korea, and Taiwan passes through South China Sea shipping lanes (ibid., p. 41). Moreover, before any oil shipments originating in the Middle East can traverse the South China Sea, they must first pass from the eastern Indian Ocean through the Straits of Malacca, one of the world's most strategic geographic features from a shipping perspective. This so-called "Malacca Dilemma" is centuries old and is what prompted the Japanese Imperial Army to gamble so heavily on control of this region during World War II. Times have changed, but the underlying imperative to secure energy supplies has not, and that imperative is of course magnified during times of military conflict.

China's maritime claims in the South China Sea are based on a so-called nine-dash line that was sketched on a 1947 map during the Republic of China era. Seen on maps, it resembles a tongue worthy of a Rolling Stones album cover. The Spratly Islands are located within this area, and these tiny scattered outcroppings have become a particularly stubborn source of contention between China and its maritime neighbors to the south, all of which have established outposts in this area. In the eyes of many, China has been particularly aggressive in converting such outposts into expanded facilities that will serve both civilian and military purposes (Rinehart, 2016, p. 240). U.S. military observers are concerned that China's plan is to take over the Spratlys without firing a shot – the "salami-slicing" strategy alluded to earlier. According to Beckley:

> China's plan faces two obstacles, however: the 2016 ruling by the tribunal in The Hague dashed China's legal claims to the area; and four other countries militarily occupy features in the Spratlys and are unlikely to budge unless China uses force…. In short, China's neighbors are firmly ensconced in the Spratlys and are backed by international law.
>
> *(2017, p. 105)*

Moreover, these Chinese airbases are themselves quite vulnerable to attack in the event of regional conflict (Goldstein, 2017). The net result of all this activity is a potentially volatile situation whereby several countries, with China most prominent among them, are jostling with each other to establish outposts in highly contentious and strategic waters that are of vital importance to all. According to Cordesman (2014, p. 473), "The potential for conflict in the South China Sea is significant and ranges from low level clashes between China and its neighbors and conflicts involving China and the US."

In evaluating the military balance, it is necessary but not sufficient to carefully assess the military assets (soldiers and materiel) available to both sides. This is analogous to chess, where the player with a material advantage in pieces typically but not always has the upper hand. Chess lore is full of delightful examples whereby the particular disposition of the pieces is such that the player with fewer pieces is nonetheless able to produce a decisive victory. For this reason, it can be highly instructive to examine realistic scenarios that are grounded in the specific context of a potential battlefield. A good example of this is a lengthy and detailed study by the Rand Corporation, at the behest of the U.S. Air Force, that focuses on two concrete scenarios – one involving the Spratlys and the other centered on Taiwan. The South China Sea scenario is set out as follows:

> The Philippines moves toward exploiting oil and gas resources in the South China Sea. China denounces Manila's "provocative behavior" and begins to harass Philippine ships and platforms. The Philippines reinforces its position in the Spratly Islands, especially on Thitu Island, and China responds by dispatching naval forces and occupying the island. With nationalist demonstrations becoming more unruly in both countries, the United States dispatches a carrier battle group to the area to reassure allies and tamp down tensions. A U.S. surveillance aircraft is destroyed by Chinese naval surface-to-air missiles (SAMs), and the United States decides to eject Chinese forces from Thitu.... The scenario assumes that both sides have deployed additional naval and air assets to bases within range of the Spratly Islands and have sortied surface and submarine elements to positions around the islands. Because of the origins of the conflict, the United States is allowed to use bases in the Philippines and Japan. Despite a desire to keep the conflict limited, both sides see their credibility at stake and are willing to strike bases that are being actively used by the other.
>
> *(Heginbotham, 2015, p. 14)*

This chilling scenario is analyzed in the Rand study using data from four different years: 1996, 2003, 2010, and 2017. Doing so enables one to assess how the military balance for the given scenario has been evolving over time. The report summarizes the analysis using a "scorecard" that assesses the relative capabilities of the U.S. and China in multiple dimensions:

1   Chinese attacks on air bases
2   U.S. vs. Chinese air superiority
3   U.S. airspace penetration
4   U.S. attacks on air bases
5   Chinese anti-surface warfare
6   U.S. anti-surface warfare

7   U.S. counterspace
8   Chinese counterspace
9   U.S. vs. China cyberwar.[5]

For the year 1996, the results for the Spratly conflict show a major U.S. advantage in capabilities in all of the above dimensions except U.S. counterspace, where China had an initial advantage.[6] For two categories, U.S. attacks on air bases and U.S. anti-surface warfare, the major U.S. advantage holds throughout 2003, 2010, and 2017. For the remaining categories there is slippage over time, where the U.S. major advantage is reduced to a simple advantage or even to rough parity. Part of this trend is attributable to the fact that the U.S. military is burdened with a global mandate and is thus unable to optimize or tailor its forces solely to a China-oriented scenario (Heginbotham, 2015). It also reflects the fact that China's military capabilities have been increasing steadily, commensurate with its overall economic growth. Finally, it reflects the fact that the closer one moves to China's shores, the further removed one is from the commons where U.S. military might remains uncontested. This becomes even more apparent as we move to examine the military balance vis-à-vis Taiwan.

The Taiwan Policy Context

Even without the myriad political and diplomatic ramifications posed by Taiwan, its geographic location as the centerpiece of the first island chain is of enormous strategic value from a military perspective. Conversely, even without these geographic and military attributes, the political and diplomatic issues surrounding the disposition of Taiwan are of core significance to the People's Republic of China. Taken as a whole, therefore, Taiwan is of paramount importance to the entire configuration of the political and military landscape in the western Pacific. This chapter focuses on the rise of China from a U.S. defense policy perspective, but it is useful to pause for a moment to consider just how important the Taiwan issue is to China, insofar as that may help assess the potential for military actions and the conditions under which they might occur.

Taiwan has been an integral part of China's effective national governance system for only four of the past 125 years. Taiwan was under Japanese colonial rule from 1895 to 1945, and subsequent to 1949 has been effectively functioning independently of the People's Republic of China. During the early decades following its decisive military defeat and effective exile to Taiwan, the Kuomintang regime vociferously voiced its rival claim as the true, legitimate ruling party of the Republic of China. Over time, with the passing of generations, that claim became increasingly untenable and divorced from reality. Gradually, but steadily and perhaps inevitably, the focus of people living on Taiwan turned more to the practical matters of getting on in the world as a de facto autonomous society with its own increasingly Western-style neoliberal political system. Meanwhile, the proportion of the population on Taiwan that self-identifies as solely Taiwanese has been rising steadily in recent decades, while the proportion that self-identifies as both Taiwanese and Chinese has been steadily diminishing. Those who view themselves as exclusively Chinese are a vanishing breed altogether.

Meanwhile, on the other side of the Taiwan Strait, official views of the People's Republic of China towards Taiwan have evolved in a reciprocal manner. No longer needing to respond to a rival regime's claims, the PRC leadership in Beijing has focused increasingly on ensuring that its territorial integrity is not violated and that its sovereignty over Taiwan is not challenged. As China asserts in its White Paper, "reunification is an inevitable trend in the course of national rejuvenation ... 'Taiwan independence' separatist forces and their activities are still the biggest threat to the peaceful development of cross-Straits relations." Preparations for conquering Taiwan consume roughly one-third of China's defense budget (Beckley, 2017, p. 84). There is every reason to believe that this is truly a core interest that the PRC is prepared to use military force to accomplish if necessary. Not only is it a matter of national pride and a bruised sense of justice, it is also intended to send a strong message to other insipient separatist movements within its realm that might be inspired by a de facto independence of Taiwan.

The U.S. Department of Defense reminds us:

The circumstances under which the mainland has historically warned it would use force ... have included:

- Formal declaration of Taiwan independence;
- Undefined moves toward Taiwan independence;
- Internal unrest on Taiwan;
- Taiwan's acquisition of nuclear weapons;
- Indefinite delays in the resumption of cross-Strait dialogue on unification;
- Foreign intervention in Taiwan's internal affairs; and
- Foreign troops stationed on Taiwan.

(DOD, 2017, p. 75)

No doubt China has concerns that the longer the status quo of de facto autonomy remains in place, the more entrenched it becomes. On the other hand, as China grows increasingly strong and influential as a global power, it has greater means of isolating or "squeezing" Taiwan internationally. The question for China becomes at what point, and under what conditions, might a swift, strong, and decisive military action lead to a successful repatriation of Taiwan under PRC rule?

Meanwhile, the United States has not been a passive observer to this ever-unfolding drama. The United States strongly favored the Kuomintang regime, and the "loss of China" in 1949 led quite directly to widespread recriminations within the United States and contributed to a virulent anti-Communist political culture that shaped foreign policy over many decades. The United States stubbornly, or loyally, depending upon one's point of view, supported the Kuomintang's claim to be the legitimate ruler of China long beyond the effective expiry date, and it continues to be the principal supplier of armaments and other military support to Taiwan. Thus, the United States is seen by China as actively committed to a Taiwan policy that is directly contrary to a core aspiration of the PRC.

U.S. policy vis-à-vis Taiwan is enshrined in the *Taiwan Relations Act* of 1979, which was enacted in tandem with official recognition of, and the establishment of diplomatic relations with, the People's Republic of China by the United States. Three sections from the Taiwan Relations Act are particularly relevant for our purposes.[7] Section 4.2.1 states: "Whenever the laws of the United States refer or relate to foreign countries, nations, states, governments, or similar entities, such terms shall include and such laws shall apply with such respect to Taiwan." In other words, notwithstanding its formal recognition of the PRC, the United States shall continue to treat Taiwan in a manner that is consistent with de facto statehood. Section 3.1 asserts that the United States "will make available to Taiwan such defense articles and defense services in such quantity as may be necessary to enable Taiwan to maintain a sufficient self-defense capability." Section 3.3 directs the President

> to inform the Congress promptly of any threat to the security or the social or economic system of the people on Taiwan and any danger to the interests of the United States arising therefrom. The President and the Congress shall determine, in accordance with constitutional processes, appropriate action by the United States in response to any such danger.

This situation contains the seeds for potential military confrontation between the United States and China, depending in part on whether the U.S. commitment to defend Taiwan matches China's determination to repatriate Taiwan, by force if necessary.

The Taiwan Military Context

The same Rand study reviewed above in the context of the South China Sea also analyzes the military balance between the U.S. and China in the context of Taiwan based on the following scenario:

> A more assertive China moves to isolate Taiwan further on the world stage, inadvertently pushing Taipei toward de jure independence. When

diplomatic pressure fails to dissuade Taipei from changing course, Chinese leaders decide to occupy the island by force. In the lead-up to war, Taiwan appeals for U.S. assistance, and, given the ambiguous circumstances of conflict, Washington decides to use military force to protect the island.... The scenario assumes that, as tensions mount, both sides prepare militarily. The PLA deploys additional combat and support aircraft to the Nanjing Military Region, sorties its most advanced submarines, and deploys its forces out of garrison to forward staging areas. The United States moves additional aircraft and ships to the region and raises alert levels. Politically, the scenario assumes that the United States is allowed to operate freely from bases in Japan, the PLA is permitted to strike U.S. bases in Japan, and U.S. forces are allowed to attack nonstrategic targets in mainland China.

(Heginbotham, 2015, p. 14)

It is instructive to compare the Rand study's summary scorecard for the Spratly and Taiwan scenarios. Of the nine categories considered, three are the same in the case of a possible Taiwan conflict versus a Spratly Islands conflict: U.S. counterspace, Chinese counterspace, and U.S. vs. China cyberwar.[8] This result is not surprising insofar as counterspace and cyberwar actions are not directly tied to the specific geographical contexts of those engagements. For each of the remaining categories, there is an unfavorable shift in the military balance from a U.S. perspective as one moves from the Spratly Islands case to the Taiwan case. The main reason for this is that Taiwan is much closer to the mainland China coastline. In two cases, Chinese attacks on air bases and Chinese anti-surface warfare, the Rand study concludes that, by 2017, it was no longer simply a case of a diminishing advantage for the United States but has already become a clear advantage for China.

While China's military resources continue to grow apace, Taiwan's military spending remains at a modest 2 percent of its GDP, and is now only one-tenth that of China's. Moreover, Taiwan's transition to an all-volunteer army has not gone as smoothly as hoped for (DOD, 2017). As the military balance continues to shift in China's favor, two important points of consensus appear in the literature. The first is that Taiwan does not have the wherewithal to counter a Chinese attack directly. According to Cordesman:

China's ongoing military modernization, combined with ... improvements in human capital, training, and military exercises, are eroding the effectiveness of the ROC's prior reliance on intangible factors. Thus, as intangible differences between the two forces are slowly decreasing, tangible factors such as force numbers are becoming more important indicators of the Taiwan Strait military balance.

(2014, p. 382)

The second point of consensus in the literature is that Taiwan's best military strategy is to rely on asymmetric warfare, to adopt what Murray (2008) has referred to as the "porcupine defense." This approach recognizes that while China may be able to establish advantages in anti-surface warfare and undermine Taiwan's air bases, effective control of Taiwan would likely necessitate a large-scale and prohibitively costly amphibious landing (Cordesman, 2014; DOD, 2017; Goldstein, 2017). This is A2/AD in reverse. Other options that China might call upon are not promising either. Beckley (2017, p. 92) observes that no blockade in the past 200 years has coerced a country into surrendering its sovereignty. A more extreme measure would be to inflict massive punishment on the civilian population to force an outright surrender. But, as Beckley notes:

> China … probably cannot compel Taiwan to give up its de facto sovereignty by raining hell on Taiwan's cities. [China] wants to reincorporate Taiwan as a prosperous Chinese province and turn Taiwan's people into loyal Chinese citizens. Reducing Taipei to a smoldering ruin and incinerating hundreds of thousands of Taiwanese civilians would not achieve that end.
>
> *(Ibid., p. 95)*

A porcupine defense strategy by Taiwan would emphasize a professional standing army equipped with mobile, short-range, defensive weapons, civil infrastructure improvements, stockpiling of basic supplies, and other investments that are designed to prolong Taiwan's ability to endure and resist an invasion. This approach would also be consistent with the U.S. proclaimed intent under the Taiwan Relations Act to provide Taiwan with military support that is defensive in nature (Murray, 2008). It buys the United States and its allies more time to formulate an effective response to any attempt by China to repatriate Taiwan by force. U.S. military responses need not entail a direct engagement with Chinese forces in the Taiwan Strait, although that is the scenario examined in the aforementioned Rand study. The U.S. military could respond indirectly to Chinese military aggression against Taiwan by, for example, interdicting oil supplies moving through the Malaccan Strait (Beckley, 2017).

Several considerations would argue against direct engagement. One is the obvious potential for a horrific war between two great powers that could reach catastrophic proportions. Indeed, the worst-case scenario is dreadful to contemplate. A related point is that it is not clear what would constitute victory for the United States or whether a successful outcome, however defined, could in fact be achieved. There are many daunting reasons for China not to attack Taiwan, but if China were to take that giant step, one can only assume that it would do so with forceful determination.

China from a U.S. Defense Policy Perspective

The United States remains the world's sole superpower militarily, but even superpowers have their limitations. This is a lesson that the United States has learned through painful experience in Vietnam, Iraq, Afghanistan, North Korea, and elsewhere. China dwarfs those other countries, so it only stands to reason that there are serious limits to what the United States could hope to accomplish through military engagement with China. But if the U.S. military has limits, so too does the People's Liberation Army. It may be able to undermine or counter U.S. efforts to project power militarily, especially in its own "back yard," but China is subject to similar constraints in any attempt to project power militarily.

As the United States continues to assume a military burden that is truly global in scope, its command over the commons is an essential advantage against any potential adversary. The commons is not static, however, nor are the contested zones that press against its fringes. Those contested zones will evolve over time, some growing while others shrink along with the fortunes of the countries involved. As China continues its rise, one should expect that it will take up more space in the world militarily, just as it does in other dimensions. How the United States and China adjust to the evolving military balance is an open question. As Graham Allison (2017) concludes in his study of what happens when established powers are confronted with rising powers, "as far ahead as the eye can see, the defining question about global order is whether China and the United States can escape Thucydides's Trap."[9]

A key factor will be the scope for mutual accommodation where overlapping core interests are at odds. For example, China's "salami-slicing" tactics in the South China are no doubt driven by the imperative to secure essential supply lines for its oil imports. The challenge is to find ways to accommodate that underlying imperative without impinging upon the equally compelling rights of freedom of passage for the United States and its allies through those same strategic sea lanes. If those opposing imperatives are construed in a zero-sum framework, the potential for conflict is higher. Likewise, in the case of Taiwan, the challenge is to somehow acknowledge and respect China's legitimate historical claims while also meeting core interests of the United States, including faithfulness to a valued ally and trusting friend. Military confrontation is neither inevitable nor unthinkable, but war between the United States and China would surely be enormously costly and perhaps catastrophic to all parties. Much depends, therefore, upon the resilience and effectiveness of the institutions and processes, both formal and informal, through which mutual accommodation might be attained. These issues are addressed in Chapter 10.

Discussion Questions

1   Non-discretionary items such as Social Security, Medicare, and interest on accumulated debt comprise 70 percent of U.S. federal budget expenditures. Of the remaining 30 percent, half is defense-related and half is everything else. In this context, can the United States increase military expenditures sufficiently to maintain its military edge relative to a rising China and other potential rivals?

2   Of the three potential "hot spots" – North-east Asia, the South China Sea, and Taiwan – which do you think is more likely to ignite a U.S.–China military conflict? If that were to happen, how should the U.S. respond?

3   If the United States does not clearly commit to coming to Taiwan's defense in the case of an attack, it might unwittingly encourage China to invade. If the United States *does* commit, it might unwittingly encourage Taiwan to declare independence, thereby provoking China to invade. How can the U.S. best resolve this conundrum?

Notes

1   Sandler and George (2016) question the value of inducting these former Warsaw Pact member states that contribute only 2.4 percent of NATO's budget while also imposing significant additional cost burdens.

2   Japan is included in this count.

3   This same CRS report sets China's actions within the broader context of so-called hybrid warfare or ambiguous warfare tactics, as also deployed by Russia and other potential adversaries.

4   See www.mofa.go.jp/region/n-america/us/q&a/ref/1.html.

5   The study also summarizes the analysis of a potential Taiwan conflict, and we review that scenario next.

6   This somewhat counter-intuitive result, giving China an early advantage with respect to U.S. counterspace operations, is based on the relatively slow start that the U.S. had in developing such systems, in part, due to political concerns regarding the militarization of space. The interpretation of the scorecard is that in 1996 and 2003 China could be relatively confident that its space-deployed military assets could survive U.S. attempts to neutralize or destroy them. By 2010 and 2017, this shifted to rough parity, reflecting improvements in U.S. counterspace capabilities. See Heginbotham (2015, Chapter 9).

7   See www.ait.org.tw/our-relationship/policy-history/key-u-s-foreign-policy-documents-region/taiwan-relations-act/.

8   To refresh the reader's memory, the Rand scorecard assesses nine categories of military conflict for both the Taiwan and Spratly Island scenarios: (1) Chinese attacks on air bases; (2) U.S. vs. Chinese air superiority; (3) U.S. airspace penetration; (4) U.S. attacks on air bases, (5) Chinese anti-surface warfare; (6) U.S. anti-surface warfare; (7) U.S. counterspace; (8) Chinese counterspace; and (9) U.S. vs. China cyberwar.

9   Graham Allison's quote is taken from MacDougall (2017, p. 113). The premise of the Thucydides's trap, where the term is inspired by the ancient historian's account of Sparta's response to the rise of Athens, is that war is a likely but not inevitable outcome of an established power being confronted with a rising power.

References

Allison, Graham (2017). *Destined for War: Can America and China Escape Thucydides's Trap?*, Boston: Houghton Mifflin Harcourt.

Beckley, Michael (2017). "The Emerging Military Balance in East Asia," *International Security*, 42(2), 78–119.

Bitzinger, Richard (2013). "China's ADIZ: South China Sea Next?," *RSIS Commentaries*, No. 219, Singapore: Nanyang Technological University.

Brooks, Stephen and William Wohlforth (2015). "The Once and Future Superpower: Why China Won't Overtake the United States," *Foreign Affairs*, 95, 91–104.

Buzen, Barry, Ed. (2004). *The United States and the Great Powers: World Politics in the Twenty-First Century*, Cambridge: Polity Press.

Chase, Michael, Cristina Garafola, and Nathan Beauchamp-Mustafaga (2017). "Chinese Perceptions of and Responses to US Conventional Military Power," *Asian Security*, 14(2), 136–154.

Cordesman, Anthony (2014). *Chinese Military Modernization and Force Development: Chinese and Outside Perspectives*, Washington, DC: Center for Strategic & International Studies.

CRS (2017a). *A Shift in the International Security Environment: Potential Implications for Defense – Issues for Congress*, CRS Report R43838, Washington, DC: Congressional Research Service. (Author's name redacted.)

CRS (2017b). *U.S. Role in the World: Background and Issues for Congress*, CRS Report R44891, Washington, DC: Congressional Research Service. (Authors' names redacted.)

DOD (2014). *Quadrennial Defense Review*, Washington, DC: U.S. Department of Defense.

DOD (2017). *Military and Security Developments Involving the People's Republic of China*, Washington, DC: Annual Report to Congress, U.S. Department of Defense.

DOD (2018). *Summary of the 2018 National Defense Strategy: Sharpening the American Military's Competitive Edge*, Washington, DC: U.S. Department of Defense.

Drea, Edward, Ronald H. Cole, and Office of the Chairman of the Joint Chiefs of Staff (2013). *History of the Unified Command Plan*, Washington, DC: Joint History Office,

Erickson, Andrew and Joel Wuthnow (2016). "Barriers, Springboards and Benchmarks: China Conceptualizes the Pacific 'Island Chains'," *China Quarterly*, 225, March, 1–22.

Goldstein, Lyle (2017). "The US–China Naval Balance in the Asia-Pacific: An Overview," *The China Quarterly*, 232, December, 904–931.

Heginbotham, Eric (2015). *The U.S.–China Military Scorecard: Forces, Geography, and the Evolving Balance of Power 1996–2017*, Santa Monica, CA: Rand Corporation.

IISS (2017). *The Military Balance 2017*, London: International Institute for Security Studies.

MacDougall, James (2017). Book review of *Destined for War* by Graham Allison, *Parameters*, 47(2), Summer, 113–116.

Murray, William (2008). "Revisiting Taiwan's Defense Strategy," *Naval College Review*, 61(3), Summer, 12–39.

Posen, Barry (2003). "Command of the Commons: The Military Foundation of U.S. Hegemony," *International Security*, 28(1), Summer, 5–46.

Posen, Barry (2012). "From Unipolarity to Multipolarity: Transition in Sight?" in G. John Ikenberry, Michael Mastanduno, and William C. Wohlforth (Eds.), *International Relations Theory and the Consequences of Unipolarity*, Cambridge: Cambridge University Press, pp. 317–341.

Rinehart, Ian (2016). *The Chinese Military: Overview and Issues for Congress*, CRS Report R44196, Washington, DC: Congressional Research Service.

Sandler, Todd and Justin George (2016). "Military Expenditure Trends for 1960–2014 and What They Reveal," *Global Policy*, 7(2), May, 174–184.

State Council (2015). "China's Military Strategy," White Paper, Beijing: The State Council, The People's Republic of China, 27 May 2015. Available at: english.gov.cn/ archive.

Swaine, Michael (2017). "Chinese Views on South Korea's Deployment of THAAD," *China Leadership Monitor*, 52(4).

Symonds, Matthew (2018). "The Future of War," Special Report, *The Economist*, January 25.

Thomas, Robert (2017). "Taking Stock of US Military Alliances in Asia," *Global Asia*, 12(4), Winter, 15–19.

Trenin, Dmitri (2016). "The Revival of the Russian Military: How Moscow Reloaded," *Foreign Affairs*, 23, May/June, 23–29.

White House (2017). *National Security Strategy*, Washington, DC: U.S. Government.

Wu, Riqiang (2016). "South Korea's THAAD: Impact on China's Nuclear Deterrent," *RSIS Commentaries*, No. 192, Singapore: Nanyang Technological University.

10

FOREIGN RELATIONS

U.S. Foreign Relations in an Evolving Global Context

During the initial years of the great American experiment, the United States held a tenuous position in world affairs as the fledgling Republic scarcely had a foothold in the world, and diplomacy was key to developing alliances and trade relations. The importance of foreign relations for the United States from the outset is reflected in the fact that, beginning with Thomas Jefferson, five of the first ten people to hold the office of Secretary of State would subsequently go on to become President of the United States.[1] By the latter part of the nineteenth century, however, as the United States began to grow and prosper, U.S. foreign policy was firmly entrenched in the "overarching principles of isolation and neutrality."[2] This began to change rather dramatically during the Spanish-American War at the end of the century, when the U.S. began to acquire colonial possessions, and more so as it entered World War I. After the failure of President Wilson's attempt to establish a League of Nations in the aftermath of WWI, the United States retreated once more into another period of relative isolation. It was during this time that the Great Depression took hold, and the world at large was wracked by economic and political upheaval, culminating in World War II.

It was a very different world that emerged after WWII. The nuclear age was upon us, and so was the Cold War. The devastation of the war and lessons from the events leading up to it persuaded the United States and its allies that a more proactive stance was needed, regarding the kinds of institutions, protocols, and policies that might manage international relations. This was the dawn of a new international order anchored ultimately in the economic and military might of the United States. The World Bank, the International Monetary Fund (IMF), and the United Nations (UN) were all established during this period, and they all had their headquarters in the United States. The initial focus of the World Bank and the IMF was reconstruction of war-torn Europe, and the Marshall Plan was the ultimate expression of this endeavor. As Western Europe got back on its feet, the focus of these institutions gradually shifted to other parts of the world, and European countries became major donor countries in their own right.

This American-led international order was not fully global, as it was challenged by an ideologically opposed system led by the Soviet Union. The ensuing Cold War pitted these two competing world orders against each other, and the U.S. State Department was on the front lines of a global policy of "containment" that was designed to respond proactively and strategically to efforts by the Soviet Union to expand its spheres of influence at our expense. Increasingly, the venue for the ideological, economic, and geopolitical competition between these two worlds took place in the so-called Third World, and armed struggles in far-flung locales were viewed as proxy battles for the two superpowers in what Ikenberry (2017, p. 157) terms the "territorialization of ideology." Ultimately, the U.S. policy of containment proved successful, as the internal contradictions of the Soviet Union led to its spectacular implosion, while signs of grassroots democratic impulses were evident in China as well. Perhaps with more confidence than was justified, a so-called "Washington Consensus" emerged during the last two decades of the century around a global order that, in addition to democratic principles and human rights, was based on the principles of neoclassical economics, according to Stephen (2017, p. 485), thereby "providing a powerful and coherent set of policy prescriptions centered on privatization, trade and financial liberalization, and fiscal conservatism."

The advent of the twenty-first century ushered in much more doubt and self-doubt about the viability, primacy, and even durability of the U.S.-led global order. Joseph Nye, in *Is the American Century Over?*, declares that "There are two great power shifts occurring in this century; power transition among states from West to East, and power diffusion from government to non-state actors as a result of the global information revolution" (2015, p. 94). The iconic Al-Qaeda attack on the symbolic heart of U.S. global dominance certainly contributed to a shaken sense of confidence and called into question U.S. invincibility. But this was only one indicator of an ebbing tide of the power of nation-states and the corresponding rise of more fluid and often transnational networks of actors coalescing around a plethora of divergent causes. In many cases, these networks are quite positive, focusing on issues of social justice, the environment, or a myriad other worthy concerns. Nonetheless, when reinforced by the growing ubiquity of social media platforms, the aggregation of these politically motivated networks gradually erodes the centrality of traditional institutions of governance at the local, national, and global scales. This in turn contributes to the sense of entropy and dissolution of any erstwhile global order.

As noted by Nye, the power transition from West to East is another factor, and China is of course central to this movement, along with other BRICS[3] countries. Institutional inertia affecting the United Nations, the World Bank, the International Monetary Fund, and the World Trade Organization (WTO) (formerly, General Agreement on Tariffs and Trade, GATT) has contributed to a growing sense that these and other Breton Woods era institutions have been slow and clumsy in adapting to these changing realities (Patrick, 2014).

The durability and coherence of any U.S.-led global order can be further undermined by dramatic and unsettling swings in U.S. foreign policy, especially when these policy shifts coincide with watershed changes in U.S. leadership such as President Trump succeeding President Obama. Dramatic reversals on globally oriented issues such as climate change, the Trans-Pacific Partnership, trade policy, military alliances, and the role of international institutions inevitably calls into question the very foundation of international relations. When global institutions, both formal and informal, are supplanted by ad hoc deal-making, how are other nations to respond? What is the nature of the global order that emerges? What guidance principles might apply? Might one realistically hope for a world order, as once evoked by President John F. Kennedy, "where the weak are safe and the strong are just"?[4]

The Belt and Road Initiative and the Asian Infrastructure Investment Bank

Of the two tectonic shifts in the evolving global order described by Nye – from West to East and from governmental institutions to non-state actors – China looms largest in the first. Its approach to monitoring and corralling non-state actors is also significant and is addressed later in this chapter. The central question here, however, is what role China will play in the larger global order. One thing is abundantly clear: China regards itself as the rightful inheritor of much of the leadership role that the United States cedes, wittingly or otherwise. China does not seek to overthrow the institutions and practices of the evolving world order so much as it seeks to exercise more global influence within existing structures (Ikenberry, 2014; Nye, 2017). This is evident in China's accession to the World Trade Organization, its increasingly prominent role in the United Nations and other multilateral institutions, its cultivation of alliances in Asia and beyond, and its leadership role in climate change negotiations. At the same time, China has demonstrated a willingness to forge new institutions and initiatives where older ones are too restrictive or no longer serve their purposes. Most notably, its Belt and Road Initiative sets out a long-term strategic vision for China's place within the emerging world order, and the Asia International Infrastructure Bank establishes an alternative to the World Bank and the Bretton Woods legacy.

Announced in 2013, initially under the rubric of "One Belt, One Road," China's *Belt and Road Initiative* (BRI) is an ambitious plan to establish a fundamental realignment of economic, political, and security ties throughout Asia and beyond. As such, its scale and scope invite superlatives.[5] As described by one observer, the projects comprise

> a series of overlapping elements – upgraded and developed transcontinental railway routes, highways, port facilities and energy pipelines. [It] potentially involves over 60 countries with a combined population of over 4 billion people, whose markets currently account for about one-third of global GDP.
>
> *(Ferdinand, 2016, p. 950)*

It has been likened to the massive Marshall Plan that was launched by the United States in the mid-twentieth century (ibid.; Yu, 2017). Both cases entail efforts of breath-taking ambition, where the initiating country seeks to create, if not a new global order, a large-scale, transnational, regional order of major global significance. In the case of the Marshall Plan, as noted earlier, the goal was to get a war-torn Europe back onto its feet, thereby achieving a mutually supporting set of economic, political, and security objectives. While the European countries were in one sense the direct recipients of these large-scale investments, the United States was clearly guided by a kind of enlightened self-interest. And, of course, the geopolitical backdrop of the emerging Cold War contributed to the essential significance of the Marshall Plan.

The parallels to the Belt and Road Initiative are indeed quite evident, but with important differences.[6] For one, the principal emphasis of BRI is *connectivity* through hard infrastructure investments spanning the Asian land mass. Like the Marshall Plan, BRI is framed conceptually in what are intended to be mutually reinforcing economic, political, and security considerations. From an economic perspective, BRI is intended to provide an outlet for excess capacity in construction and related sectors of the Chinese economy (Dollar, 2015; Sit et al., 2017). Once the infrastructure links are in place, it will provide conduits for trade. BRI also seeks to foster a web of international political ties based on mutuality of interests but with China as the de facto centerpiece.[7] Its westward orientation from China also is designed to reduce China's reliance on trade with the United States and to establish its own sphere of influence extending throughout and beyond the Asian land mass. These political ties are reinforced by an invocation of the historic and cultural legacies of the ancient Silk Road (Winter, 2016). From a military and security perspective, BRI is designed to integrate the troublesome (from Beijing's point of view) Xinjiang region more fully into China's broader economic development goals while countering any incipient separatist tendencies there. The initiative also establishes alternative routes to secure energy and other essential supplies while reducing its potential vulnerability to hostile interventions by the United States or others, especially in shipping lanes through and about the Strait of Malacca and the South China

Sea. In this context, Sit et al. (2017, p. 37) provide an interesting perspective on the Belt and Road's geopolitical significance, with a quote from the English geographer Halford John Mackinder that seems eerily prescient one hundred years later:

> "who rules the Heartland commands the World-Island [Asia]; who rules the World-Island commands the world." In practice, however, it is still necessary to coordinate control of land routes with maritime transportation along the coast of this World-Island.

To spearhead financing of the extensive investments required to realize the Belt and Road vision, China created the Asian Infrastructure Investment Bank (AIIB) together with 56 other Signatories to the AIIB charter from Asia, Europe, Africa, South America, Australia, and Oceania. Although the AIIB insists that "there is no reference to the Belt and Road in any of the institutional rules or operational policies of the Bank [and that conformity] with Belt and Road objectives is not a consideration in AIIB's evaluation of investment proposals," the AIIB Charter does set out flatly that the purpose of the AIIB is to "foster sustainable economic development, create wealth and improve infrastructure connectivity in Asia" (Sanders, 2017, pp. 368, 370). China is the largest investor in the AIIB, and with a voting share of more than 26 percent, it is the only country with effective veto power, as the founding Articles of Agreement stipulate that a total of three-quarters of all votes are required to amend those Articles (Yu, 2017).[8] Upon its founding, the initial authorized stock of AIIB was US$100 billion. The aggregate lending power of the AIIB – together with other financial institutions founded by China for related purposes, including the New Development Bank and the Silk Road Fund – is expected to exceed that of the World Bank and IMF combined (Overholt, 2015). Thus, both by virtue of its very existence and in consideration of the magnitude of resources at its disposal, the AIIB is the potential harbinger of a post-Bretton Woods multipolar financial order.

How one views these developments and their impacts on U.S. interests depends on several considerations. One question is whether there is a "crowding out" effect by which financial capital flowing to the AIIB, for example, might be at the expense of capital investments that would otherwise be funneled through the World Bank. To put this into some perspective, we observe that total financing from all facets of the World Bank Group[9] – including all loans, grants, equity investments, and guarantees to partner countries and private businesses – approached $59 billion in FY 2017.[10] In comparison, a recent World Bank report finds that total private sector foreign direct investment flowing to developing countries is in the order of $700 billion annually. That same report bemoans the fact that this FDI volume still falls far short of what would be needed to attain the United Nations Sustainable Development Goals.

McKinsey (2016) reports that for more than two decades through 2013, China has devoted 8.6 percent of its GDP to infrastructure investments. No other country comes close. The worldwide average is 3.5 percent while the United States, Western Europe and Latin America hover at a mere 2.5 percent. In certain respects, this is not surprising. Countries like the United States had set down their basic infrastructure in earlier decades, whereas newly developing countries, such as China, India, and those in Eastern Europe may be still catching up. Stated another way, the effective economic rate of return to infrastructure investments may be lower where there is a relative abundance of infrastructure already in place. Conversely, that rate of return is higher where the relative lack of infrastructure is the source of costly bottlenecks. Investments that remove or ease tightly binding constraints are, *ceteris paribus*, more likely to be cost effective. Central Asia has long been notable for its relative paucity of infrastructure, and this limitation has been compounded by relatively ineffectual institutions of governance and finance. To the extent that the Belt and Road Initiative fosters productive new infrastructure investment opportunities of global significance, that is a good thing, especially where such opportunities are made available to a wide range of investor countries through the auspices of the Asian Infrastructure Investment Bank. Moreover, at least in the initial stages, the AIIB will be partnering with the World Bank, the Asian Development Bank, and other such institutions – in part because AIIB needs to develop its institutional capacity in this regard. This is less a question of crowding out and more a matter of expanding the pool of productive investments.

Another angle from which to consider the policy implications of the Belt and Road Initiative and the Asian Infrastructure Investment Bank for the United States is to consider the reverse situation. Would one consider the World Bank, for instance, to be an institution that undermines China's global and strategic objectives? If not, then one must ask why it should be different in the reverse direction. Are there are some fundamental asymmetries such that the World Bank and its companion Bretton Woods institutions are essentially benign while the Asian Infrastructure Investment Bank and related institutions in the context of the Belt and Road Initiative are not? Some would indeed argue that BRI is nefarious. The U.S. Department of Defense states flatly, in its summary of National Defense Strategy, that "China is a strategic competitor using predatory economics to intimidate its neighbors" (DOD, 2018, p. 1). What may well be the case is that the BRI and AIIB developments signify an emerging World Order 2.0 characterized by competing spheres of influence centered primarily around the United States and China. This is an issue to which we shall return later in this chapter.

China's Territorial Extent and Integrity

No geopolitical consideration is more central to China's core interests than its national geographical integrity. This applies to Xinjiang, Tibet, and Hong

Kong, of course. But above all others, the Taiwan issue is paramount. In each of these cases there are corresponding dueling narratives that underpin tension between China and the United States, where the Chinese narrative is one rooted in historical legitimacy and national integrity while the counter-narratives favored by the United States emphasize self-determination and freedom from oppression.

Taiwan

The scenario is by now a familiar one. After a prolonged and divisive regime-changing civil war in China, the losing side retreats to Taiwan, suppressing local resistance on the island and vowing to reclaim the Mainland in the name of the ousted regime. While this scenario immediately brings to mind the Kuomintang's retreat to Taiwan in 1949, the same scenario applies equally well to Zhang Chenggong's[11] bid to restore the Ming Dynasty as it fell to the Qing three centuries earlier. Indeed, from the early 1600s until now, Taiwan has seen a regular procession of ruling regimes. Ironically, it was the period of Dutch colonialism on Taiwan from 1624 to 1662 that set the stage for subsequent Chinese rule. As described in the engaging account by Andrade (2008), the Dutch deliberately encouraged Chinese traders, especially those from Fujian Province, to settle on Taiwan as part of a process that he terms "co-colonization" of the Austro-Polynesian aboriginal peoples. Its location was ideal for facilitating trade in silver from Japan, silk from China, and natural resources from Taiwan (Tse, 2000). Following the Dutch colonization (1624–1661) and a brief rule by Zhang's family, the Manchus ruled over Taiwan until their Qing Dynasty was defeated by Japan in 1895.

Reinforced, no doubt, by Taiwan's geographical status as a relatively large oceanic island, this succession of ruling regimes has led to a corresponding succession of old-timers versus newcomers. After 1949, there was a sharp distinction between the newly arrived Mainlanders and the local population who, for the most part, could trace their ancestral roots to Fujian Province but had been schooled over the past half century within Japanese colonial structures (ibid.). Over time that situation has changed, as only a small and rapidly dwindling minority of Taiwan residents now think of themselves primarily as Mainlanders. Seventy years of de facto autonomy vis-à-vis the People's Republic of China has inculcated an increasingly distinctive sense of cultural, economic, and political identity among Taiwan denizens. This trend continues, and has been reinforced through several electoral victories on Taiwan favoring the independence-minded Democratic Progressive Party (DPP) over the more traditionally-oriented Kuomintang.

From China's perspective, however, the issue is clear-cut, and its position has been consistent for decades: Taiwan was rightfully returned to China after World War II. Both sides in the ensuing civil war agreed upon that fact, but disagreed over who ruled China. That latter question was resolved decisively in 1949 with the victory by military forces of the Communist Party over their Kuomintang counterparts and the establishment of the People's Republic of China. For China, there is no recourse other than eventual reunification by any means necessary, but preferably through peaceful means. Any attempt by de facto authorities in Taiwan to seek independence would be tantamount to treason and would constitute a "red line" justifying military action to repatriate Taiwan forcibly. Any interference by the United States or other third party would be a wholly unacceptable intrusion into China's vital domestic affairs and national security.

The People's Republic of China steadily gained diplomatic recognition as the sole legitimate representative of China, especially after the passage of Resolution 2758 by the United Nations General Assembly on October 25, 1971, which read in part:

> The General Assembly.... Decides to restore all its rights to the People's Republic of China and to recognize the representatives of its Government as the only legitimate representatives of China to the United Nations, and to expel forthwith the representatives of Chiang Kai-Shek from the place which they unlawfully occupy at the United Nations and in all the organizations related to it.

The United States followed suit on January 1, 1979, and by 2020 no more than 15 rather minor nations (relatively speaking, of course) have official diplomatic relations with the erstwhile Republic of China, compared to more than 175 that recognize the People's Republic of China.

Many countries, however, including the United States, maintain robust unofficial relations with the government on Taiwan. As noted in Chapter 9 [*Defense Policy*], the legal basis for United States relations with the government on Taiwan is set out in the *Taiwan Relations Act* of 1979 that states, in part: "Whenever the laws of the United States refer or relate to foreign countries, nations, states, governments, or similar entities, such terms shall include and such laws shall apply with such respect to Taiwan."[12] This effectively marked the beginning of an important shift by the United States away from the central question of which government represents China and towards an implicit assertion of Taiwan's autonomy and presumed rights to self-determination. In doing so, it underscored a counter-narrative to China's firmly held view that Taiwan is an inalienable part of China that must and will eventually return to the fold.

The counter-narrative is rooted in the precept of a people's right to self-determination. There is of course some basis in international law for such a right. Chapter I, Article 1 of the United Nations Charter declares that one of the purposes and principles of the United Nations is to "develop friendly relations among nations based on respect for the principle of equal rights and *self-determination of peoples*, and to take other appropriate measures to strengthen universal peace" (emphasis added). This seemingly laudable principle, however, cannot be translated so readily into universally supported norms of practice. An obvious point of contention is what constitutes "a people." In some cases, such as the Quebec referenda of 1980 and 1995, or the Scottish referendum of 2014, the legal right for voters to decide the issue was not contested by the "parent" entity, Canada or the United Kingdom. But in many other cases, the very premise of a right to decide is violently opposed. Ironically, U.S. history itself presents a case in point, where our country was founded on the basis of self-determination and independence from England, while a mere "four score and seven years" later that same United States avowed that the Union was sacred and refuted absolutely the right of *its* rebel States to secede. It may give one pause to note that in both cases the issue of self-determination was not decided through negotiation or in courts of law but through forcible means on the field of battle.

In recent decades, a kind of "dynamic stalemate" has evolved. I use this somewhat oxymoronic term intentionally. The stalemate arises where neither side can make a decisive move: Put starkly, Taiwan cannot overtly move toward independence while the Beijing authorities do not find it prudent to forcibly compel Taiwan to return to the fold. To a certain extent, this standoff is encapsulated in the so-called 1992 Consensus, which refers to an implicit accord that has facilitated a wary co-existence between the two sides of the Strait. This stalemate is dynamic, however, in the sense that the relevant political, economic, diplomatic, and military context is steadily evolving. For both sides, the passage of time is a double-edged sword. On the one hand, China's strength continues to increase in all dimensions, so the longer Taiwan waits, the stronger its potential adversary will be. On the other hand, the longer China waits, the more likely it is that the people of Taiwan become increasingly alienated from China and hence more resolute in their quest for autonomy. It is a perfect case of an increasingly irresistible force encountering an increasingly immovable object.

The central question for our purposes is what the U.S. policy interest is or should be. To what extent does the eventual outcome, one way or the other, impact our core interests? There are several facets to this question. A core issue, one that is both moral and strategic, concerns the extent to which the United States stands by its allies. For better or worse, rightly or wrongly, the people and the government of Taiwan over many decades already have come to rely on the United States for political, economic, and military support. While past U.S. policy has been to maintain a strategic ambiguity regarding the extent to which we would intervene in a cross-Straits conflict, there may well come a time when our response must be unambiguous one way or the other. Yet, if the U.S. were to strongly pronounce its support for the democratic aspirations of the people of Taiwan, it could lead, inadvertently or otherwise, to more brash action on the part of its government, thereby bringing about a potentially very dangerous military conflict. Ironically, one possible outcome of such a conflict is that the people of Taiwan would lose much of the political freedoms they have cultivated in recent decades. Conversely, a tepid expression of support for Taiwan could embolden China to act. This dynamic stalemate is indeed fraught with tension and latent danger.

Overlaying this dynamic stalemate is the broader, over-arching military and geo-strategic context as described at some length in Chapter 9. Even if Taiwan were an uninhabited island with no political or historical entanglements, because of its location, it is of enduring geo-strategic importance, and its disposition one way or the other could substantially affect the balance of military power in the Pacific. This in turn raises the fundamental question of whether it is a *core* interest of the United States to maintain the extent of our purview and reach to the western edge of the Pacific Ocean. To assess this, it may be instructive to engage the counter-factual hypothesis. Suppose that 20 years from now that, by whatever means, Taiwan will have been fully repatriated to the People's Republic of China, so that it would join Hainan as one of two island provinces of the PRC within hailing distance of the mainland. It would seem that much depends on the disposition of both sides. Is the relationship between the United States and China destined to be an antagonistic one where shadow warfare lurks just beneath the surface at all times? Surely, we have a choice. Both sides have agency; neither is fated to geographic determinism nor to the musings of ancient Thucydides (Allison, 2017a).[13]

When in Hong Kong, Please Mind the Gap

Hong Kong has one of the finest subway systems in the world. Throughout the system, announcements are made in Cantonese, Mandarin, and English, where the latter include regular reminders to "Please, mind the gap." While one should indeed be mindful of the gap between the train doors and the station platform, another, more daunting gap has been growing steadily in Hong Kong – and that is the cultural, economic, and political gap between Hong Kongers and mainland Chinese. More precisely, it is an *identity gap* between how Hong Kongers perceive themselves and how mainland Chinese, and especially the political leadership in Beijing, perceives Hong Kong.[14] This identity gap, in turn has been fueled by dueling narratives about what Hong Kong is and who Hong Kongers are. The tragedy is that both narratives are correct, yet they appear to be mutually irreconcilable.[15]

China's Hong Kong narrative is rooted in a painful national history and international law. That historical perspective is summarized concisely in the first paragraph of the Preamble to the *Basic Law of the Hong Kong Special Administrative Region of the People's Republic of China* (hereafter referred to as the Basic Law):

> Hong Kong has been part of the territory of China since ancient times; it was occupied by Britain after the Opium War in 1840. On 19 December

1984, the Chinese and British Governments signed the Joint Declaration on the Question of Hong Kong, affirming that the Government of the People's Republic of China will resume the exercise of sovereignty over Hong Kong with effect from 1 July 1997, thus fulfilling the long-cherished common aspiration of the Chinese people for the recovery of Hong Kong.

Article 1 of the Basic Law, which is the ultimate legal foundation for Hong Kong's Special Administrative Region (SAR), puts that Preface into legal force, stating starkly that, "The Hong Kong Special Administrative Region is an inalienable part of the People's Republic of China."

The narrative that unites many Hong Kongers, especially the younger generation, is also compelling. Hong Kong is unique and highly distinctive, and this is reflected in the self-identity of those who live there. Most university students in Hong Kong were born after Hong Kong was already repatriated, yet they do not identify as Chinese. On the contrary, they feel alienated culturally, economically, and politically from China. As one writer put it, "for many Hongkongers, the transfer from one empire to another hardly felt like a homecoming." (Cheng, 2019).[16] Ironically, many of the very measures that China has taken to integrate Hong Kong into the larger Pearl River delta region have led to a growing sense of disenfranchisement among the generation of Hong Kongers that is now coming of age. Cross-border ties generally benefit local businesses and property owners, but can be disadvantageous to employees and tenants. A vast pool of labor across the border keeps downward pressure on wages in Hong Kong, yet housing prices rank among the most expensive in the world.[17] Young adults seeking to establish themselves strain to do so with modest wages. Rather than bringing about convergence, close cross-border interactions seem to have magnified perceived differences in language, culture, behaviors, and social mores. These micro-level differences are compounded by the vastly different political and societal structures as sustained through the "One Country; Two Systems" formula set out in the Basic Law. The 50-year horizon for this formula when it was put into effect in 1997 has by now shortened considerably, and the year 2047 somehow does not seem so far off anymore. Young Hong Kongers fear a loss of their own identities and thus, in a very real way, a loss of themselves and of their future.

Perhaps more fundamentally, their narrative is about liberty and the freedom to be who they believe themselves to be. This identity question is addressed in recent research by Steinhardt et al. (2018), who use a dual rating scale, with separate questions to measure the strength of local (i.e., Hong Kong) and national (Chinese) identities. The dual scale overcomes the limitations of a single scale with Hong Kong identity at one end and Chinese identity at the other. The single scale approach implicitly imposes a "zero-sum gain" condition whereby increasing strength in one identity necessarily comes at the expense of the other. The dual scale allows more flexibility where, for example, the strength of both Hong Kong and national identities may (but need not) both rise and fall together.

Indeed, those authors do find that during the early 2000s, shortly after Hong Kong's repatriation, the strengths of *both* Hong Kong and Chinese identities were on the rise. This demonstrates that strong local and national identities in Hong Kong are not intrinsically incompatible. This began to change during the second decade, as local identity strengthened while national identity began a notable decline, especially among the younger generation. Further empirical analysis by Steinhardt et al. (ibid.) finds that the declining national identity among Hong Kongers was correlated with a self-reported diminished political trust of the central government among Hong Kongers. Those survey results were obtained before the dramatic events of 2019.

The massive outpouring of protests in Hong Kong in 2019 were sparked by a proposed bill introduced by the China-appointed leader of the Hong Kong SAR that would have opened the door under certain circumstances for the extradition to China of some criminals. With its rather ominous title, the *Fugitive Offender and Mutual Legal Assistance in Criminal Matters Legislation (Amendment) Bill 2019* was met with an uproar that demonstrates clearly how most people in Hong Kong perceive the gap between its own judicial system and that of China's. While China has alluded to "dark hand" conspiracies by foreign powers with malicious intent, it is fully apparent to most observers that the outpouring of massive protests was based on genuine popular sentiment.

What is the core interest of the United States in a Hong Kong where "One Country, Two Systems" is being superseded in Hong Kong by "one place, two irreconcilable narratives"? On the one hand, the United States is (or should be) committed to a global order where international agreements between sovereign nations are adhered to and respected. It is a foundational belief in the rule of law, including the international laws that are implicit in agreements such as the one reached between Britain and China in 1984 on the *Joint Declaration on the Question of Hong Kong*. China has, on the whole, kept its side of the agreement. It is generally in the national interest of the United States within the international arena to stand for the rule of law. Certainly, within the United States, there is general consensus that one must abide by all laws, even those that one does not agree with. If anyone can pick and choose which laws apply to them, it undermines the entire social contract. Only under the most extreme circumstances would one be justified to argue for civil disobedience by appealing to a higher moral authority.

At the same time, the United States has traditionally stood for liberty and freedom from oppression. No other nation in history has been that "shining city on the hill" in the same way that we have. Whether we have in fact earned it or not, the United States is perceived by many around the world as a beacon of hope, especially by those who are oppressed. From this perspective, it would diminish our moral authority not to heed the appeal of those who seek liberty and self-determination, including young people in Hong Kong who may abhor becoming subsumed by what in their eyes – if not in the eyes of international law or by China itself – is an alien entity.

The Periphery Is Core

Zhong Guo (中国) is the Central Kingdom. China is at the center of its world. It is the periphery of that world that is worrisome to the Chinese leadership. Whether it is in Xinjiang, Tibet, Taiwan, Hong Kong, or elsewhere, the potential for an unraveling of the ties that bind is abhorrent, so the impulse to bind more tightly is primal. And if a steady, malicious nibbling away at the periphery is perceived by the Chinese leadership to be the work of hostile forces, the defensive reaction is sure to be even more pronounced. While this was stated just now in terms of the geographic center and periphery, it is also true at the ideological and governance levels. The notion of core leadership within the Chinese Communist Party (CPP) is a central premise, with the Party itself at the core of all facets of the Chinese national agenda. As in the geographical context, encroachment upon this core is not to be tolerated. Ideology is the root expression of this proposition within China. In the post-Mao era, the fundamental premise has been an implicit social contract between the Party and the population at large, where the former delivers material prosperity, stability, and national resurgence while the latter offers obeisance.[18] During the Xi Jinping era, the CPP's political rhetoric has ratcheted upwards with a more strident insistence on correct thinking.

While these developments are primarily China's domestic matters, and in this sense not of immediate consequence for U.S. foreign relations policy, they do have a bearing on China's efforts to position itself as a sober and benign steward of global affairs. The same principle applies more broadly insofar as the United States and China may represent alternative leadership visions of an evolving world order. While the United States could forge its way alone in the world, one should not underestimate the value of trusted allies and general goodwill among peoples and nations. This is true for China as well, and so both countries could stand to benefit from such *soft power*. China exercises its soft power through diplomacy, including major strategic initiatives such as the Belt and Road Initiative discussed above. It has also undertaken a major effort to spread its cultural influence through the establishment of Confucian Institutes throughout the world, as part of what Shambaugh (2015) describes as China's "discourse war" with the United States.

Notwithstanding such efforts, and despite some unsettling changes in American foreign policy over recent years, China still lags behind the United States in this regard. Results from a recent survey in 25 countries from around the world undertaken by the Pew Research Center show that a strong majority of those surveyed consider China to have boosted its stature more as a global leader. There is a fairly even divide among those surveyed regarding which country, China or the United States, is the more dominant economic power. Nonetheless, an overwhelming majority believe the world would be better off with the United States as the world's leading power, not China. As Shambaugh states, soft power cannot be bought; it must be earned.

China @ World Order 2.0?

The most fundamental question for U.S. foreign policy in this context is what kind of world order we want to strive for, and what is the nature of U.S.–China relations in that world? As defined by Ikenberry, "Order refers to the settled arrangements – rules, institutions, alliances, relationships, and patterns of authority – that guide the interaction of states. Order reflects the organizational principles and rules that shape and direct state relationships" (2016, p. 5).

As noted earlier in this chapter, the Bretton Woods-era institutions and associated norms have had a remarkable run but are struggling to maintain their relevance and effectiveness in a global context that is very different from that of the post-World War II era in which they were conceived. China's role within that order has also evolved over the past four decades. In a very focused and strategic way, it has managed to develop and thrive by adapting to its external world order.

Over the most recent decade, however, coinciding especially with the Xi era, China has become more assertive in challenging the parameters of the U.S.-led global order. As Shirk describes it (2017, p. 20), "In recent years, China has started throwing its weight around." In trade policy, it has been more overt in applying laws that strongly favor state-owned enterprises and other Chinese firms at the expense of erstwhile foreign competitors. In the geopolitical sphere, it has defied international law in its aggressive stance in the South China Sea. And the ruling Communist Party of China has also been more aggressive in asserting its primacy over any political discourse within (and even beyond) the country, and has dismissed Western liberal norms as misguided, naïve, and not applicable to China. Brands and Cooper (2019) observe with biting irony:

> The most glaring contradiction at the heart of America's post-Cold War strategy toward China [is] the fact that the United States has long sought to contain China's ability to challenge the American-led world order while simultaneously helping China build the economic and military wherewithal to mount such a challenge.

Bipolar Disorder?

Ikenberry (2016) provides a thoughtful analysis of how this challenge might unfold, focusing on East Asia as a harbinger for how China is likely to operate globally as its growing strength permits it to do so. He argues that what is emerging in East Asia is a dual hierarchy, with an economic order that is centered on trade with China and a security order that is based on U.S. military strength in the region. This dual hierarchy is effectively replacing the former unitary hierarchy of the prior era where the United States held sway in terms of both economic and military dominance. China's growing economic dominance in East Asia compared to that of the United States is evident in Figure 10.1. In 2001, when China was joining the WTO, exports from the U.S. and China to the rest of the EAP[19] region were of a comparable scale, while U.S. imports from the region were twice those of China's. By 2017, however, China's imports from EAP were more than double those from the United States, and its exports were more than triple.

China also has the largest military presence in the region, so without the United States as a counterbalancing force, it is likely that the regional order within East Asia would be emphatically Sinocentric. Without the presence of the United States, China would in effect assume the position within the region previously enjoyed by the United States as the dominant economic and military presence. The continued presence of the United States in the region, therefore, is highly significant not just in numeric terms, but qualitatively as well. As

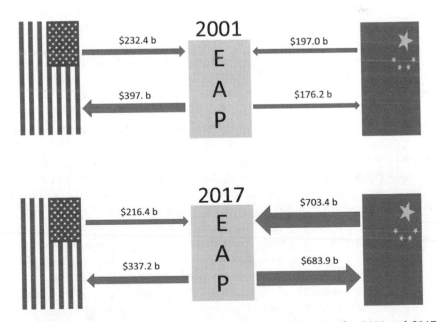

FIGURE 10.1   China and U.S. trade with East Asia and the Pacific, 2001 and 2017 (in constant 2010 $)

Source: Compiled using data from World Integrated Trade Solution, the World Bank, and converted to constant 2010 dollars using global GDP deflator, World Bank.

Ikenberry (2016) points out, under the right conditions, this kind of dual hierarchy could actually be quite stable and enduring, even as all countries in the region continue to evolve, but much depends on the United States itself. Several observers have noted that no country in the region would want to be compelled to choose between the United States and China.[20] Those countries are highly dependent on China for economic trade, yet they worry about China's potential military dominance. China, in turn, is limited in how overt it can be militarily without provoking a defensive backlash from countries within the region.[21] The United States has an incentive to retain an active presence within the region, for to do otherwise would in effect acquiesce to a unitary hierarchical order within East Asia centered firmly on China. The concern, however, from a U.S. policy perspective, is whether the cost of maintaining an effective presence is sustainable.

Who Needs Friends?

This is where the durability of alliances and the effectiveness of region-based institutions are of crucial importance. Absent the United States, countries within the region would find it challenging to forge coordinated, collective responses to China's initiatives. It would be difficult for any single country to take on a leadership mantle, especially in light of historical differences and even animosities between some of these nations. Any egregious move by China to assert itself could prompt an across-the-board response, but China could and does make steady inroads through patient and deliberate strategic initiatives, such as the Belt and Road Initiative as discussed earlier in this chapter. Only the United States is in a position to provide a countervailing initiative by virtue of its economic reach, its military presence, and related considerations. The Trans-Pacific Partnership (TPP) initiated by the Obama Administration, but abruptly abandoned by the Trump Administration, was one example of how this might be done.

The reneging of the TPP by the United States gives a boost to more China-centered multilateral trade clusters such as the Regional Comprehensive Economic Partnership (RCEP). Some might argue that the United States is better off negotiating bilateral trade agreements rather than working through cumbersome regionally based partnerships, while others see opportunities for more comprehensive agreements through multilateral efforts (Williams and Fergusson, 2017). From a longer-term geopolitical perspective, however, curtly abandoning such regionally based initiatives can undermine confidence in the United States by our allies in the region and thus move them closer to China. As one prominent observer noted, "We know that China will be our neighbor in 1,000 years' time. We don't know if the Americans will be here in 100 years' time."[22]

Cold War 2.0?

By all accounts, the United States won the Cold War with the Soviet Union. Is Cold War 2.0 inevitable, winnable, or desirable – this time with China as the adversary? Related questions have been raised in the context of the "Thucydides's trap." Thucydides, an ancient Greek historian, stated that "It was the rise of Athens and the fear that this inspired in Sparta that made war inevitable," (Allison, 2017b, p. 81). In the contemporary context this is an expression of power transition theory (Mazarr et al., 2018). The question is whether the rise of China and the fear that it inspires in the United States make war inevitable. To a significant extent, this is up to us. As much as or more than China or any other nation, the United States can help shape the world today that we all find ourselves in and respond to tomorrow. If we leave the door open to China, it is conceivable that China may respond affirmatively. If, however, we predicate our policy on the assumption that China is our enemy, China will no doubt respond in ways that affirm that assumption for us. This sentiment is expressed well in an open letter to President Trump and to Congress entitled "China is not the Enemy" published in July 2019 in the *Washington Post*, and signed by a large and impressive group of scholars, policy-makers, and other experts.[23]

Brands and Cooper (2019) set out four fundamental approaches the United States might assume in its relationship with China. From friendliest to most hostile, these are: accommodation, collective balancing, comprehensive pressure, and regime change. They quickly dismiss accommodation as being too naïve regarding China's intentions; and they likewise dismiss attempts by the United States to provoke regime change within China as both infeasible and wrought with peril. Collective balancing hinges on regional alliances as a counterweight to China, much as we have discussed above. Comprehensive pressure is more akin to the grand strategy of containment of the Soviet Union during the Cold War era. It is premised on a mutual hostility but with sufficient restraint on both sides to avoid mutually destructive warfare. Perhaps somewhat predictably but reasonably, Brands and Cooper (2019) opt for a middle ground that they term collective pressure.

A host of other scholars and policy-makers (Feigenbaum, 2017; Mazarr et al., 2018; Schell and Shirk, 2017) have independently called for a similar approach whereby the United States should be proactive in working with regional allies to help shape a regional order that can reasonably accommodate the legitimate aspirations of all, and that China be welcomed to play a meaningful, substantive and constructive role. The corollary of this approach is that if China continues to "throw its weight around" in a manner that undermines such an arrangement, then the United States should work with its allies in the diplomatic, economic, and military arenas to respond firmly and resolutely. Such an approach is inherently challenging. To the extent that Xi Jinping and the Chinese Communist Party succeeds in subordinating all activities within China to realize its

China Dream, China may enjoy a natural advantage in terms of comprehensiveness and streamlined coordination across all domains. In comparison, the United States may struggle just to reach consensus on such issues domestically, let alone across a highly diverse set of regional allies.

Soft Authoritarianism?

There were 18 Commissioners on the first United Nations Commission on Human Rights, including Eleanor Roosevelt of the United States, who chaired the Drafting Committee that produced the Universal Declaration of Human Rights (UNDR) that was adapted by the United Nations on 10 December 1948.[24] That Declaration, with its 30 articles itemizing specific rights to which every human being is entitled, represents a landmark in human affairs. While providing a conceptual anchor, philosophical rationale, and legal basis for establishing such rights, the UNDR does not in itself bring about the fulfillment of human rights. Furthermore, while those declared human rights may be universal, there is ample room for reasonable parties to have differing views on how human rights might be attained in different contexts, and how tradeoffs between specific elements are to be weighed. In particular, there is an unavoidable tension between the rights of the collective and the rights of individuals. Each society grapples with this. In the United States, a familiar credo is "life, liberty and the pursuit of happiness," while just to the north, the Canadian counterpart is "peace, order and good government." And, indeed, those sentiments are very much in evidence in their respective countries. If such differing viewpoints are to be found between two friendly neighbouring[25] countries that have many shared cultural affinities, it is surely more likely when we compare the United States and China, which are in many ways of two different worlds.

This issue of the universality of human rights, versus an assertion of cultural relativism, received prominent attention during the 1990s, with then-President Bill Clinton and Singapore's leader Lee Kuan Yew arguing their respective sides (Barr, 2000). The Singaporean model of "soft authoritarianism," for some, exemplifies good governance that is reflective of and consistent with Asian values. And while no one would mistake China for Singapore, one detects a "rhetorical alliance" between the two in this regard, as echoes of Lee Kuan Yew can be heard in Chinese refrains (Roy, 1994). A key difference between Singapore and China is how "soft" their respective versions of authoritarianism are.

Each year, the U.S. State Department in accordance with laws passed by Congress, submits a set of *Country Reports on Human Rights Practices*.[26] These are intended to inform Congress, broadly, in its conduct of foreign policy. The first page of its *2018 Country Report for China* enumerates a litany of human rights violations, most notably: "mass detention of Muslim minority groups in [Xinjiang, where] authorities were reported to have arbitrarily detained 800,000 to possibly more than two million Uighurs, ethnic Kazakhs, and other Muslims in internment camps designed to erase religious and ethnic identities." China also continues to devise and implement what, for some, is an Orwellian social credit system using Artificial Intelligence applied to massive social media, financial, and other big data sources (Hvistendahl, 2017).

Meanwhile, China has taken it upon itself to issue parallel reports about human rights violations in the United States. As China's Xinhua news agency describes it:

> The 12,000-character report exposes the human rights violations in the United States of different areas: the severe infringement on citizens' civil rights, the prevalence of money politics, the rising income inequality, worsening racial discrimination, and growing threats against children, women and immigrants, as well as the human rights violations caused by the unilateral America First policies.[27]

Cultural relativism, indeed.

Putting Our Own House in Order

The role of the United States in shaping a world (dis)order depends not just on the world outside our borders. Ultimately, it depends on US. It depends on who we are, collectively as a nation, and what we stand for. Any nation – however great it purports to be – that is deeply polarized internally and that is debasing its own institutions of governance and civil discourse, cannot inspire others to help build a world order that any of us would hope to live in. Yet despite our woes, the United States continues to be a nation with a magnetic draw.[28] The same deeply rooted individualism that sometimes makes our collective seem chaotic and dysfunctional is the bedrock of American identity. The United States is *THE* place where individual freedom is celebrated and where each person has not only the right but the moral obligation to become his or her true self in harmony with others. Individual liberties are the bedrock, but our institutions are the key and a just society is the best litmus test of what works and what does not. If we can demonstrate those principles at home, we have a better chance of applying them abroad.

Discussion Questions

1   Is the Belt and Road Initiative inimical to U.S. core interests? If so, would this imply that there is a "zero sum game" whereby any geopolitical initiative that works to China's benefit is necessarily at the expense of the United States? Is there any way to turn the BRI into a "win–win" proposition for both the U.S. and China?

2   What are the core interests of the United States with respect to the status of Hong Kong as a Special Administrative Region of the People's Republic of China? As a signatory to the 1984 Sino-British Joint Declaration, does the United Kingdom continue to have special standing on these issues relative to other countries outside China? What standing does the United States have compared to any other country outside China regarding Hong Kong matters, and what is its basis?

3   Is the post-World War II (Bretton Woods) world order still viable? Is it possible to formulate a "World Order 2.0" that can accommodate the core national interests of both the United States and China, as well as the vast majority of countries in the world? If not, what is the default option for the United States? Can America and China escape Thucydides's trap?

Notes

1   The first five Secretaries of State (and their order of appearance in that role) who subsequently went on to become President are Thomas Jefferson (1), James Madison (5), James Monroe (7), John Quincy Adams (8), and Martin van Buren (10). John Buchanan (17) is the only other person to have done so thus far, although more recent notables including William Jennings Bryan (41), Hillary Clinton (67) and John Kerry (68) did secure their Party's nominations for President at some point in their careers.
2   Office of the Historian, U.S. Department of State.
3   The common acronym refers of course to Brazil, Russia, India, China and South Africa – significant emerging voices in shaping any emerging global order.
4   The JFK quote is from Ikenberry (2014, p. 90).
5   Among other superlatives, BRI has been described as "a gargantuan project unprecedented in history" (Shambaugh, 2018, p. 96) and "the greatest project of the age" (Sanders, 2017, p. 367).
6   I scrupulously avoid here the temptation to refer to the Belt and Road Initiative as a "Marshall Plan with Chinese characteristics."
7   Professor Barry Naughton, the well-known expert on China's political economy, observed that the Belt and Road is actually more of a hub and spoke. (remarks at a seminar held at USC in March 2018). See also Breslin (2016, p. 67).
8   China's effective veto power within AIIB mirrors the U.S. example in the context of the World Bank and IMF. See, for example, www.brettonwoodsproject.org/2016/03/imf-world-bank-decision-making-and-governance-existing-structures-and-reform-processes/.
9   Institutions comprising the World Bank Group include the International Bank for Reconstruction and Development (IBRD), the International Development Association (IDA), the International Finance Corporation (IFC), the Multilateral Investment Guarantee Agency (MIGA), and the International Centre for Settlement of Investment Disputes (ICSID).
10   Figures on total financing provided by the World Bank Group taken from http://pubdocs.worldbank.org/en/982201506096253267/AR17-World-Bank-Lending.pdf.
11   Zhang Chenggong was known by the Dutch and other Western contemporaries as Koxinga, a transliteration of the Fujian pronunciation of Zhang's honorific title, "Kok Seng Ia," 國姓爺, bestowed by a Ming prince. See Andrade (2008, Chapter 10).
12   *Taiwan Relations Act*, section 4.b.1.
13   As explained later in this chapter, Thucydides was an ancient Greek historian whose

comments have had some currency in recent debates about China as an emerging rival to the United States.

14 There is a cruel irony in this metaphor as the result of the Mass Transit Railway itself coming under attack from Hong Kong protesters.

15 Overholt (2019) provides an interesting, albeit somewhat personalized, account of how these two narratives became increasingly opposed.

16 Chris Patten, Hong Kong's last British Governor, stated the same sentiment less delicately: "Promised a share in President Xi Jinping's China dream, all Hong Kong's citizens could see was a nightmare" (*Project Syndicate*, 30 September 2019).

17 Hong Kong is by far the least affordable major urban housing market in the international survey conducted annually by Demographia. See www.demographia.com/dhi.pdf.

18 Mazarr et al. (2018) refer to this arrangement as "performance-based legitimacy."

19 The East Asia and Pacific (EAP) region as defined by the World Bank includes China plus 14 other countries: Cambodia, Indonesia, Korea, Laos, Malaysia, Mongolia, Myanmar, Pacific Islands, Papua New Guinea, the Philippines, Singapore, Thailand, Timor-Leste, and Vietnam.

20 Dollar (2015); Ikenberry (2016); Schell and Shirk (2017).

21 Ikenberry (2016, p. 3) refers to this as China's problem of "self-encirclement."

22 Singapore's Kishore Mahbubani, a retired senior diplomat and former dean of the Lee Kuan Yew School of Public Policy. Quoted in Shambaugh (2018, p. 109).

23 See www.openletteronuschina.info.

24 See www.un.org/en/universal-declaration-human-rights/index.html.

25 I intentionally use the Canadian (British) spelling here.

26 See www.state.gov/reports/2018-country-reports-on-human-rights-practices/.

27 See www.xinhuanet.com/english/2019-03/14/c_137894687.htm.

28 I myself am an immigrant, so I know first-hand about the draw that the United States has on those from abroad.

References

Allison, Graham (2017a). *Destined for War: Can America and China Escape Thucydides's Trap?*, Boston: Houghton Mifflin Harcourt.

Allison, Graham (2017b). "China vs. America: Managing the Next Clash of Civilizations," 96, *Foreign Affairs*, 80–89.

Andrade, Tonio (2008). *How Taiwan Became Chinese: Dutch, Spanish, and Han Colonization in the Seventeenth Century*, New York: Columbia University Press. Accessed through Gutenberg-e project at www.gutenberg-e.org/andrade/index.html.

Barr, Michael (2000). "Lee Kuan Yew and the 'Asian Values' Debate," *Asian Studies Review*, 24(3), 309–334.

Brands, Hal and Zack Cooper (2019). "After the Responsible Stakeholder, What? Debating America's China Strategy," *Texas National Security Review*, 2(2), 68–81.

Breslin, Shaun (2016). "China's Global Goals and Roles: Changing the World from Second Place?," *Asian Affairs*, 47(1), 59–70.

Cheng, Yangyang (2019). "A Birthday Letter to the People's Republic," *Chinafile*, September 28.

DOD (2018). *Summary of the 2018 National Defense Strategy: Sharpening the American Military's Competitive Edge*, Washington, DC: U.S. Department of Defense.

Dollar, David (2015). "Regional and Global Power: The AIIB and the 'One Belt, One Road'," *Horizons*, Summer, 162–172.

Feigenbaum, Evan (2017). "China and the World: Dealing with a Reluctant Power," *Foreign Affairs*, 96, 33–40.

Ferdinand, Peter (2016). "Westward Ho – the China Dream and 'One Belt, One Road': Chinese Foreign Policy under Xi Jinping," *International Affairs*, 92(4), 941–957.

Hvistendahl, Mara (2017). "Inside China's Vast New Experiment in Social Ranking," *Wired*, 14 December 2017.

Ikenberry, G. John (2014). "The Illusion of Geopolitics: The Enduring Power of the Liberal Order," *Foreign Affairs*, 93, 80–90.

Ikenberry, G. John (2016). "Between the Eagle and the Dragon: America, China, and the Middle State Strategies in East Asia," *Political Science Quarterly*, 20(20), 1–35.

Ikenberry, G. John (2017). "Recent Books: Political and Legal," *Foreign Affairs*, 96, 156–157.

Mazarr, Michael (2017). "The Once and Future Order: What Comes after Hegemony," *Foreign Affairs*, 96, 25–32.

Mazarr, Michael, Timothy Heath, and Astrid Cevallos (2018). *China and the International Order*, Santa Monica, CA: RAND Corporation.

McKinsey (2016). *Bridging Global Infrastructure Gaps*, New York: McKinsey Global Institute.

Nye, Joseph (2015). *Is the American Century Over?*, Cambridge: Polity Press.

Nye, Joseph (2017). "Will the Liberal Order Survive?: The History of an Idea," *Foreign Affairs*, 96, 10–16.

Overholt, William (2015). "One Belt, One Road, One Pivot," *Global Asia*, 10(3), Fall.

Overholt, William (2019). "Hong Kong: The Rise and Fall of 'One Country, Two Systems'," Cambridge, MA: Ash Center, Harvard Kennedy School.

Patrick, Stewart (2014). "The Unruled World: The Case for Good Enough Global Governance," *Foreign Affairs*, 93(1), 58–73.

Roy, Denny (1994). "Singapore, China, and the 'Soft Authoritarian' Challenge," *Asian Survey*, 34(3), 231–242.

Sanders, Gerard (2017). "The Asian Infrastructure Investment Bank and the Belt and Road Initiative: Complementarities and Contrasts," Letter to the Editors, *Chinese Journal of International Law*, 367–371.

Schell, Orville and Susan L. Shirk (2017). *U.S. Policy Toward China: Recommendations for a New Administration*, Task Force Report, New York: Asia Society Center on US China Relations and UC San Diego 21st Century China Center.

Shambaugh, David (2015). "China's Soft-Power Push: The Search for Respect," *Foreign Affairs*, 94(4), 99–107.

Shambaugh, David (2018). "U.S.–China Rivalry in Southeast Asia: Power Shift or Competitive Coexistence?," *International Security*, 42(4), Spring, 85–127.

Shirk, Susan (2017). "Trump and China: Getting to Yes with Beijing," *Foreign Affairs*, 20, 20–27.

Sit, Tsui, Erebus Wong, Lau Kin Chi, and Wen Tiejun (2017). "One Belt, One Road: China's Strategy for a New Global Order," *Monthly Review*, January, 36–45.

Steinhardt, H. Christoph, Linda Chelan Li, and Yihong Jiang (2018). "The Identity Shift in Hong Kong since 1997: Measurement and Explanation," *Journal of Contemporary China*, 27(110), 261–276.

Stephen, Matthew (2017). "Emerging Powers and Emerging Trends in Global Governance," *Global Governance*, 23, 483–502.

Tse, John Kwock-Ping (2000). "Language and a Rising New Identity in Taiwan," *International Journal of the Sociology of Language*, 143(1), 151–164.

Williams, Brock and Ian Fergusson (2017). "The United States Withdraws from the TPP," *CRS Insight* (IN10646), Congressional Research Service, May 23, 2017.

Winter, Tim (2016). "One Belt, One Road, One Heritage: Cultural Diplomacy and the Silk Road," *The Diplomat*, March 29.

Yu, Hong (2017). "Motivation behind China's 'One Belt, One Road' Initiatives and Establishment of the Asian Infrastructure Investment Bank," *Journal of Contemporary China*, 26(105), 353–368.

11

SYNTHESIS AND CONCLUSIONS

Linked policy domains

Having taken everything apart, it is now time to put the pieces back together again. The premise of this book has been that there is no single U.S. policy perspective on China, but there is instead a multiplicity of valid and substantive policy perspectives as have been analyzed in considerable detail in the preceding chapters. Ultimately, however, U.S. policy must be more than a collection of fragmented perspectives. This final chapter explores how these distinct – and at times mutually contravening – policy perspectives towards China's rise are linked together, traded off against one another, and potentially reconciled.

Figure 11.1 provides a notional view of how these diverse policy perspectives are related to one another. While necessarily subjective, it does help to focus our attention on key linkages, and is amenable to alternative representations, so anyone with a differing view can use this same device as they please.[1] Each of the nine policy realms reviewed in the previous chapters is represented in Figure 11.1 by a node (a larger colored dot). Because the diagram is topological, and not topographical, the location of those nodes has no bearing on the analysis.[2] Symbolically, however, it is convenient to place them all on a circle equidistant from some center point. They are also linked by economic, sustainability, and geopolitical perspectives, and shared perspectives are grouped together. The arrows in Figure 11.1 indicate notable flows of influence between policy domains and the thickness of each arrow indicates the strength of the corresponding linkage.

Trade policy immediately jumps out as the only policy domain depicted there with multiple strong lines of influence impacting other policy domains.[3] No other policy domain has more than one strong outward linkage, while trade

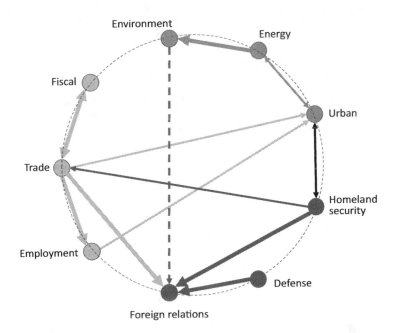

FIGURE 11.1   Linked policy domains

has strong direct impacts on fiscal policy, employment, and foreign relations. Trade, in turn, is also impacted directly by fiscal policy, so that linkage is represented by a two-way arrow. In Chapter 2 we saw how trade deficits are intrinsically linked – via national income accounts – to countervailing surpluses or deficits in the government and private sectors. Trade also impacts employment directly, as we saw in Chapter 4, and this was indeed a key issue in the 2016 presidential election, as Trump and others blamed our trade deficits with China for job losses in America. We have also seen trade dominate much of U.S. foreign relations, not just during the Trump presidency, but also in earlier administrations where the Trans-Pacific Partnership or NAFTA were contentious issues. The linkage between trade and urban outcomes is a weaker influence, but noteworthy nonetheless, especially in port cities. There is also the indirect influence that trade has on cities through employment effects. Jobs are city-builders.

In this same vein, we see that urban policy also displays a complex set of influences. Although they are not as strong as those of trade policy, they are richly multifaceted. This reflects the fact that cities embody not just single-sector perspectives but, as we saw in Chapter 6, they are truly microcosms of society at large. While urban outcomes are influenced by trade and employment activity, the way cities are designed also impacts energy consumption. That linkage is bi-directional, as energy prices also impact commuting choices and building designs. There is also a bi-directional linkage between cities and homeland security, as cities are the likely foci of potential security threats, and those potential dangers in turn compel us to rethink how we design our cities.

Another notable policy node in the context of Figure 11.1 is foreign relations, with strong linkages from trade policy, homeland security, and defense. Notice that all three arrows are directed toward foreign policy, so it is domestic concerns that drive foreign policy rather than the other way around. Defense and homeland security deal directly with transborder threats, so it is no surprise to see strong linkages between those two geopolitical policy issues and foreign relation concerns. Likewise, the focus for trade policy is also intrinsically transnational, so the strong direct link to foreign relations is understandable. Another reason for the strong link between trade policy and foreign relations is that trade policy is also a proxy of sorts for fiscal policy and employment policy insofar as they have strong links to trade but relatively weak links to foreign relations. Finally, Figure 11.1 also shows a moderate link between trade and foreign investment activities and homeland security concerns. As we saw in Chapters 3 and 8, these concerns are embodied in review mechanisms such as the Committee on Foreign Investment in the United States (CFIUS) and the Bureau of Industry and Security's Export Administration Regulations (EAR).

To recap, what we have seen is two strong policy clusters, one pertaining to economic issues and the other to security concerns. Both of these in turn have strong links to foreign relations. Indeed, this depiction accords with the two principal lines of strategic dialogue between the United States and China that have run in one form or the other through the past several administrations. What is notably absent in Figure 11.1 is any strong link between the sustainability cluster (urban, energy and the environment) and foreign relations. As noted already, urban policies are quite multifaceted and thus have diverse linkages to other policy domains. We have also noted strong links between energy and environmental policies. Notice, also, that environmental policies as depicted in Figure 11.1 are relatively isolated from the other broad policy domains, although the indirect impacts over the longer run may be very substantial. As we saw in Chapter 5, climate change is intrinsically global in nature, yet the established links between environmental policy and foreign relations is much weaker than those of trade, defense, or homeland security. This is especially true after the Trump Administration withdrew from the Paris Climate Accord. The dotted line linking environmental policies with foreign relations is indicative of this lamentably tenuous connection.

Lessons Learned

Economic Policies

The preceding analysis points to the need for a more comprehensive approach to a U.S. policy perspective on China. Beginning with the economic cluster, we have seen that trade policy is important not only in its own right but also in terms of its strong links to other sectors. We tend to over-emphasize trade policy in our dealings with China, when it is the economy as a whole that is of vital importance. As we saw in Chapter 2, trade deficits are more an *outcome* of our fiscal policies rather than a fundamental cause of economic imbalances. Put another way, the best way to restore trade balance with China may be to restore fiscal discipline at home. In terms of the fundamental national income accounting identity

$$(M-X) = (G-T) + (I-S)$$

if the private sector is in balance, so that investments (I) are fully funded by savings (S), we see that an excess of imports (M) over exports (X) is a *necessary* condition if government expenditures (G) are to exceed taxation (T) and related revenues. It is a fact that can be obfuscated or misconstrued, but it cannot be avoided. If we are unable to alter the right-hand side of this identity through our fiscal or related policies, the trade deficits on the left-hand side will remain – whether they be trade deficits with China or some other countries. The converse is also true: if we can alter the right-hand side through fiscal and related policies, the trade deficits will necessarily respond accordingly.[4]

The other crucial facet of our economic policies is employment and income. As depicted in Figure 11.1 and as described in considerable detail in Chapter 4, trade does have an important impact on this policy domain. But here again, we need not cast ourselves as victims of trade. It is within our capacity to address employment and income in a comprehensive way. Growing income inequality in the United States is a worrisome trend, and its causes are manifold. Ultimately, however, it is the structural foundation of our own political economy that enables and even fosters growing income inequality here. Technological change is a vitally important factor. Trade is another. Even more fundamental, however, is the fact that we appear to accept deep social inequalities as tolerable or perhaps even inevitable, just as we accept that many in our community do not have access to vital health care or other essential services. This is as much a question of our own political ethos as it is about the technical aspects of service delivery or of employment generation. As shown in Chapter 4, the aggregate benefits from trade – primarily in the form of lower prices for goods purchased by American consumers – likely outweigh the costs of employment dislocation. That fact, however, is of little solace to those who are displaced. If our overall policy ethos were oriented more toward ensuring that we all had a reasonable share in those benefits, trade imbalances would not be so highly charged emotionally and politically.

Sustainability Policies

The sustainability cluster is another policy locus that can prompt us to think more comprehensively about our domestic priorities and how they pertain to our relationship with China. A priority for the United States should be to strengthen the link between environmental policies and foreign relations – that thin dotted line depicted in Figure 11.1 *ought* to be a thick solid line. By engaging more proactively with China and other countries on climate change, we also could help to rebalance our foreign relations policies to reflect a whole-of-government perspective through its direct and multifaceted linkages to the communities we live in and the lifestyles we lead. This approach also introduces a perspective that is more intrinsically cooperative and based on mutual self-interest, so that our entire foreign relations outlook with China need not be premised wholly on rivalry or enmity.

Geopolitical Policies

The locus of geopolitical policy areas in Figure 11.1 is one where a premise of rivalry might more justifiably apply. Vigilance is the foundation of defense and security policies, and responsible planning in these policy domains necessarily entails "what if" scenarios that must guide our preparations. Planning for an earthquake does not mean that we want or even expect one, but it is nonetheless the responsible thing to do in light of the realistic possibility of such an event. A similar reasoning applies to public health (i.e., pandemics), security and defense issues, but with the important distinction that earthquakes themselves are completely oblivious to our undertakings, while that is not true of potential adversaries. Put in the language of social sciences, earthquakes are exogenous shocks while China's behaviors are to a significant extent determined endogenously. That mutual determination is the fundamental premise of game theory, where the strategic behaviors of either party depend in significant measure on the actions of the other.

Several implications can be derived from this observation. One is that our security and defense policies should not be gratuitously provocative; nor should they countenance dangerous provocations from China or other potential adversaries. While this principle is easy to articulate, it may be more difficult to translate into finely calibrated policy responses. A subtle example is raised by the Schell and Shirk (2017) report, which points out that it is a mistake for the Department of Defense to broadcast the operational details of freedom of U.S. navigation exercises in the South China Sea because doing so undercuts the argument that these are routine maneuvers rather than military provocations on our part. Another example of an unnecessary provocation on our part is when the Obama Administration vociferously sought to dissuade our allies from participating in the China-led Asian Infrastructure Investment Bank (AIIB). This ultimately unsuccessful bid squandered precious political capital and helped undermine the strength of our important alliances. Moreover, from a neutral or disinterested perspective, as argued in Chapter 10, if it is reasonable and even enlightened on the part of the United States to provide leadership for the World Bank and other Bretton Woods institutions, it should not be unreasonable for China to embark on a similar project. What may appear to be a provocation by one could reasonably be viewed by another party as simply a normal and reasonable exercise of an emerging country's growing capacities and developmental aspirations.

It is not difficult to find examples of over-reach on the part of China, however. Perhaps the most egregious example lies in China's territorial claims (the "Nine-Dash Line," as discussed in Chapter 9) vis-à-vis the South China Sea. Other examples are in the field of trade and intellectual property rights, where all indications are that China's disregard for and violations of fair-trade practices have been systemic. As seen in Chapter 8, cyberspace is another realm in which China's actions appear to have been highly invasive. In such cases, it would be derelict for the United States *not* to respond firmly and consistently. While these examples are quite diverse in one sense, they have in common an imperative for the United States to delineate between the normal expansive, but reasonably benign, exercise of growing strength and capabilities of a rising nation versus egregious and unacceptable intrusions into legitimate core interests of the United States.

An Institutional Perspective

Institutions, both formal and informal, can be a constructive means of working toward these policy objectives. For this to be the case, however, much depends on institutional design. Ultimately, the litmus test for an effective institution should be that it yields from the whole something that is more valuable than the mere sum of its constituent parts. Conversely, an ineffective institution is one where some or all of the individual components would be better off on their own, without such institutional encumbrances. The Brexit movement in the European Union is an important contemporary example of this tension in institutional design – and of the challenges in getting it right. A good institutional design accomplishes at least two important things. One is to codify a set of protocols, regulations, principles, and/or guidelines that helps all parties establish common benchmarks for what constitutes reasonable conduct. Important examples are the United Nations Convention on the Law of the Sea (UNCLOS), the World Trade Organization (WTO) and the United Nations Framework Convention on Climate Change (UNFCCC) – each of which provides for a codification of protocols and mechanisms for adjudicating disputes within the context of those rules. The value of these or other institutions is diminished if they become too cumbersome, costly, clumsy, corrupt, or co-opted.

An alternative is for the United States to eschew such international institutions altogether. If any country can go it alone, surely it is the United States, which, despite its woes, remains the wealthiest and most powerful country in the world. This *is* an option, and it is one that the Trump Administration has tilted heavily toward. If we follow this path, however, we effectively invite China and others to do likewise. International relations become ad hoc and intensively transactional in piecemeal bits. As with traffic rules or criminal justice, the absence of any agreed-upon guidance for what is acceptable and what is not inevitably devolves to a more chaotic state. Some may thrive under such conditions, but it is unlikely that the system as a whole would perform better than it would under any reasonably designed set of agreed-upon protocols and enforcement mechanisms. None of us wishes to have limitations placed upon our own actions, but we are loath to live in a world where there are no limitations on the actions of anyone else. That is the fundamental basis for social contracts, and it is formal and informal institutions that are the embodiments of those explicit or implicit contracts.

A vexing yet unavoidable challenge with any such institutional arrangement, however, is monitoring and enforcement. In the cyber domain, especially, it can be very difficult to ascertain where violations may have occurred or who the perpetrators are. But similar monitoring challenges arise in most other realms also. In the military sphere, the use of proxy forces or other forms of hybrid warfare can obscure facts on the ground, as the Russians have amply demonstrated in the Crimea. Likewise, regarding trade agreements, a country may profess to engage in fair trade practices while impeding trade by indirect means. Even in policy spheres, such as climate change, where there is a relatively strong basis for mutual benefit, it is necessary to have mechanisms in place to avoid free-riding and for ensuring that agreed-upon commitments are met. Ultimately, *intent* is a crucial factor in determining the degree to which institutional arrangements can succeed. If the parties to an agreement do so in good faith, there is always a reasonable basis for hope. If the underlying intent is malevolent, however, institutional masking is unlikely to succeed. Intent reveals itself over time. As a general principle, the United States should be most proactive in establishing and maintaining effective institutions together with partners that have demonstrated good intent on a consistent basis – and of course we should demonstrate that same good intent and consistency through our own actions.

A Club Goods Perspective

The emphasis on institutions as described above is, in effect, a prescription for the joint production and enjoyment of what are known in the public choice field as *club goods*. While the underlying theoretical framing of the club goods literature does have a strong technical aspect,[5] at an intuitive level, a club goods arrangement is a fairly straightforward proposition by which multiple parties derive benefits through mutual association. Expanding club membership can be a worthwhile undertaking, provided that those additional members do not begin to undermine the benefits of the original members. Security or defense alliances may be usefully viewed as clubs, as can free trade regions or the set of countries that ratifies a climate change accord. Calling something a club does not alter the thing itself, but it can help to add analytical clarity to a messy world. Because of China's enormous size and growing clout, the United States and associated allies cannot be indifferent about having it join such clubs. On the whole, China over recent decades has shown itself willing to join existing clubs while also seeking to modify or perhaps bend club rules to better suit its own purposes. In some ways, that is not so very different from our own approach to international affiliations. In any event, clubs may also evolve along with the context in which they operate. It is not only China's size that makes its erstwhile membership in global clubs potentially problematic for the United States and others, it is also the fact that the Chinese political economy is hard-wired in a very different way from ours. In effect, the United States and China have two highly distinct operating systems.

Competing Operating Systems

While one should be wary of relying too heavily on metaphors to guide one's analysis (first clubs, now operating systems), much analytical work in economics, public policy, and related fields does use models as devices for making complex problems tractable. If the models are well chosen, such mathematical or other abstract representations of a phenomenon can help us focus on the essential elements. Conversely, models that are too simplistic or reductionist can be dangerously misleading. Likewise, with metaphors. With that caveat firmly in mind, it is instructive to think of the compatibility of the United States and China in terms of their underlying "operating systems." In some areas, especially that of homeland security, this analogy applies both literally and figuratively. As the Internet-of-Things (IOT) becomes more core to daily life, the operating systems that underpin the internet comprise increasingly core critical infrastructure. Protocols that underpin IOT are codified in machine language. As detailed in Chapter 8, just within the United States we struggle to find an appropriate balance between legitimate security concerns that may justify intrusive data collection by the National Security Agency and other government agencies – versus the looming possibility of an Orwellian drama at home. If surreptitious code from China or other foreign entities were to be hard-wired into our telecommunications systems, the possibilities are even more unsettling. Europe may be more on the right track, as it puts in place its General Data Protection Regulation (GDPR). In the United States, we have scarcely begun to sort out a robust policy frame.

The metaphor of competing operating systems can also be applied more broadly. The political economies and governance systems of the United States and China are also akin to divergent operating systems. This does not necessarily mean that they are incompatible, but "applications" designed for one platform may not always function smoothly on the other. They are, in effect, different club goods in the economic sense of the term as defined above, and so this brings us full circle. As more members are drawn to a particular platform, the potential for club benefits may grow, depending upon its design features. This applies to trade groupings, security and defense alliances, and climate change accords, as noted earlier. For some club goods, agglomeration effects are strong so that benefits increase with the quantity of members. This is particularly true for network-based economies, and it is why social media platforms (Facebook or WeChat) can become so pervasive. For other types of club goods, it is the quality rather than the quantity of members that is the key to benefits. This is true of elite social clubs and gated communities. The European Union may also be an example, although not everyone in the United Kingdom would agree. Hybrid clubs may be more the norm, where both the quantity and quality of members can enhance the club experience for all members – up to a point.

Welcome to the Club, China

While these analogies to clubs and to operating systems may seem esoteric, there is in fact a substantial, rigorous, and credible scholarly literature in these areas that can help to inform policy analysis vis-à-vis China. This kind of transference of models from one scholarly field to another is in fact quite common as one can see, for example, from the widespread use of "gravity" or "entropy" models from physics usefully applied in economics. As a general rule, the United States should promote associations ("clubs") with other nations that share similar aims, and it should be willing in principle to welcome China into any of these, provided that its joining would not undermine, intentionally or otherwise, the benefits of the original membership. It is likely that China's membership in a climate change accord would be highly beneficial, whereas the benefits of its membership in a security or trade alliance might be less certain. The United States should also be open in principle to showing some flexibility regarding the terms of membership for China in specific cases, thereby allowing for the possibility, as appropriate, for "membership with Chinese characteristics." In contemplating Chinese membership terms in one club or another, the United States must also think through, carefully and thoroughly, the counterfactual hypothesis. That is, if China were not to join, then what? The example of the Asian Infrastructure Investment Bank (AIIB) is a good reminder that China, too, can create clubs.

The club perspective also underlines the importance of allies – there is little point in having a club with no members. In the area of climate change, only a global effort can hope to succeed, and even then the challenges are immense. With regards to trade policy, a strong trade group such as initially envisioned for the Trans-Pacific Partnership could accomplish several objectives. In addition to boosting markets for U.S. trade and its partners, it could also be a positive inducement for China to join on terms that are mutually agreeable and beneficial. This is in turn could help extend the reach of a more conducive "operating system." If the United States does not engage with a bloc of trading partners in this way, it becomes more likely that protocols for trade will emerge in the region that are less well suited to U.S. interests.

In the context of defense, we should also recognize that the cost of projecting military power increases with distance. As China continues to grow, its military reach will do so also. The cost to the United States of countering China's growing capabilities in the region with our own will also increase, placing further strain on our fiscal solvency. Here too, strong alliances can be a game-changer. Countries in the region have as much or more at stake as the United States does, and the prospect of an Indo-Pacific region that is dominated militarily and economically by China will surely give each country pause. If our allies there share our interests and commitments, they can help compensate for the geographic remoteness of the United States from the region. The United State may well be the only country that could provide effective leadership in this regard, and even so, the challenges of effective and reliable coordination are formidable.

Shaping the World by Defining Ourselves

This book advocates for a positive, proactive role for the United States in helping to give shape to a world that is more conducive to our own future and the future of those who join us in that effort. Even if we choose an alternative path of relative isolation, decoupling or shunning of global institutions, China will remain an increasingly significant part of the evolving global order and hence the world we live in. U.S. economic, sustainability, and geopolitical policies will still need to contend with the consequences of China's rise. All indications are that China does not seek enmity with the United States, but it does intend to assert itself more boldly in pursuit of what it sees are its own legitimate aspirations. As argued above, institutionalized alliances that work to the mutual advantage of the United States and those who partner with us are key. Faithful allies are the best means by which the United States can work in partnership with others to extend the domain within which our core values are adhered to. For this to happen, we need to clarify what those core values are, communicate those effectively to ourselves and to others, and demonstrate our commitment to those values through our own actions. Ultimately, the task is for us to define who we are as a nation, for those values and aspirations will infuse our global undertakings, including our relationship with China and with our allies.

What Has Trump Wrought?

The range of U.S. policy issues that are impacted by China's rise are largely the same for any incoming administration. How they respond to those issues, however, can vary significantly from one administration to the next. It is why this book has concentrated on a framing of the policy issues themselves rather than on the to-and-fro of the political process by which decisions are ultimately arrived at. The analysis in the nine preceding substantive chapters are intended to be a useful guide for any interested reader, regardless of her personal political views. It is also why the book has refrained from casting the analysis in terms of a scorecard regarding one administration or another. The ushering in of the Trump Administration, however, has compelled a reconsideration of this approach because it is not just another administration. Instead, it marks a watershed moment in the American political landscape that will retain its significance, for better or worse, long after the Trump Administration has passed.

This book emphasizes the importance of institutions, enduring alliances with like-minded partners, and reasoned policy discourse. The advent of the Trump Administration has seriously undermined all of these through a vociferous debasing of civil discourse and a disdain for truthfulness. Our democracy rests on institutions that have endured thus far for almost a quarter of a millennium, but they should not be taken for granted. Institutions are akin to infrastructure in that we sometimes forgot how valuable they are until they begin to crumble. Likewise, one may forget how valuable enduring friendships are until they begin to dissolve in acrimony.

Open, reasoned civil discourse is a foundation of democracy. It is nurtured by the premise that those who hold differing views from us might be right, and even if they are wrong, we should accord them respect. As political discourse in the United States becomes increasingly polarized and partisan in nature, reasonable middle ground has given way to an unreasoned muddled round of recriminations and castigations. A regrettable consequence of these developments is that it impedes our ability to respond to the diverse policy challenges posed by China's rise. Instead of a thoughtful policy framework that has strong bipartisan support, decisions of major consequence are being reduced to ephemeral transactions that lack any enduring basis. Rousing the American public to demonize China is profoundly detrimental to our own interests. Ironically, this does not mean that Trump is wrong about everything. We *do* have a problem with persistent trade deficits. We *are* losing manufacturing jobs that once were the basis of a solid working middle class. The United States *is* bearing an oversized financial burden in support of an erstwhile world order. None of these problems will be resolved, however, by debasing civil discourse.

We the People

It is too easy to point an accusatory finger at President Trump or to politicians at large. In a democracy, however, we ourselves must bear the ultimate responsibility. We cannot lead a global discourse if we cannot engage in civil discourse with each other. We cannot help shape a world order that is positively inclusive if we define ourselves through acts of primitive tribalism at home. We cannot persuade other nations that we value their right to prosper when we tolerate growing inequality among ourselves. We cannot expect to reach a reasonable accord with those whom we demonize.

There is much that we *can* do, however. As we have seen throughout these chapters, the rise of China has significant implications for the full range of economic, sustainability, and geopolitical policy domains. In each of these areas there are positive steps we can take to mitigate the negative consequences and to capitalize on opportunities for constructive engagement. Thoughtful policy analysis cannot relieve of us of tough choices, but it can help us make the most of the options we do have. By addressing these challenges in a mature and responsible manner, without casting blame on scapegoats, we will enhance our capacity to align with our allies and with China. We can also continue to inspire others. No country, especially among those in the Indo-Pacific region, wants to be compelled to choose between the United States and China. They may be inclined, however, to lean more one way than another. And it is not just the leadership of those countries that matters; popular sentiment may well be more decisive. There is something truly inspirational about the creative energy of individuals who are free to pursue their own destinies in accordance with their own beliefs. The United States holds a special place in the world not just because of the size of its economy or the capabilities of its military. Ours is a country that spawns dreams, and encourages each one of us to realize those dreams for ourselves. As we move forward with policies that respond constructively and effectively to China's rise, we must clearly understand the differences between values, ideologies, and partisanship. Either way, it is up to us. As we seek to make America great again, this would be an excellent place to begin.

Notes

1 I deploy a somewhat similar technique in Heikkila (2007).
2 In a topological representation, it is the logical connections between nodes that matters, not the precise placement. A common example is a social network analysis, where it is the *linkages* between individuals that have meaning.
3 Fiscal policy exerts influence across the board, but that is in terms of defining overall constraints rather than impacting the substance of other policy domains directly. The linkage between fiscal policy and trade policy is an important exception.
4 The (I-S) term representing private sector imbalances is a complicating factor, but it does not negate the fundamental point.
5 See, for example, Cornes and Sandler (1996).

References

Cornes, Richard and Todd Sandler (1996). *The Theory of Externalities, Public Goods, and Club Goods*, Cambridge: Cambridge University Press.

Heikkila, Eric J. (2007). "Three Questions Regarding Urbanization in China," *Journal of Planning Education and Research*, 27(1), 65–81.

Schell, Orville and Susan L. Shirk (2017). *U.S. Policy Toward China: Recommendations for a New Administration*, Task Force Report, New York: Asia Society Center on US China Relations and UC San Diego 21st Century China Center.

INDEX

Page numbers in **bold** denote tables, those in *italics* denote figures.

Acemoglu, Daron 57–9
ADIZ *see* air-defence identification zone (ADIZ)
Advanced Persistent Threat, Level 1 (APT-1) 143
AI *see* Artificial Intelligence (AI)
AIIB *see* Asian Infrastructure Investment Bank (AIIB)
air-defence identification zone (ADIZ) 160
Alameda Corridor projects 97, 99
Allison, Graham 169
AML regime *see* anti-money laundering (AML) regime
anti-access/area denial (A2/AD) defense strategies 153
anti-money laundering (AML) regime 25–6
Arab oil embargoes 120
Archibugi, Daniele 44
arms race 152
Artificial Intelligence (AI) 144, 191
Asian Infrastructure Investment Bank (AIIB) 8, 177–8, 200–1, 204
authoritarianism 190–1
automobiles 94–5, 111, 113–14, 142
Autor, David 56–7, 64–5
Ayyagari, Meghana 26

Baldwin, Robert 43

banking system 25–6; creditworthiness of 13
Baumeister, Christiane 114–15, 117
Beckley, Michael 157, 159–60, 162, 165, 168
Belt and Road Initiative (BRI) 8, 175–6, 178, 185, 188; policy implications of 178
Bergsten, C. Fred 26–7, 38
Bernanke, Ben 26
Bernard, Andrew 56–7
bioterrorism 133, 140–3; threats of 141
bi-partisan commission 18
Bobashev, Georgiy 139–40
Bogich, Tiffany 137–8
borderline vigilance 131–3
Bowles–Simpson Commission 17, 18
Bracmort, Kelsi 83
Brands, Hal 186, 189
Bretton Woods institutions 8, 175, 178, 186, 201
Brexit movement in European Union 201
BRI *see* Belt and Road Initiative (BRI)
BRICS consortium 48
British thermal unit (Btu) 111–12
Brooks, Stephen 153, 155, 158
Btu *see* British thermal unit (Btu)
budgets 4, 16–20

CAA *see* Clean Air Act (CAA)

cabinet-level appointments 2
California 93, 95, 97, 100
cap and trade 80–2, 84–7, *85*
capital investments 177
capitalism 52–3
carbon: intensity 76; interagency working group on social cost of **79**; social cost of 78–80
carbon capture and sequestration (CCS) 83
carbon dioxide (CO$_2$) emissions 3, 79, 95; emissions *73*; US-China comparisons *4*
carbon tax *85*; *vs.* cap and trade 80–2, 84–7
cargo container route shares 97, *98*
cargo movements 99–100
Carson, Rachel 71
CCS *see* carbon capture and sequestration (CCS)
CDM *see* Clean Development Mechanism (CDM)
Chenggong, Zhang 179
China/Chinese 155; American visitations to 137; attacks on air bases 167; CO$_2$ emissions in 3; defense strategy 158; domestic economy 22; economic dominance 187; economic impacts of 3; economic policy perspectives on 5–6; for economic trade 188; energy security 121; financial institutions 101; food items imported from 136; foreign reserves 20–2; geopolitical policy perspectives on 7–8; global energy prices 117–18; immigration 102; import exposure 59; import penetration 59; membership in climate change 204; military expenditures 4; military modernization 157, 167; military posture and general strategy 157; military resources 167; military strategy 156; missile strike capacity 158; money laundering 25–6; national cybersecurity 145; national oil companies (NOC) 121; national security agencies 145; negative impacts of imports from 62; oil production 115; overview of 3–4; political economies and governance systems of 204; political risk in 102; primary oil suppliers 121; public health effort within 138; rapid urbanization 137; real estate 101; relationship with 205; sustainability policy perspectives on 6–7; territorial claims 201; trade

balance with 199; trade cargo 99; trade port 98; trade with East Asia 187, *187*; U.S. policy perspective on 196
China Investment Corporation (CIC) 22
Chinese Communist Party (CPP) 52, 185
CIC *see* China Investment Corporation (CIC)
civil discourse 206; institutions of 191
Clarke, Richard A. 141, 143, 146–7
Clean Air Act (CAA) 78, 81
Clean Development Mechanism (CDM) 82
climate change 8, 72–4, *73*; carbon tax *vs.* cap and trade 80–2, 84–7; causes and consequences of 71; China's impact on U.S. environment 74–5; effective global response to 6; environmental consciousness 71–2; geoengineering options for 83–4; global burden of 6; mitigating 95–6; movement 92; negotiations 175; social cost of carbon 78–80; Trump Administration's denial of 92; urban regions and 93–4
club goods: perspective 202–3; theoretical framing of 202–4
Codex Alimentarius Commission 135–6
CO$_2$ emissions *see* carbon dioxide (CO$_2$) emissions
Cold War 176, 189–90
collective balancing 189
collective policy 2
collective security 121
Committee on Foreign Investment in the United States (CFIUS) 198
communicable diseases 132, 141; public health capabilities for 137
comprehensive pressure 189
Congressional Budget Office 14, 17
Congressional Research Service (CRS) 2, 55–6, 118
conventional trade theory 55–6
Coolidge, Calvin 33
Cooper, Zack 186, 189
Cordesman, Anthony 167
counterfactual hypothesis 58, 204
COVID-19, 7, 100, 136, 138; emergence of 138–9; epidemic 100–1; global dimensions of 139; outbreak 139; pandemic 137
CPP *see* Chinese Communist Party (CPP)
creditor, co-dependence of 23
creditworthiness 13–16

Crimea 155, 202
critical infrastructure 133, 143–6, *144*
cross–border ties 183
cross-Straits conflict 181
CRS *see* Congressional Research Service (CRS)
crude oil: global demand for 114–15; price of 115; prices 109, *109–10*
currency: devaluation cum industrial policy 41; exchange 15; and trade 40
current account deficit 26
cyberactivists 143
cyber attacks 133, 141
cyber defense 146–7
cybersecurity: responsibility for 147; strategy 147
Cybersecurity and Infrastructure Security Agency (CISA) 143
cyberspace 201
cyberspies 142
cyberterrorists 142
cyberthieves 142
cyberwar 147
cyberwarriors 143

debtor, co-dependence of 23
decision makers 94–5
decision making, unified locus of 6
de facto autonomy 179
defense 198; expenditures, by country 154, **154**
defense policy: China's evolving military strategy 156–9; historical and global context of U.S. military 151–3; hot spots in Western Pacific Region 159; North-east Asia 159–61; South China Sea 161–4; Taiwan military context 166–8; Taiwan policy context 164–6; U.S. perspective 169
deficit hypothesis 16
democracy 9, 207; foundation of 206
democratic governance 9
Department of Homeland Security (DHS) 131–3
di Giovanni, Julian 65
digital infrastructure 144
Dilemma, Malacca 162
diplomatic recognition 180
disenfranchisement 183
dispute settlement process 43
dissolution, sense of 174
Dixit, Avinash 64
Dodd–Frank Act 19–20

domestic production 135
Drafting Committee 190
Dutch colonialism 179
dynamic stalemate 181

East Asia 187; unitary hierarchical order within 188
ecological systems 83
economic/economy: activity, level of 73; development objectives 47–8; growth 76; imbalances, fundamental cause of 199; inequality 54; policies 1, 198–9; power 186; processes, consequence of 6; theory 5, 56; uncertainty 17–18
education 102; programs, cost-effectiveness of 5
electricity generators 78
electronic reporting system 137–8
embodied emissions in trade (EET) 74
empirical analysis 56
employment 54–5; direct impacts on 197; generation 199; human capital and U.S. labor force 60–3; labor 52–4, **54**; laborers/consumers 63–5; manufacturing *55*; trends in 5; United States "exporting" jobs to China 54–60, *55*
Employment and Training Agency (ETA) 61
energy: agreements 121; consumers of 120; consumption 112–13, 197–8; demand 112–14, *113*; economy 123; energetic overview 108–9; and environment 118–19; environmental costs 118; essential and strategic nature of 119–20; as lynchpin 123–4; paradox 119; prices *109*, 109–12, *110*, 117; production, dimensions of 117; security 119–22; shifts, demand for 6–7; supply 114–16
energy-efficient technologies 114
Energy Information Administration 116
Energy Organization Act of 1977 108
energy policies: implications for 4; lynchpin role of 6
energy products 116; quantity of 114
enforcement: issues 5; mechanisms 202; outcome-based approach 134; production-based approach 134
environmental consciousness 71–2
environmental degradation 118
environmental justice 71–2
environmental movement 6

environmental perspective 6
environmental policies, and foreign
   relations 200
Environmental Protection Agency (EPA)
   71, 78
ethnic minority 97
exchange rate policy 21

FDI *see* foreign direct investment (FDI)
federal budget 17
federal deficit 14, *14*, 26
Federal Tax Code 27
Feldstein, Martin 25
Filippetti, Andrea 44
finance 178
Financial Action Task Force (FATF) 25–6
financial capital 18–19, 177
financial crisis 14–15
financial institutions 19, 177; in China 26
Financial Stability Oversight Council
   (FSOC) 19
fiscal policy 46–7; budgets and
   stakeholders 16–20; China and U.S.
   asset bubble 25; China foreign reserves
   20–2; co-dependence of creditor and
   debtor 23; creditworthiness 13–16;
   deficit disorder 16; direct impacts on
   197; outcome of 199; parables 23–5
fiscal solvency 205
5G internet technology 145
5G technologies 142
food 7; assurance programs 135
foodborne diseases 133–4
food for thought 133–6
Food Safety Modernization Act (FSMA)
   134
foreign direct investment (FDI) 54–5
foreign exchange 21
foreign investment 198
foreign relations: Asian Infrastructure
   Investment Bank 175–8; Belt and Road
   Initiative 175–8; China's territorial
   extent and integrity 178–9; direct
   impacts on 197; environmental policies
   and 198, 200; in evolving global
   context 173–5; Hong Kong 182–5;
   importance of 173; soft authoritarianism
   190–1; Taiwan 179–82
foreign reserves 21–2
Frank, Andre Gunder 35
free trade agreements 33–4
Freund, Caroline 64
fuel consumption 111–12

game theory 200
gasoline, price of 111
General Agreement on Tariffs and Trade
   (GATT) 42–3
General Data Protection Regulation
   (GDPR) 203
"general equilibrium" effects of Chinese
   imports 57
geopolitical policy 1, 198, 200–1, 207
geo-strategic importance 182
global demand curve 119
global emissions 95
global energy 108–9; consumption 112;
   demand 114; markets 119; supply 114,
   124
Global Epidemiological Model 140
global institutions 205
globalization 134
global order 175
global pandemics 131
global production 135
global self-sufficiency 119–20
global shipping 98
global value chains (GVC) 5, 53
global warming 74–5
Goldstein, Lyle 158
governance 178; institutions of 191
government expenditures 199
Great Depression 173
greenhouse gases (GHGs) 49, 72;
   emissions 72–9, 81–2, 91, 123–4
gross domestic product (GDP) 3;
   US-China comparisons *4*
Gulf of Aden 120

Harvey, David 53
Health Powers Act 140
heaters 142
Hipgrave, David 138
Holmes, Thomas J. 59
homeland security 198; bioterrorism
   140–3; borderline vigilance 131–3;
   concerns *132*; cyber defense 146–7;
   food for thought 133–6; Huawei and
   critical infrastructure 143–6
Hong Kong 182–5; dueling narratives
   about 182; local and national identities
   in 184; and national identities 184;
   protests in 184; Special Administrative
   Region (SAR) 183; United States in
   184; university students in 183
Hornbeck, J.F. 42
household decisions 94

Huawei 145; and critical infrastructure 143–6; Cyber Security Evaluation Centre 145
human capital 60–3
human rights 190; universality of 190
hybrid clubs 204
hydrological fracturing technologies 123

Ikenberry, G. John 186–8
IMF see International Monetary Fund (IMF)
import penetration ratio 55, *55*
income disparities 5, 53–4, **54**
income, employment and see employment and income
income inequality 53–4
increasing returns to scale (IRTS) 34
individualism 191
industrial control system (ICS) networks 144
industrialization 76
infectious diseases 132–3
infectiousness 132
informationization of war 156
infrastructure investments 178
institutions/institutional 47, 201–2; alliances 205; denigration of 9; design 201; entity 14–15; of governance and civil discourse 191; importance of 206; masking 202; perspective 201–2; traditional 174
insurance rates 75
intellectual property rights (IPR) 36–7; formal international recognition of 44
intended audience 9
Intergovernmental Panel on Climate Change (IPCC) 72; Working Group III 92
international affiliations 203
International Bank for Reconstruction and Development (IBRD) 15, 42–3
international banking 15
international institutions 202; role of 175
International Monetary Fund (IMF) 8, 15, 23, 38, 173–5, 177; provision of 41
international offsets 82
international order 174
international relations 173, 202
International Trade Organization (ITO) 42–3
internet connectivity 60
Internet-of-Things (IOT) 145, 203; interconnectivity of 142

IOT see Internet-of-Things (IOT)
IOUs 24
IPR see intellectual property rights (IPR)
island chains 157–8
isolation, measures 139
ITO see International Trade Organization (ITO)

Japanese colonial structures 179
J-curve effect 39
Jefferson, Thomas 173

Kaska, Kadri 143, 145
Kennedy, John F. 175
Knake, Robert K. 141, 143, 146–7
knowledge spillovers 139
Korean War 152
Krugman, Paul 34–5
Kuomintang 164, 166, 179–80

labor 52–4, **54**; market 102
laborers/consumers 63–5
labor movement 5, 52–3; overview of 5
Lambert, Bruce 99
Landis, John 95
land use, transformation of 99
Latino minority 102
Lattanzio, Richard 83
Lawrence-Zuniga, Denise 103
Lee Kuan Yew 190
linked policy domains 196–8, *197*; competing operating systems 203–4
Los Angeles (LA) 104
lynchpin 123–4

Mackinder, Halford John 177
macroeconomic debates 33
maritime domain awareness 158
market reforms 138
Marshall Plan 176; essential significance of 176
Marucheck, Ann 136
Marx, Karl 52
medical devices 142
merchandise trade deficits 36
Metropolitan Planning Organizations (MPOs) 93, 95
micro-level differences 183
military: assets 163; balance 163; capabilities 164; conflict 156; confrontation 169; power 205; provocations 200; strategy 158–9
mitigation response, category of 83

Monios, Jason 99
Monterey Park 102–3
Morrison, Wayne M. 39
MPOs *see* Metropolitan Planning
	Organizations (MPOs)
multilateral institutions 175
municipal design review processes 104
Murdock, Charles 20

National Association of Realtors 100
National Climate Assessment (NCA) 74–5
National Commission on Fiscal
	Responsibility and Reform 18
National Energy Commission 120
national geographical integrity 178–9
National Income Accounts 28–9
National Research Council study 95
National Security Agency 203
national transportation strategy 99
NATO 156; alliance 154
natural gas (NG) 116
neoclassical economics, principles of 174
network-based economies 204
networked computers 142
New Development Bank 177
North American Free Trade Agreement
	(NAFTA) 97, 197
North-east Asia 159–61; military balance
	in 161
North–South accord 77
nuclear energy 112
nuclear energy plants 118–19
nuclear hazards 118–19
Nye, Joseph 174–5

Obama, Barack 74, 78, 175, 200
objective analysis 8
objectivism 8
oil: demand for 112; deposits 116;
	products 117; supply curve for 116
One Belt, One Road 175
"One Country, Two Systems" formula
	183–4
operating systems 203–4; metaphor of
	competing 204
Organization of the Petroleum Exporting
	Countries (OPEC) 108
organized criminal activities 25
Ortega, David 135

Panetta, Leon 146
Paris Agreement 75, 92
Paris Climate Accord 198

Park, Jooyoun 62
Patent Cooperation Treaty 44–5
payments, fiscal dimensions of 3
Peersman, Gert 114–15, 117
People's Liberation Army 169
People's Liberation Army (PLA) 156
Permanent Normal Trade Relations 58
Pew Research Center 185–6
pharmaceuticals 7; product 133
Pigovian tax 80
plant capital 56
policy: analysis 1–2, 8; broad spectrum of
	1; clusters 198; of containment 152;
	domestic transfer payments 3; issues 2;
	perspective on China 196; realms 196;
	tradeoffs, balance of 1–2
policy domains 2–3, 196–7; of United
	States 3
political discourses 152, 186, 206
political economy perspectives 96, 203
polluting rights 81
porcupine defense 168
production-based approach 74
production, modes of 5
public debt 14
public health: conditions 138;
	infrastructures 140
Public Health Emergency of International
	Concern (PHEIC) 136
public policy discourse 3

quantitative easing 25
quarantines 136; measures 139
Quebec referenda of 1980 181

RAND study 140
Rand study's summary 167
real estate markets 100
"rebalancing" plan 157
rebound effects 114
refrigeration 142; units 142
regime change 189
Regional Comprehensive Economic
	Partnership (RCEP) 188
Regional Greenhouse Gas Initiative
	(RGGI) 92
regional trade agreements 47
region-based institutions 188
regulatory institutions 19
renminbi (RMB) 21; exchange rate policy
	5; valuation of 22
Ricardian principle 34
Rodrik, Dani 40

Roosevelt, Eleanor 190
Russia: defense expenditures 154; natural gas exports 121; resurgence of 153–4; warfare methods of 155

"salami-slicing" strategy 162
SAMs *see* surface-to-air missiles (SAMs)
SARS 7, 136–7, 139
Saudi Arabia 111, 116–17, 154
savings deficit 27
SCC *see* social cost of carbon (SCC)
science, technology, engineering and mathematics (STEM) 63
SCO *see* Shanghai Cooperation Organization (SCO)
security threats 198
self-determination 181
Shanghai Cooperation Organization (SCO) 121
Silk Road 176
Silk Road Fund 177
social contracts 185; fundamental basis for 202
social cost of carbon (SCC) 79
social distancing 136
social insurance 65
social justice 71–2, 174
Social Policy Research Associates (SPR) 61
society, microcosms of 197
soft authoritarianism 190–1
South China Sea 161–4; maritime claims in 162; potential for conflict in 162
Spanish–American War 151
Spratly conflict 164
S-shaped energy 113, *113*
S-shaped trajectory 113
stakeholders 16–20
state-owned enterprises 26, 186
Stevens, John J. 59
Stiglitz, Joseph 64
Straits of Malacca 120
strategic ambiguity 181
strategic behaviors 200
strategic geographic importance 157
strategic thinking 156
surface-to-air missiles (SAMs) 163
surveillance web 142
sustainability cluster 198, 200
sustainability policies 1, 200
Sustainable Development Goals 123
"swine" flu virus 136

Taiwan 159–60, 179–82; autonomy of 180; de facto authorities in 180; Democratic Progressive Party (DPP) 179–80; effective control of 168; geographical status 179; military context 166–8; military strategy 168; policy context 164–6; porcupine defense strategy by 168; repatriation of 165; "squeezing" 165
Taiwan Relations Act 165
Taiwan Strait 165, 167
tax revenues 111–12
telecommunications 60, 203
telephones 142
Terminal High Altitude Area Defense (THAAD) 161
toxic environments 71
trade: agreements 188; deficits, chronic balance of 123; groupings 204; investment 198; principal economic drivers of 34; victims of 199
Trade Adjustment Assistance (TAA) Program 5, 61–2
trade policy 8, 196–8, 205; blocs as clubs 47; currency manipulator 38–42; and developmental trajectories 47–9; intellectual property rights 43–5; tricks of 33–6; unilateral action 45–7; U.S. merchandise trade deficits 36–8; World Trade Organization (WTO) 42–3
Trade-Related Aspects of Intellectual Property Rights (TRIPS) 5, 43–4
traditional institutions of governance 174
training, cost-effectiveness of 5
Trans-Pacific Partnership (TPP) 188, 197, 205
transportation policies 3; implications for 4
transportation systems 99–100
TRIPS Agreement 44
Troubled Asset Relief Program (TARP) 25
Trump, Donald 38, 45–6, 76–7, 175, 189, 202; Administration's denial of climate change 92; effect 8–9; trade deficits with China 197
tuberculosis (TB) 136
"twin deficits" hypothesis 26

UN *see* United Nations (UN)
Unified Command Plan 151
unilateral action 45–7

United Nations (UN) 173–5, 190;
Commission on Human Rights 190;
General Assembly 180; purposes and
principles of 180–1; Sustainable
Development Goals 177
United Nations Convention on the Law
of the Sea (UNCLOS) 201
United Nations Framework Convention
on Climate Change (UNFCCC) 75–6,
92, 201; broader agreement within 77–8
United States 191, 201; anti-surface warfare
164; and China 182; colonial power 151;
command of the commons 152; defense
policy perspective 169; deficits 26;
energy consumption in 112; energy
exports and imports *117*; "exporting"
jobs to China 54–60, *55*; foreign
relations policy 185; geographic
remoteness of 205; global dominance
174; global order 186; infrastructure
investment 6; interest rates 25; labor and
employment in 52; labor force 60–3;
labor markets 57; merchandise trade
imbalances 35, **35**; metropolitan region
93; military balance 167; military deaths
151; military expenditures 153; military
strength 7; policy interest 181; policy
issues in 9; policy makers 9, 122; policy
perspective 3, 135, 188, 196, 198–9;
policy realms **2**, 2–3; policy responses 3;
political economies and governance
systems of 204; residential real estate 100,
101; counter-measures of war 155–6;
stature and position of 7; trade deficit 24;
trade with East Asia 187, *187*
United States-Mexico-Canada Agreement
(USMCA) 97
United States Trade Representative's
(USTR) 36–7
Universal Declaration of Human Rights
(UNDR) 190
urbanization 96; magnitude of 91
urban policy: China, U.S. cities, and
climate change **91**, 91–6, *94*; by land,
by sea, and by air 96–100, *98*;
neighborhood 100–4, *101*
urban population **91**, 91–2
urban regions, and climate change 93–4
Uruguay Round: final agreements 43; of
GATT negotiations 43–4
U.S.–China relations 158–9, 161, 186

vaccination programs 139
Venezuela 112
Vietnam War 152
vigilance 200

wages: economy 56; purchasing power of
63
Warren, Elizabeth 19
Warsaw Pact 154
Washington Consensus 174
Wei Li 103
welfare effect 65
Western Climate Initiative 92
western democracies 145
Western liberal norms 186
Wohlforth, William 153, 155, 158
World Bank 8, 173–5, 177, 201
World Health Organization (WHO) 136
World Trade Organization (WTO) 5,
35–7, 40, 42–5, 47–9, 58, 175, 201;
agreements 100; dispute mechanism 46;
Dispute Settlement Body 43;
framework 45; mechanisms 41;
membership 45; provision of 41
World Urban Forum 96
World War I 173
World War II 48, 162, 173, 179–80
WTO *see* World Trade Organization
(WTO)

Xi Jinping 185, 189–90

Yergin, Daniel 108, 112

"zero-sum gain" condition 183–4
Zhong Guo 185